PROTEST:

Sacco-Vanzetti and the Intellectuals

PROTEST:

Sacco-Vanzetti and the Intellectuals

by DAVID FELIX

INDIANA UNIVERSITY PRESS
BLOOMINGTON AND LONDON

Library of Congress catalog card number: 65–19707
Manufactured in the United States of America

ACKNOWLEDGMENT

I am indebted to Harry Kressing for editorial counsel

CONTENTS

PHOTOGRAPHS

(following page 38)

PROTEST:

Sacco-Vanzetti and the Intellectuals

1. In Dedham

ON the sunny morning of April 9, 1927, a little group of men stands on Dedham Common. Dedham is a town of white frame houses and wide green lawns just to the southwest of Boston. It might be a Sunday group of worshipers; nearby, on High Street, you could see the chaste steeples of the Unitarian and Congregational churches, and two of the men are formally and almost sumptuously dressed in dark suits and velvet-collared coats. But then your eye would pick out the loops of handcuff chains. The Italian anarchists Nicola Sacco and Bartolomeo Vanzetti are going to climb the steps of Dedham courthouse to be sentenced to die for a crime committed seven years ago.

Dedham glances at the men and goes about its business. It believes it knows all there is to be known about them. Dedham cannot understand why the world outside should claim to know more from a distance.

The eyes of the men are crinkled in the sunshine. The men are bareheaded at the request of photographers who want to show all of their faces to the world. The faces are alien in this Puritan town, but each is sharply different from the other; the men refuse to become interchangeable victims of injustice. Both men are smiling, and the smiles are also different. Sacco is a dully handsome workingman of almost thirty-six; he smiles with great effort.

Vanzetti, who will be thirty-nine in two months, has a scythe of thinning hair, domed forehead, strong nose, long sweep of mustache, and heavy chin. His deep smile reaches out to anyone who would receive a friendly offering. The lines in the faces show how much the men have aged during seven years of imprisonment but give the faces a power that had been absent when Sacco and Vanzetti were free and unknown.

The men had undergone a thorough education in the psychology and sociology of prison life. They had also filled in the years with book learning, and they would make use of this more formal training to master the court scene. Through the study of English with women sympathizers they got into the habit of writing letters to their new friends. The letters became famous. Sacco's progress had remained modest because of his slow mind and his sense of hopelessness, but Vanzetti used the language with great fluency to communicate his feelings and argue his case in legal syllogisms. A friend of his remarked to me that Vanzetti had been an ignorant workingman when he went to prison: "It was a miracle, the case was a miracle, that made a thinker out of him. He was just a simple worker and he became this great writer. The case was like that, how it changed men, what it did to this man!"

At the courthouse, a handsome granite building with four Doric columns, some two hundred persons stand quietly among the parked automobiles. They represent the concern of the world for Sacco and Vanzetti, who are alien only in Massachusetts. Seven years before, on a sunny April day like this, a holdup gang had robbed a shoe factory of its payroll and killed two men. Sacco and Vanzetti were anarchists, that is to say, men with a vision of a world ruled by justice, a world, thus, ruled entirely without force, and they had been accused of participating in the murders. Millions of people could not see the connection between the theory of anarchism and the practical art of payroll robbery.

They expressed their doubts through Sacco-Vanzetti liberation committees and, right now, in mass meetings in Paris and London, in Stockholm and Berlin, and in scores of other cities. In Buenos Aires, bakers and taxi drivers had begun a protest strike, and radical groups had become so threatening in Geneva that police set a heavy guard around Hugh Gibson, the American ambassador to Belgium, who was in Switzerland to represent the United States in League of Nations disarmament talks. A little later the protests would become even angrier. Thousands of demonstrators would attack American embassies; there would be bloody battles with the police, broken heads and bomb explosions, and Americans abroad would fear for their lives and the honor of their country. Here in Dedham, the friends of the prisoners helplessly and dumbly let them pass into the courthouse.

In the courtroom, officers of the law formed an important part of the attendance. A few women sympathizers, bearers of distinguished Massachusetts names, were gathered unobtrusively off to one side. More important, several reporters, including representatives of the wire services and the New York City press, prepared to communicate the sense of the proceedings.

The court crier bawled: "Hear ye!" Judge Thayer, who had arrived by automobile from his Worcester home fifteen miles away, entered the courtroom now, a few minutes after the prisoners, and ascended the dais to take command. A man of sixty-nine, he had a square, stony New England face with a gray mustache and thin lips; his robes covered a brief, weightless body. He had not troubled to conceal his abhorrence of the prisoners.

The defense had collected damning evidence of Thayer's feelings. Thus Professor James Richardson of Dartmouth, Thayer's college, deposed that the judge had said to him: "Did you see what I did with those anarchistic bastards the other day? I guess that will hold them for a while. . . ."* And if anyone might accuse Richardson of a liberal bias in remembering what he did, a conservative Boston lawyer and former city treasurer named George U. Crocker recalled this from a conversation in the University Club:

> The points which Judge Thayer talked to me about, and which I remember, were the failure of the defendants to establish an alibi, the fact that they were draft dodgers and anarchists and entitled to no consideration, although he said that the matter of their being anarchists, etc., was lugged in by the defendants and not by the Government, and some evidence about their identification. . . . I remember that in particular he talked about counsel for the defense and the argument for the defense. He pulled out of his pocket a paper which he said was part of his charge, and said, "Now, Moore said so and so yesterday in his argument to the jury, and I want to read you a part of the charge I am going to deliver. That will hold him. . . ." He conveyed to me by his words and manner the distinct impression that he was bound to convict these men because they were "Reds." I remember that Judge Thayer in substance said to me that we must stand together and protect ourselves against anarchists and "Reds."**

New England but not New England taciturn, Thayer had volunteered his opinions to a large number of people. He even permitted one determined Boston lady, a defense sympathizer, to debate with him on the verdict, but a Boston lady is a special case. He was, however, a different man in the courtroom, and it was harder to find fault with him in a strictly legal sense. Thayer

* *The Sacco-Vanzetti Case: Transcript of the Record of the Trial of Nicola Sacco and Bartolomeo Vanzetti in the Courts of Massachusetts and Subsequent Proceedings. 1920–1927.* (5 vols.) *With a supplemental volume on the Bridgewater case.* (New York: Henry Holt, 1928–29), vol. 5, p. 5418. See *Note on Sources.* Hereinafter referred to as *Transcript,* this record is the source for statements cited in this book from the trials, hearings, and affidavits, unless otherwise indicated.

** *Transcript,* vol. 5, p. 4947.

spoke little on April 9, 1927. It was a time for Sacco and Vanzetti to speak.

Judge Thayer was a manikin on his high bench. District Attorney Winfield M. Wilbar rose and recited the request for imposition of sentence. He suggested that the week of July 10 might accord with the judge's discretion in setting a time for the execution. With this courtroom idiom, the district attorney was presenting an abstraction of death and giving it an automatic character that removed its agents from feeling or responsibility. But there was another formal matter to be got through. The clerk of Dedham court asked Sacco if he had anything to say.

Sacco leaped to his feet before the clerk had come to the period of his part. "Yes Sir!" he cried. The abstractions vanished. "I am not an orator. It is not very familiar with me the English language, and as I know, as my friend has told me, my comrade Vanzetti will speak more long, so I thought to give him the chance." With these words Sacco had immediately ranged himself as second to Vanzetti.

Yet Sacco had his own force and he struck hard: "I never know, never heard, even read in history anything so cruel as this Court. After seven years prosecuting they still consider us guilty." His face, working with the effort to tell what he felt, became less stolid, and the words began moving more easily. All other sounds in the courtroom died down and the women sympathizers leaned forward. The lawyers, who often overwhelm the real protagonists, were quiet. They had nothing to say this morning.

Sacco said: "I know the sentence will be between two class, the oppressed class and the rich class, and there will be always collision between one and the other. We fraternize the people with the books, with the literature."

Sacco cried: "You persecute the people, tyrannize over them and kill them. We try the education of people always. You try to put a path between us and some other nationality that hates each other. That is why I am here today on this bench, for having been the oppressed class. Well, you are the oppressor."

An unkind observer could point out that Sacco was dealing in art as well as the truth of his situation. The statement was, of course, an arrangement of appeals to sympathy. Even the awkwardness was effective. Yet a man has a right to defend his life as well as he can, and Sacco was aware that he represented more than himself. He had his duty to perform. If he addressed himself ostensibly to Thayer, he meant to reach all the world outside.

Having made his general charge, Sacco got down to Thayer: "You know it Judge Thayer—you know all my life, you know why I am here, and after seven years that you have been persecuting me and my poor wife, and you still today sentence us to death."

Sacco was brief: ". . . and I will give my friend a chance."

He sat down, but Vanzetti whispered to him and he jerkily rose again and made another effort: "I forgot one thing which my comrade remember me. As I said before, Judge Thayer know all my life, and he know that I am never been guilty, never—not yesterday nor today nor forever."

The clerk said: "Bartolomeo Vanzetti, have you anything to say why sentence of death should not be passed upon you?"

Vanzetti said: "Yes. What I say is that I am innocent, not only of the Braintree crime, but also of the Bridgewater crime. That I am not only innocent of these two crimes, but in all my life I have never stole and I have never killed and I have never spilled blood. . . . Not only am I innocent of these two crimes, not only in all my life I have never stole, never killed, never spilled blood, but I have struggled all my life, since I began to reason, to eliminate crime from the earth."

Calm and often smiling, Vanzetti dominated the courtroom with an eloquence that impressed the reporters. From time to time he consulted notes that were penciled on two scraps of paper, twisting and turning the leaves until they were creased and damp.

But his voice was steady. One of the women began to weep while Vanzetti rejoiced that the greatest men on earth were trying to save him from the electric chair.

Vanzetti held out his arms: "Everybody that knows these two arms know very well that I did not need to go into the street and take money and kill a man."

He went back to the case origins: "We were tried during a time that has now passed into history, when there was resentment and hate against people of our principles, the foreigner and the slacker."

To make sure that everyone understood, he went over all of the ground Sacco had covered. Then he discussed various aspects of the case at length, almost in the manner of a university lecturer. Again and again, however, he would return to the statement of innocence with which he had begun. He analyzed his motives. Why should he steal? He argued that he had a prosperous father, that he had proved his ability to earn a living, that if he had refused to make more money, it was because business was exploitation. He was willing enough to admit his faults: "some sins. . . ." There were, however, carefully drawn limits: ". . . but not crimes." Beyond that: "I struggled all my life to eliminate crimes."

With more force than Sacco, he made the charge that the authorities were preparing to kill two idealists because of their ideals: ". . . and if there is a reason why I am here as a guilty man, if there is a reason why in a few minutes you can doom me, it is this reason and no one else."

Vanzetti again asserted his own person: "You see it is seven years that we are in jail. What we have suffered during those seven years no human tongue can say, and yet you see me before you, not trembling, you see me looking you in your eyes straight, not blushing, not changing color, not ashamed or in fear."

Then, like Sacco, he attacked Thayer directly. Leaning across the prisoners' cage toward the judge, Vanzetti spoke out an absolute condemnation in gentle tones: "We have proved that there could not have been another judge on the face of the earth more prejudiced and more cruel than you have been against us." He referred to Thayer's out-of-court remarks. "We know that you have spoke yourself and have spoke your hostility against us and your despisement against us with friends of yours on the train, at the University Club of Boston, on the Golf Club of Worcester, Massachusetts." Inserting a regard for Thayer's age, Vanzetti went on to indict the old man under sanctions that were as rigorous as those he and Sacco faced. "I am sure that if the people who know all what you say against us would have the civil courage to take the stand, maybe your Honor—I am sorry to say this because you are an old man, and I have an old father—but maybe you would be beside us in good justice at this time."

The speech, however, gave evidence of an undisciplined mind. Vanzetti insisted on resolving complex issues with flat statements: "We have proved. . . ." Nor could his sense of proportion keep him from wandering off into distant tangents. Thus he lost himself in an attack on the trial prosecutor revolving around the question of who might have poisoned a well in the interest of the Germans during the war. The effect of all these arguments was to set an unreal frame of the anarchist imagination around a real New England event.

But then Vanzetti concluded to the point. "I am suffering because I am a radical and indeed I am a radical; I have suffered because I am an Italian, and indeed I am an Italian; I have suffered more for my family and for my beloved than for myself; but I am so convinced to be right that if you could execute me two times, and if I could be reborn two other times, I would again to do what I have done already."

Vanzetti said: "I have finished. Thank you." He had spoken for forty-two minutes.

"I am suffering because I am a radical." Vanzetti's cry held one group of Americans. Each of them could say: "I am suffering because I am . . . an intellectual."

They suffered because all intellectuals of all times must suffer. Knowing too many possibilities they could not accept things as they were. Toynbee has said: ". . . an intelligentsia is born to be unhappy." Yet the American intellectuals had their unique unhappiness. The Europeans could take comfort from acceptance and recognition; the Americans had neither. They existed, ignored or despised, in a country impatient of thought and busy organizing its physical resources. Ezra Pound saw them: ". . . a helpless few, a remnant enslaved, astray, lost in the villages, mistrusted, spoken against. . . ."—and escaped to Europe.

The American intellectuals did not have to call themselves radicals to respond to Vanzetti. Very nearly all of them were liberals, and they could easily sympathize with an idealist in rebellion against the Philistines and Pharisees. Even more, they could identify themselves with him.

The intellectuals had been aware of themselves as a class only since the turn of the century. Looking back from 1927 they could see their brief history as a series of defeats. They had learned to be disillusioned with the progress achieved under Theodore Roosevelt and Woodrow Wilson; they had been helpless against the succeeding waves of reaction. During the war, a gross patriotism had thrown pacifists and Socialists into prison and threatened independent thought. The postwar situation had been bad. Returning veterans had mobbed radicals in the early days and then gone on to join the reactionary American Legion. The Ku Klux Klan, revived in 1916, was growing swiftly and invading the Middle West. Meanwhile, a confused and irritated country rejected the League of Nations and turned its back on Europe. In 1919 the great steel strike was broken, leaving the steelworkers to the twelve-hour day and seven-day week. During the first half of 1920 the Red raids, organized by Attorney General A. Mitchell

Palmer, resulted in the arrest of thousands of radicals and the deportation of about 500 of them. To the intellectuals the increasing prosperity of the twenties was a doubtful palliative. In 1927, the best year of the period, the intellectuals knew that they and the nation deserved better.

One of the intellectuals later tried to put their contribution to the Sacco-Vanzetti case into historical perspective. In the *New Republic* of November 6, 1935, Malcolm Cowley wrote: "There were several new features of the case that stirred the intelligentsia profoundly . . . innocence endangered . . . radicals . . . arrested during the Palmer raids . . . high smugness of Massachusetts officials . . . international interest. . . ." This was not, however, the complete explanation. The intellectuals were more than exponents of social virtue; they were human: "Those were the days . . . when the intellectuals were trying to save their private souls by love and psychoanalysis and running away from the machine age. Their only group manifestations were literary teas; their only political platform was a cocktail tray." But then the Sacco-Vanzetti case called them to something more important. Here was injustice. Here, moreover, was an opportunity to do something about it. In this matter they need not be helpless, as they had been in the face of the physical force of the war or union-busting action. Saving Sacco and Vanzetti, they might save much more.

In 1927 the American intellectuals were united and effective as they had never been before. With the sentencing they would move into full-scale action. Some would use their professional skills in strategic functions: writing editorials, articles, and pamphlets, organizing publicity and making speeches. Others would write letters to the editor, sign protest petitions, and join in demonstrations. And in the next months a number of intellectuals would come to Boston to confront their enemies directly. So much depended on saving Sacco and Vanzetti.

The case left its mark on many of the intellectuals. For John

Dos Passos, it was an important stage in his development as a novelist. The critic Alfred Kazin wrote: "It transformed his growingly irritable but persistently romantic obsession with the poet's struggle against the world into a use of the class struggle as his base in art." In 1927, Dos Passos wrote "Facing the Chair," one of the most widely read pamphlets for the defense, while he would bring the case into his trilogy, *U.S.A.*, as a major episode in the struggle for a better world. About the columnist Heywood Broun, his son, Heywood Hale Broun, said: "The case . . . represented . . . a very definite turning point. It would be overstating the case to say that he made overnight a conscious decision which changed him from a light essayist into a fiery crusader . . . but for the first time he ran into public apathy on a large scale and realized . . . that injustice is not knocked out in one round." In the summer of 1927 Broun would write the angriest and most brilliant articles of the Sacco-Vanzetti case literature, denunciations of Massachusetts authority in the tradition of Zola's "J'accuse" of the Dreyfus case. He would go on to become one of the clearest liberal-radical voices of the depression thirties and also the militant leader of the New York Newspaper Guild. In the case of the two radicals, these two intellectuals, Dos Passos and Broun, gave and received much.

Other intellectuals, who may have been less profoundly affected, were more important in practical matters than the novelist and the newspaperman. Felix Frankfurter, then a Harvard Law School professor, was a leading member of the Sacco-Vanzetti Defense Committee and the author of the most authoritative article on the case. Walter Lippmann, Broun's superior as editor of the *New York Evening World*, would write the most widely influential articles in the form of *World* editorials. And long before 1927 Roger N. Baldwin, executive director of the American Civil Liberties Union, was contributing the A.C.L.U. resources to the cause.

Many of the brightest names of the twenties gave their support in one form or another. There were women like Dorothy Parker, Edna St. Vincent Millay, and the suffragette, Ruth Hale, who was Broun's wife. There were ministers like John Haynes Holmes of New York's Community Church and Rabbi Stephen Wise, professors like Robert Morss Lovett, Arthur M. Schlesinger, and Samuel Eliot Morison, the literary historian Van Wyck Brooks, and the philosopher John Dewey. In the summer months of 1927 they would rouse the world for Sacco and Vanzetti.

Against Sacco and Vanzetti, against the intellectuals and the world, Judge Thayer defended himself coldly on April 9, 1927. They had accused him of having infected the forms of the trial with his prejudice, that without official responsibility for the verdict, he had nevertheless helped guide the jury to it. To this he gave a complete answer that said nothing. He recited the legal fact: "Under the law of Massachusetts the jury says whether a defendant is guilty or innocent. The Court has absolutely nothing to do with that question. The law of Massachusetts provides that a Judge cannot deal in any way with the facts. As far as he can go under our law is to state the evidence." The explanation offered, Thayer turned to Sacco:

"First, the Court pronounces sentence upon Nicola Sacco. It is considered as ordered by the Court that you, Nicola Sacco, suffer the punishment of death by the passage of a current of electricity through your body. . . . This is the sentence of the law.

"It is considered and ordered by the Court that you Bartolomeo Vanzetti—"

Vanzetti shouted: "Wait a minute, please, your Honor. May I speak for a minute with my lawyer, Mr. Thompson?"

After a moment Thayer went on: "I think I should pronounce the sentence—Bartolomeo Vanzetti, suffer the punishment of death—"

Now Sacco leaped to his feet and cried: "You know I am innocent. That is the same words I pronounced seven years ago.

You condemn two innocent men." A ring of police officers closed toward the prisoners' cage and Sacco fell back silent.

Thayer's voice continued evenly: "—by the passage of a current of electricity. . . . This is the sentence of the law.

"We will now take a recess."

The law permits the prisoner to speak freely before he is sentenced. It is a meaningless procedure because the judge listens with his response written out before him. Within the courtroom the speeches of Sacco and Vanzetti had changed nothing. Yet the law does not protect the judge as man against the prisoner as man. We are a democratic country and we accord the unjustly accused full protection as he condemns his judge.

Thayer later permitted himself an informal defense among his friends. In his chambers he denied the accusation of prejudice and insisted again that the trials had been fair. He announced: "I am ready to meet my Maker this minute." He meant every word. Thayer feared God and trusted in his own judgments.

Court had opened at ten o'clock; it was now eleven and Sacco and Vanzetti walked back into the April sun. A week before the sentencing Vanzetti had written to a devoted correspondent: "Another little bit of squishing and of crushing and I will become so sweet and suave to not even demostate at my autopsy. . . ."

2. Moore

THE Sacco-Vanzetti case belonged to the intellectuals. Yet they had only recently discovered it. In fact, they got the force to win the world for the cause from their shocked surprise. In the spring of 1927 the case was seven years old, but for most of the intellectuals it was weeks or months old. Why had they failed to see it earlier?

Begin with the commonplace that need seldom speaks for itself. Someone had to bring the case to the attention of the intellectuals. Few people realized what he had done; fewer people spoke of him now. But the case had once belonged to Fred Moore.

Fred H. Moore was not an intellectual. He was not a man to think deeply about ideas; his way was to recognize an idea quickly and do something with it. He was a lawyer, but the law was only his starting point. No intellectual and no conventional lawyer could have done what Moore did. He made the Sacco-Vanzetti case.

In October 1920, when Moore came into it, the case was a shabby thing about a pair of mute, unknown anarchists. Thousands of radicals were in trouble at the time, but Moore saw Sacco and Vanzetti in 1920 as the intellectuals and the world did not see them until 1927. He saw the idea right away.

Seeing the idea so clearly and dominating the case so absolutely, Moore imposed himself on it to the end, long after he was out of it. His image of the prisoners became the image of the intellectuals and the world. His arguments became the arguments of his successors. The evidence he discovered was mined again in subsequent appeals, while the new evidence was found by following his directions. His witnesses and his experts continued to testify. In 1927 the defense simply fitted on the last links of Moore's logic. Only one new element was added, and the person of Moore, if not his initiative, was responsible for it. In his efforts to save the men he had committed acts which could be criticized. Now in 1927, the defense would argue that Moore's actions had driven Thayer deeper into prejudice, that his incompetent handling of the case had betrayed the innocence of his clients. Through this last humiliation the case belonged to him all the more.

In his late thirties when he entered the case, Moore was a short, stocky, long-jawed Westerner with brown hair running straight back from a sharp widow's peak. He brought with him an air of casualness and prairie-wide freedom that expressed itself in the way he dressed, talked, gestured, and even sat. In a well-buttoned Massachusetts courtroom he was a shirt-sleeved stranger who might take his shoes off. A successful railroad attorney with a brilliant career ahead of him, he had walked out of the office one day to defend a labor union acquaintance; he never came back. From then on he found himself fighting for labor rebels in hostile courtrooms. As a labor lawyer he found the freedom his spirit demanded, wandering about the country to engage himself totally and temporarily in desperate causes. In his private life Moore required the same freedom, going enthusiastically from one attractive woman to the next, spending money hugely when he had it, and freely giving himself day and night to his task or suddenly disappearing for reasons unknown even to himself. He was a rebel with a succession of causes and good times.

Moore's way with women and money is remembered nostalgically or apologetically by his old associates. The old anarchist treasurer of the Sacco-Vanzetti defense group pays tribute to his services—"I'll say this for him, he brought labor into the case"—but shakes his head over the thousands Moore spent. A friend tries to calculate how many times Moore was married: "He was always engaging pretty secretaries, cooling off on the wife he had, and marrying the secretary." The friend adds the detail that the castoffs, wives and unpromoted secretaries, bore Moore and each other no ill will and, indeed, formed a "kind of club." A copy of a letter that Moore carelessly left behind in his office correspondence also gives witness to his method. Apparently written by Lola Darroch, the wife contemporaneous to the Sacco-Vanzetti trial, it began with muted recriminations about money; the writer had evidently not received the promised sum for a legal errand in the West: "As a wife who has her husband's welfare at heart I should naturally have believed your cry of poverty, but unfortunately, Fred, when one is up against it for money one doesn't have theatre parties for several people or have young lady guests in out-of-town cities, nor pay bills for young ladies who desire to attend Art School. . . . The biggest curse that you have been inflicted with is a pleasing personality and a glib tongue."* If this was not enough of a distraction from the needs of the case, his friend recalls that Moore's rebellion would lead to recondite drinking episodes. Moore disappeared at a moment when he was particularly needed and his wife, having already traced the pattern, found him steeped in books in a private library in New York. It was no mere drunk; Moore always ended such fugues with literature. He was no mere rebel.

You go back from 1927, a vintage year of prosperity, to the moment the postwar depression fell upon the country, from Coolidge to the stricken Wilson (right now, in October, Harding and Coolidge are running against Cox and Franklin Roosevelt), from

* Dated December 19, 1922. Sacco-Vanzetti Miscellany. Sacco-Vanzetti Collection, Treasures Room, Harvard Law Library. (See Note on Sources.)

knee-high skirts to skirts around the ankles, from the great speak-easy culture to the early catch-as-catch-can months of Prohibition. You go back to the time when the I.W.W. meant something.

Fred Moore was an I.W.W. lawyer, and the great days of the Industrial Workers of the World were just ending, another of those defeats which the intellectuals would unhappily celebrate. The I.W.W. was a loose federation of Western unions that somehow combined a frontier spirit with a European theory of anarchosyndicalism; it proposed to organize the country into "one big union" that would function without such restraints as policemen or jails. In the years just before the war, the I.W.W. had unionized Western miners and even invaded mill towns in the East against the resistance of feudal business. Both sides in the struggle were bitter and unscrupulous. The war patriotism became another enemy of the I.W.W., and its members, called "Wobblies," were going to jail on loose charges of criminal syndicalism. All this gave Moore rounded experience in a situation where a courtroom was one of several fields for the play of power.

The I.W.W.'s Western tactics were not as irrelevant to Boston as one might think. Actually, both the I.W.W. and Moore had been active in Massachusetts before, the I.W.W. having organized a strike in Lawrence in 1912, with Moore successfully helping out in a trial resulting from it. Although Moore had functioned as investigator, while a local lawyer represented the strike leaders in court, the Lawrence case, which combined such matters as the use of dynamite and the violent death of a working girl, was excellent preparation for the Sacco-Vanzetti defense.

Moore went on to participate in important trials in Kansas and the state of Washington. Before coming to Boston he had been chief defense counsel in an Oklahoma case, where he got an acquittal for a Wobbly accused of dynamiting the home of an oil company official. Later he would write his old client, who had risen to a good union post in Pennsylvania, to ask him to repay the service by supporting Sacco and Vanzetti: "You know that for a long time I was in doubt with reference to yourself, equally for a long time I was in doubt with reference to them. Now I know, and I pledge you my word, that they do not know anything more about this crime than you did about the Pew job."*

When Moore arrived in Boston wearing a Western sombrero, he found a situation as desperate as any he had known. Vanzetti had already been convicted of a lesser crime and sentenced to a long prison term. Together with Sacco he would then stand trial for the payroll murders. The friends of the prisoners, comprising less than a score of local anarchist comrades, were almost helpless. Isolated in Boston, they could, however, call on other anarchists elsewhere, and it was this fact that brought them Moore himself. When they had sought aid in New York, the anarchist leader Carlo Tresca had remembered Moore, an old friend of his, and persuaded him to take the case. As in the I.W.W. cases, Moore could see, there was a tangle of legal and extralegal problems. Whatever the purer elements of justice in the situation of Sacco and Vanzetti, the defense needed everything: money, connections, and publicity. Moore had to work at all three at one time; money meant publicity and connections, connections meant more money and publicity, and publicity meant . . . and so on. The situation was desperate but familiar.

Moore's most important connection was the American Civil Liberties Union. In November the A.C.L.U. leaders listened to a report by a left-wing writer named Mary Heaton Vorse (the publicity element, also; she would write sympathetic articles in national magazines) and gave their cautious support to the defense effort. Roger N. Baldwin, the A.C.L.U. executive director, who happened to be a philosophical anarchist, would give more than official assistance; he would give his personal warmth, and more, his friendship to Vanzetti. Locally, Moore won the interest

* Undated letter, Sacco-Vanzetti Miscellany.

of the New England Civil Liberties Union, and through it, the help of a number of proper Boston ladies: a connection to the power centers in Boston. The brothers, uncles, and cousins of these ladies managed Boston. Among the women was Mrs. Elizabeth Glendower Evans, a member of both the A.C.L.U. and the N.E.C.L.U. and a widow of a Harvard Law classmate of Supreme Court Justice Louis Brandeis. (During much of the crucial period she would live in the Brandeis Boston home.) Thus the civil liberties connection was both local and national. Felix Frankfurter, who had been one of the founders of the A.C.L.U., would also help in both areas, although he did not become active in the case until much later. Meanwhile, Moore had very quickly established effective relations with respectable power.

Of course Moore used his labor connections to the utmost. The American Federation of Labor would have given him enormous strength, but its national leaders were suspicious of both the lawyer and his clients. At its Cincinnati national convention in June 1922 the A.F. of L. passed a resolution asking for a new trial, but this was very nearly the total of its official support. Moore did get more cooperation from second-rank leaders like John Van Vaerenwyck, the vice president of the A.F. of L. Massachusetts branch. Also, A.F. of L. locals, frequently over the opposition of headquarters, contributed money and carried prodefense articles in their newspapers. Moore's I.W.W. did all that it could, but it lacked money, respectability, and power in the right places. From it, however, Moore drew personnel and all kinds of services. Moore's old friend recalled "a number of roughneck Wobblies whom Moore had saved from jail or the noose at various times and who hung around like faithful dogs in the hope of serving him." One Wobbly performed a double function at the Sacco-Vanzetti trial, acting as an assistant for nonlegal tasks and testifying in court about the holdup. In view of the A.F. of L. inhibitions and the I.W.W. weaknesses, Moore's use of organized labor was a brilliant tour de force.

Money was always a critical subject. According to copies of his correspondence in the Harvard Law Library, Moore begged bravely from a wide range of organizations and individuals. He wrote hundreds of letters himself and also charged friends to attempt Sinclair Lewis, Eugene O'Neill, and Walter Lippmann, whom he defined as "good touches." Moore was cheerfully poor when the defense was poor and lightheartedly openhanded when contributions began rising. He did not always make a clear distinction between his account and the cause's, but it was an arrangement that worked both ways.

Moore was acutely aware of the importance of publicity. At the Oklahoma trial he had been helped by a young newspaperman named Eugene Lyons (the old friend cited above, and in recent years a senior editor of the *Reader's Digest*), and he brought Lyons to Boston. Lyons was not surprised to discover that Moore could not pay him, but he was an idealistic socialist; he got a job on a Boston newspaper to support himself. Sometimes he stood by silently as his city editor threw away a press release he had written for the defense. Besides Lyons, Moore had another socialist journalist, John Nicholas Beffel, on his publicity staff, and a Beffel article appearing in the *New Republic* of December 29, 1920, was one of the first writings in a national publication. Week after week Moore's writers sent out releases offering new details, correcting negative impressions, and reminding a distracted country about the outcasts who were experiencing Massachusetts justice.

All this was not in the area of legal operations, but Moore was more than a lawyer. He was, to use a fair approximation in one word, a promoter. He was more. Combining connections, money, and publicity, he could move men and circumstances physically. He was a wielder of power.

Moore was an idealist, but one after his own fashion. Ideals needed stern protection in the world of the I.W.W. Lyons told me: "Moore had no conscience once he decided his client was innocent. He would stop at nothing, frame evidence, suborn witnesses, have his people work on witnesses who had seen the wrong things—I pity anyone he went after." Moore's I.W.W. assistants were appropriate to these tactics, as Lyons has related in his book, *Assignment in Utopia*. After describing their doglike loyalty, he added: "These latter were not too fastidious about the nature of their service, nor was Moore himself too finickey." Lyons goes on: "But Fred Moore saw [the Sacco-Vanzetti case's] magnitude from the start. His legal tactics have been the subject of dispute and recrimination. I think there is some color of truth, indeed, to the charge that he sometimes subordinated the literal needs of legalistic procedures to the larger needs of the case as a symbol of class struggle. If he had not done so, Sacco and Vanzetti would have died six years earlier, without the solace of martyrdom."

Moore's skills won the admiration of Upton Sinclair, who described them under a thin fictional veil in his novel, *Boston*, the most explicit fictional treatment of the case. Sinclair obviously approved of what Moore did to thwart the defenders of the capitalistic system, but he realized that the world might not understand hard proletarian necessity. Accordingly, he created one Lee Swenson as the man who carries out the questionable acts of the real Moore and later inserted a pale character named Moore who does nothing untoward in the novel. Sinclair's Swenson talks about the Lawrence trial: "I could name several laws of your great Commonwealth we broke in putting that job across. . . ." Swenson is a good journalistic likeness of Moore.

The testimony, factual or fictional, of Lyons and Sinclair cannot be submitted as proof of Moore's actions. It is a fact, however, that his labor connections, his I.W.W. associates, and his Boston anarchists gave him real and even frightening power. This was evident in the case of George T. Kelley, superintendent of the plant where Sacco had worked, who tried to back out of a statement that tended to incriminate Sacco. At the trial Kelley admitted having said to the investigating officers: "I have my own opinion . . . but I don't want a bomb up my ass." The record indicates that some people *thought* that Moore and his associates could hurt them.

Moore's actions within the legal area itself occasionally betrayed the fact that he put more emphasis elsewhere. At times he permitted his witnesses to say things that were better left unsaid, and he appears not to have prepared himself too well in some technical matters. Nevertheless, as Lyons said, Moore got the point of the case and built the best possible defense around it. The point was radicalism.

The point had its legal and extralegal uses. First, it was the central element in the logic of the defense case. Thus Sacco and Vanzetti had been acting in a strange fashion on the evening of their arrest, and if they could not explain their actions as part of their radical activities, the jury could be brought to see them as fitting into payroll robbery operations. This was discouragingly evident in Vanzetti's first trial, where his lawyer, deciding that radicalism was too risky a subject, had excluded it entirely. The strategy had failed, but there was no reason to suppose that a reversal of it would work. Audacious but not foolhardy, Moore believed that it would: the chance had to be taken. In the final review of the case in 1927, one of Moore's lawyer associates, while criticizing him for his effect on Judge Thayer, agreed that the strategy was correct. After the lawyer had mentioned the radical activities of Sacco and Vanzetti, he was asked: "Do you mean by this, that if the radical purposes of the prisoners don't account for their conduct, there would be no question of their being innocent?" He replied: "There wouldn't be any defense in my mind. No explanation." The issue was not as clear as that when the trial began, but Moore saw it well enough.

Moore would go much further than offer an explanation within the limits of the case logic. At best, that would mean canceling out one prosecution argument. His opponent would have other weapons, and Moore meant to disarm all of them. A reporter who covered the trial heard the prosecutor's complaint at one point that Sacco was memorizing a radical speech written for him by Moore: Moore would rub in radicalism. He would make the issue of radicalism so clear and hard that Massachusetts justice would be forced to retreat from its prejudices in the face of national opinion. With his publicity operations, he would make sure that everybody knew what was going on. We recall Vanzetti's words at the sentencing: ". . . and if there is a reason why I am here as a guilty man . . . it is this reason and no one else." The reason and the issue were radicalism.

Moore almost succeeded. He gave four years of his life to the attempt. Through his failure, he lifted the Sacco-Vanzetti case into American history.

3. The Beginning

HOW could it have happened? Later faultfinding to the contrary, Moore had been able enough. With his allies and his use of publicity, with his power, he should have succeeded. Why was Boston so stubborn about killing this pair of outcasts?

A good answer requires facts, and the moment of the sentencing is far from the facts. The facts go back beyond Moore. From 1927 they go beyond 1920, when Moore arrived, back into 1919.

In 1919, in the backwash of the war, the nation was experiencing odd crimes and violences. There was a police strike in Boston, which Coolidge broke so skilfully that he won the Republican vice-presidential nomination. In California forty-six Wobblies were convicted on charges arising out of the dynamiting of the governor's home. About that time a score of bombs, presumably of anarchist origin, were mailed to such prominent Americans as Justice Oliver Wendell Holmes, J. P. Morgan, and Attorney General Palmer. Sixteen of them were stopped by a mail clerk, but another went to a Georgia senator, blowing off the hands of his Negro maid. In still another initiative thirteen bombs were delivered personally to other addresses, including Palmer's home, where one of them damaged the building and annihilated the bearer. Among these events an attempted robbery in Massachusetts on the day before Christmas was hardly noticed.

It occurred in Bridgewater, some twenty-five miles south of Boston. With a population of 8,000, Bridgewater was the peaceful center of an area specializing in poultry and dairy products. What kind of criminals would have selected Bridgewater for their operations? Where might they have come from?

At 7:20 A.M. an early rising college student saw a large automobile halt by his house without apparent purpose and drive away as mysteriously a few minutes later. After a few minutes more, a housewife, who was walking to the railroad station with her five-year-old son, crossed Broad Street near the station and noticed a large Buick directly in front of her. She later remembered that the driver had been watching her intently in a manner she described as "very severe." Whatever his thoughts might have been, they were directed toward the arrival, occurring after a few more minutes had gone by, of the payroll truck of the L. Q. White Company, a shoe manufacturer.

At perhaps 7:40 A.M. the truck, carrying a safe with $33,113.31, appeared on Broad Street and advanced in the direction of the parked Buick. In the truck were Earle Graves, twenty-four, the driver, Benjamin F. Bowles, forty-seven, a Bridgewater policeman, and Alfred E. Cox, Jr., the paymaster. The Buick then started up and swung left in face of the oncoming vehicle, turning into a cross street and parking at the corner immediately after having made the turn. Leaving the driver and perhaps another man in the car, three men descended, one of them carrying a shotgun and the other two armed with pistols. The action was joined.

It was a low comedy in the style of the slapstick movies which were then becoming popular. The weather had been cold and the street was slippery. The shotgunner began running, promptly lost his balance and his slouch hat, and fell on hands and knees. One of the pistol-bearers nearly fell. As the paymaster Cox later recalled: "He had one hand in the air and the other hand as though he did not know where it was himself. The hand with the revolver was up in the air."

The shotgunner scrabbled to his feet hatless and, running, shouted, "Stop!" and fired a first blast.

The guard Bowles responded: "What do we want to stop for?"

The shotgunner shouted another "Stop!" He was shooting at the truck, Bowles later recalled, and not directly at him and he had a "stary look in his eyes, a glary look," while his hair, freed of his hat, "stuck up a little on top."

The senseless interchange of words between attackers and attacked continued. Bowles retorted to the second "Stop!" with "Nothing doing," and shouted to the driver Graves, "Step on the gas!" One of the other assailants, a cap pulled over his ears, was also firing his pistol, and it seemed to Bowles that this man, unlike the shotgunner, was aiming directly at him.

As the shotgunner ran, he passed a pedestrian, a salesman named Frank W. Harding, at a distance of three or four feet. Observing the melodramatic actions, Harding thought he had indeed walked into the middle of a film scene. Who would shoot anyone in Bridgewater? In any case, remaining rapt with the problem of the moving payroll truck, the holdup men paid no attention to the unengaged stranger, nor to a fourteen-year-old newsboy who was observing everything with an interest natural for his age.

With the paymaster Cox also urging him on, the driver Graves accelerated his vehicle and passed by the shotgunner at a distance of ten to fifteen feet. Cox later recalled the "scared expression" of the man and the bright blaze issuing from the shotgun muzzle. At that moment a new defense for the embattled payroll truck appeared in the form of a streetcar, which had preceded the truck down Broad Street and was now halted near the scene. Graves had the wit or desperation to swerve the truck to the left of the streetcar as he drove past the attackers. Thus protected by the streetcar bulk, the truck sped on down Broad Street away from the point of attack. Optimistically or despairingly, the shotgunner launched new salvos after the vehicle but he had not improved his aim. The driver Graves and the policeman Bowles disagreed about the subsequent action. Graves, who died in February 1920, deposed that Bowles had grabbed the wheel in his fright. Bowles claimed that the driver had slipped to the floor and released the wheel, leaving him to guide it with a desperate left hand. In any case the truck slewed off the road and crashed into a tree. Here, suddenly, was a new opportunity for the holdup men.

But, maintaining their incompetence to the end, the assailants clambered into the Buick, which started off down the cross street and disappeared. The episode ended in no casualties and trivial damage.

And that is all there was to it: a crime so incompetent that it was harmless. Yet, to the police, that itself suggested an unpleasant threat. Here was no professional crime pattern that might lead to the discovery of the holdup men or the taking of anticipatory measures. The dangerous fools might strike anywhere, any time.

Meanwhile Attorney General Palmer, obliged to do something about the anarchist bombings, countered with the Red raids. There were two preliminary raiding operations in 1919, on November 7 and December 29. Then, on January 2, 1920, a climactic raid gathered in 2,500 persons in 33 cities, including 16 Massachusetts communities—Boston and Bridgewater among them—and more raids were carried out during the first half of 1920. Palmer's objective was to prevent future bombings by arresting and deporting radical aliens. This wholesale approach was obviously inefficient, and on September 16, 1920, a bomb exploded across from the J. P. Morgan offices in New York's financial district, killing 34 and injuring 130 persons. The authorities were being harassed by conservative citizens demanding more effective police action and by liberals citing violations of civil liberties. It was a disorderly period of senseless crimes, police brutality, and unresolved irritations.

The Bridgewater crime was followed by a more earnest affair in

South Braintree, which is fifteen miles north of Bridgewater. At 8:15 on Thursday morning, April 15, 1920, a coal wagon driver sees a strange Buick and another, smaller, and equally strange automobile. He thinks little of them. Yet today is payday for the 400 employees of the Slater & Morrill shoe factory, and the Bridgewater holdup occurred less than four months ago. Shelley A. Neal, the American Railway Express agent, has less excuse for his little thought. He should have seen a connection between the strange Buick manned by rough-looking men and his duty to receive the payroll money. Indeed, when he is returning from the 9:18 train laden with $30,000 comprising the payrolls of two factories, he takes particular note of the appearance of the vehicle's driver. Neal later testified: "He struck me as a man who had either been through some severe sickness or under a great strain." In fact, Neal is brushed by a presentiment that something is going to happen, but nothing does, and he fails to mention his suspicion.

Located ten miles south southeast of Boston, Braintree with East and South Braintree had a population of 10,000 in 1920. Although it had two shoe manufactories—the Rice & Hutchins Company as well as Slater & Morrill—it could not be called a factory town; it was then and remains today, despite the doubling of population, a pleasant country town. Time has treated it casually, and most of the structures important to this narrative are still there: the minuscule railroad station, now inoperative, the lower Slater & Morrill plant building, and the neighboring Rice & Hutchins building, the latter two now under the sign of the Atlantic Abrasive Company. Enough, thus, of the scene remains to suggest now what was true more than a generation ago, that South Braintree was most inappropriate to robbery and murder.

Had the holdup men acted at the first moment, when Neal received the money shipment, they would have been rewarded with both payrolls. A moment after he entered his office, in the upper Slater & Morrill building across Railroad Avenue from the railroad station, Neal heard the Buick start up and he dismissed his apprehensions as he separated out the money. But the vehicle and its occupants, having again blundered into notice while failing the best opportunity, compounded their incompetence by arousing notice again and again throughout the morning and early afternoon. Remaining unscathed by active suspicion, their progress was plotted in this wise:

After 10 in the morning, Harry E. Dolbeare, a South Braintree piano tuner, saw a large automobile with five men in it driving about town. He particularly noticed one of the back-seat passengers, a man with a mustache. Asked at the trial what had caught his attention, he said: "I hardly know how to express myself. I know how I felt at the time. I felt it was a tough-looking bunch."

After 11 A.M., Mrs. Lola R. Andrews of Quincy, a woman with a past who called herself a practical nurse, saw a large automobile and two men in front of the lower Slater & Morrill building. One of the men was sitting in the back seat and the other was bending over the hood, apparently trying to repair the motor. Mrs. Andrews, who was looking for work, spent an unproductive quarter of an hour in the S. & M. plant and, on departing, found the presumed mechanic in the act of crawling out from under the automobile. At this moment she took the opportunity to ask the man where she could find the factory office. Inasmuch as she had just emerged from the lower S. & M. factory office, she evoked the counter-question: what factory did she mean, the S. & M.? No, she had just been there, she meant the Rice & Hutchins office. The man obligingly indicated the R. & H. plant just a few feet up Pearl Street.

At about 11:40 A.M. William S. Tracy, a South Braintree real estate dealer, saw two rough-looking men, one of them leaning against the front of the Torrey drug store on Pearl Street. His concern rendered acute because he owned the building, he drove past the drug store three times and took specific note of the men.

About noontime, William J. Heron of Cambridge, a railroad

police officer, was occupied with a loiterer who had made trouble at the station newsstand. Heron failed to concern himself actively with a lesser misdemeanor. At the trial, he testified that he had noticed a man smoking against the rules. The man, he said, was speaking Italian with a companion and both seemed nervous.

It was a lovely spring day, sunny and breezy. At about three o'clock Frederick A. Parmenter, the Slater & Morrill paymaster, and Alessandro Berardelli, the guard, entered the office in the upper S. & M. building, across from the railroad station. Parmenter, forty-four, had been with the firm for twenty years and also functioned as its chief bookkeeper. For six months a Braintree resident, he had previously lived in Avon, six miles to the southwest, where he had been a prominent citizen and a member of the Board of Selectmen. He had a wife, Hattie, a son, Richard, ten, and a daughter, Jeanette, eight. Berardelli, twenty-eight, was also married and the father of two children, Michael, seven, and Ida, five. Ill for three or four days, he had returned to work only today. But his daughter Ida was sick with scarlet fever in the Homeopathic Contagious Hospital in Brighton, a Boston suburb, and Berardelli's wife, Sarah, had sent Michael off to school and then gone to the hospital to see Ida. Two small-town family men on a routine day.

Margaret Mahoney, Parmenter's office assistant, had the payroll money, S. & M.'s $15,775.51 out of the total of $30,000 received, ready for him. The money was in two metal boxes, each weighing about five pounds, 24 by 12 by 8 inches in size, Parmenter and Berardelli each carrying a box. Parmenter was apparently unarmed; despite defense efforts to contest the point, Berardelli must have been armed but he carelessly carried the box in his shooting hand. The men sauntered from the upper S. & M. building the few feet to Pearl Street, turned left, and walked down Pearl Street and across the tracks. Parmenter took the time to stop James P. Bostock, an S. & M. millwright, and tell him to repair a pulley in the lower S. & M. plant. This was the end of the afternoon's innocence.

When Parmenter and Berardelli had about fifty yards to go to reach their destination, the lower S. & M. plant, they approached two men in dark clothes, who were leaning against a fence in front of the Rice & Hutchins building. Paymaster and guard were walking on the right side of Pearl Street and both buildings were on their right, while across the street, facing the R. & H. building, a group of Italian laborers were working on an excavation for a new restaurant. A double-horse team that had been bringing material to the job was waiting at the excavation, and two automobiles were down by the lower S. & M. building. One was the strange Buick and two men were with it, apparently still engaged in making repairs or adjustments. Lewis Wade, an S. & M. shoe worker who was also in charge of the company gasoline supplies, was filling up the other automobile, the property of the plant owner. The action began at 3:05 P.M. After speaking to Bostock, Parmenter had moved on ten or fifteen yards with Berardelli. At that moment the paymaster and guard were opposite the lower corner of the R. & H. building. One of the dark-clad men, who had moved from their position by the fence, initiated a new dialogue following the exchange between Parmenter and Bostock. The man spoke to Berardelli, who may have recognized him as an acquaintance, and he seemed to put a hand on Berardelli's shoulder. Pistol shots sounded.

Bostock started for the scene. It seemed to him that Berardelli knew the men and was begging them not to shoot him. John E. McGlone, the teamster on the excavation job, shouted: "Look out, look out!" The laborers scattered and dodged into the excavation. Carlos E. Goodridge, a salesman with a police history, was playing pool in a Pearl Street poolroom on the other side of the tracks beyond the upper S. & M. building; he stepped out on the street when he heard the shots. Mary E. Splaine, an S. & M. bookkeeper, ignoring the shots and the excited announcement of another employee, "There's a shooting!," went on working. Louis Pelser, 22, a Jewish shoecutter in the Rice & Hutchins plant, was at work by a window that overlooked the scene from a distance of seven feet. Opening the window after he heard three shots, he had the presence of mind to take down the crime automobile's license number accurately, despite the fact that one of the holdup men fired two shots just above that window. Berardelli had been struck in that first moment. He dropped into a crouching position, a hand vainly waving about. One witness thought the guard was trying to protect his head against the bullets; another thought he was trying to pull out his revolver. In another act a moment afterward, a holdup man fired two shots at Bostock as he was approaching. Bostock prudently turned around and ran back toward the railroad tracks.

At the first spate of shooting Parmenter dropped the money box and began to run across Pearl Street. Before the paymaster got more than a step or two away from the group he was struck in the back. He staggered across Pearl Street, one hand pressed against his back, and fell near the double-horse team.

A third holdup man, carrying a rifle or shotgun, had materialized near the scene, perhaps brought there by the smaller automobile. One of the men attacking Berardelli signaled down Pearl Street and the two men who had remained with the Buick jumped into the vehicle, which started slowly up the street.

Some witnesses reported a senseless crisscross of action. The rifleman or shotgunner seems to have fired at the fallen Parmenter and then moved toward Berardelli, firing then at the guard. The victims, however, suffered nothing but pistol wounds. Meanwhile one of the original shooting pair followed Parmenter across the street, counter to his colleague's course, and fired another shot into the paymaster. At the same time the other member of the pair, his cap falling to the ground, continued shooting at Berardelli.

All the marksmen were inaccurate. Estimates of the number of shots fired at the victims ranged from twelve to twenty, but the inquest established the fact that only six hit the mark. Additionally, several shots were fired at the bystanders, probably without specific intent to kill or wound.

The Buick with its two men had now pulled up by the engaged group. First, the killer who had remained by Berardelli picked up the money box the guard had dropped and lifted it into the vehicle. (A trial defense witness remembered he saw a shiny weapon in the man's left hand as he swung the box with his right, and the prosecution theorized that this was Berardelli's revolver, which was not found at the crime scene.) Then one of the other holdup men put Parmenter's money box into the Buick, and all three got in. The automobile continued up Pearl Street with its five holdup men.

Michael Levangie, the one-legged gate-tender, had just let down the gate in anticipation of a train arrival. One of the men pointed a gun at his head and shouted: "Up, up!" He fired at Levangie, who raised the gate as fast as he could while bullets whistled past his head. Keeping in memory the mustache of one of the gunmen, Levangie plunged into the protection of the gate-tender's shack, but the assailants were no longer interested in him. In the office of the upper S. & M. building, Mary Splaine yielded to the curiosity she had suppressed and went to the window, which was about twenty yards from the track crossing. She arrived in time to see the holdup men threaten Levangie; another bookkeeper, Frances J. Devlin, also saw the approach of the Buick. Further up Pearl Street, Goodridge, the pool-playing salesman, watched the vehicle advance toward him until it got close enough for one of the gunmen to take umbrage specifically at him. The man waved his pistol at Goodridge, and the salesman ran back into the poolroom.

Its motor running irregularly, as if a cylinder or two were dead, the Buick was still moving slowly as it bumped over the tracks and continued westward along Pearl Street. It was a seven-passenger touring car with a canvas top, and one of the curtains on the left side was loose and flapped as the vehicle jounced along. A rifle or shotgun barrel projected through the rear window.

Berardelli was still in a crouching position when Bostock got back to him. At the trial the millwright remembered: "I wiped his mouth out, and he lay in my arm, and as he lay in my arm, I thought he died in my arm." But the guard had another few moments of life and he was moved, the blood welling out of his mouth, into a house on Pearl Street just beyond the excavation, where he died. The medical examiner found four .32 caliber bullets in his body: in the lung, in the chest below the left nipple, inside the hip bone on the left side, and low in the bowel muscle. The last bullet had a vertical track, apparently having been fired while Berardelli was crouching. It had entered the body near the shoulder blade, cut through the large vein at mid-body and continued through the intestines. It was defined as the fatal bullet, although one other bullet might also have had fatal effect.

Parmenter was first carried to the house where the guard died and then taken to the Quincy Hospital. The bullet that had entered his back at the belt line went straight through the body, tearing open a wound in the abdomen. The other bullet penetrated the left side of his chest and lodged in the vena cava, the large vein that brings blood to the right atrium—chamber—of the heart. A vena cava wound is invariably fatal, but Parmenter regained consciousness in the hospital and cheerfully made convalescence plans. He died at 4:45 the next morning.

The active Bostock performed one more service relevant to the case's history. Noticing four empty shells ejected from the killer's pistol, he picked them up and gave them to Thomas Fraher, the S. & M. superintendent. Fraher passed on the shells, which were unfairly entitled the "Fraher shells" at the trial and appeals, to the head of the State Police.

The gang's shooting pattern would seem to be indicated partially by the inquest findings. Three of the four bullets in Berardelli and both bullets in Parmenter came from a .32 Savage automatic. The other bullet in Berardelli, the fatal one that had cut through his body from shoulder to bowel, came from a .32 Colt automatic. Thus the one reasonably competent marksman, although he also wasted shots, was the man with a Savage, who had fired three shots into the guard and one into Parmenter during the first moments. It would be the Savage man who followed Parmenter across Pearl Street to give him the coup de grace near the horse team. Meanwhile the rifleman or shotgunner went vainly from Parmenter to Berardelli, while the member of the original shooting pair continued firing at the guard, losing his cap in the process. The result of this last action was just one bullet, the fatal Colt bullet.

Moving along Pearl Street, the Buick picked up speed as the motor apparently consented to work properly. Beyond South Braintree, its flight was plotted by seven witnesses; their descriptions of the Buick—size, color, flapping curtain, and its passengers—agreed so well that there was no serious doubt that they were observing the same automobile. Scattering and gathering dust, it made a rough half circle around Brockton, five miles south of South Braintree, in a little more than an hour. It was last seen in Matfield Crossing, which is a mile or two north of Bridgewater.

The Buick arriving at the crossing almost simultaneously with a train, the crossing tender, Austin T. Reed, put up his stop sign. Although the automobile had no gate in its path, the train reinforced Reed's official warning. Nevertheless one of the men shouted to him, Reed testified at the trial: "What to hell I was holding him up for?" When the train had passed, the impatient man reiterated: "What to hell did you hold us up for?" The Buick plunged over the tracks, went a short distance and swung around. Back in three minutes, the driver having reconsidered his direction, it recrossed the tracks and disappeared in the direction of West Bridgewater, whence it had come.

I was discussing the case on a spring day in 1958 with Robert E. Riordan, city editor of the *Brockton Enterprise-Times.* While we were talking, Charles L. Fuller, the newspaper's publisher, lay dying in a Brockton hospital. Fuller and a friend, Max E. Wind, a

Brockton leather merchant, had been out riding on Saturday, April 17, thirty-eight years before. That day they found the Buick in Manley Woods in the northerly part of West Bridgewater; it was resting on an unfrequented path just over the Brockton line and about a mile from Matfield Crossing, where it had last been sighted during its looping flight. It had arrived at a point but eight miles distant from the South Braintree start in its tour of thirty to forty miles.

At that moment the Buick represented more unknowns than information. The dusty vehicle yielded up to curiosity a loose-hanging window curtain, a shabby fur robe, and a few coins, but no license plates. Near it, however, police found the tracks of another vehicle, which could lead, if nowhere geographically, to some possibly useful conjectures. Was this vehicle, for example, the companion automobile of the crime day? Might it be insouciantly driving about the public ways? But, for the moment, theory had little supporting substance besides the Buick, which had been stolen five months previously from an honorable citizen, and a phantom vehicle or two.

The new crime was worth front page headlines for a day or two. Unlike the Bridgewater affair, although equally inept, it had been a success, and the death of two men had given it point. Another twenty days, however, would go by before any new facts could attempt to explain it. Still more time would be required to give the crime a character more distinguished than that provided by money and death.

Brown Brothers

Nicola Sacco

Brown Brothers

Bartolomeo Vanzetti

Wide World

Judge
Webster B.
Thayer

Wide World

Governor
Alvan T.
Fuller

Wide World

Doctor A.
Lawrence
Lowell

Wide World

The death watch: this crowd gathered in Union Square, New York, a few hours before Sacco and Vanzetti were executed

Wide World

The funeral procession (part of which is shown here): a silent cortege escorted the bodies through eight miles of Boston's streets, while thousands looked on

Wide World

London: a crowd estimated at 10,000 in a memorial demonstration in Trafalgar Square, during which a spectator tore down an American flag

Wide World

Buenos Aires: a crowd in the Plaza del Congreso protests the execution of Sacco and Vanzetti

Wide World

Memorial meeting in Union Square, New York: the miniature tomb was intended for the ashes of Sacco and Vanzetti, which did not arrive

American Heritage

Ballistics evidence that Sacco's pistol was in action at the South Braintree crime scene. This is a composite photograph of a shell found at the scene (*left*) and a test shell (*right*) fired in Sacco's pistol. Every pistol leaves distinctive markings like these scratchy lines imprinted at the moment of explosion by the breechblock and the characteristic indentation of its firing pin. Note the similarity of these markings—as if this were a single shell and not two different ones.

4. A Detective Story

IN their first efforts to solve the mystery, police and Pinkerton detectives found nothing except the Buick's legitimate owner and useless rumors. Chance, however, produced an interesting lead.

On April 16, the day after the holdup, Police Chief Michael E. Stewart of Bridgewater received a telephone call concerning an anarchist named Ferrucio Coacci, whom he had arrested two years previously on behalf of the Federal Immigration Service. Charged with advocating the violent overthrow of the government, Coacci was subject to deportation as an alien. Indeed, Stewart had assumed that the man had long since returned to Italy, but Coacci had secured a postponement from the authorities until the day before, the memorable April 15. He had failed to appear, however, and now, a day late, he had called the Immigration Service with the excuse that his wife was ill. Conventionally suspicious, the immigration officer thereupon called Stewart to ask his company when he personally verified the Coacci explanation that evening. To Stewart this was the revival of a routine matter, as unimportant now as it had been two years ago when the man was one of a half dozen shabby aliens he had obligingly detained for the federal officers. Stewart had another, pleasanter engagement that evening, and he resolved the matter by detailing his night patrolman to receive the immigration man, an Inspector Root.

It was, of course, no surprise to discover, as Inspector Root and Night Patrolman Frank LeBaron did, that Coacci had been lying: his wife was not at all ill. The surprise occurred when Coacci showed himself entirely content to be found out and, in consequence, made subject to immediate deportation. Furthermore, the unpredictable anarchist insisted upon it to the personal inconvenience of Inspector Root. The Inspector lived in Wollaston, south of Boston, and he had been planning to go home directly from West Bridgewater. He would have much preferred to let Coacci report to the Boston office on his own initiative. The anarchist prevailed and achieved his deportation on April 18. It was, on the face of it, a ridiculous story.

Stewart gave the matter some thought and on April 20, two days after Coacci's departure from the United States, undertook a visit himself to the man's residence. Accompanied by Lieutenant Albert Brouillard of the State Police, he was agreeably surprised to find someone there. The suspicions, justified too late in regard to Coacci, might just possibly be redirected toward this small man with a gaunt face, prominent aquiline nose, small dark mustache, and deep-set hazel eyes. Introducing himself as Mike Boda, he talked freely, volunteering the fact that Coacci's wife had left earlier that day. He also announced that he himself did not like Coacci, who, he said, had "bad" friends. It was rather a strange statement since Boda said he himself had persuaded the Coaccis to rent the house with him the previous November. If Coacci's case was confusing, Boda was also a problem.

Stewart received an untidy number of statements and impressions. Besides Boda's past, which was well worth studying along with Coacci's, one might deeply ponder the man's admission, cheerfully substantiated, of the ownership of a .32 caliber Spanish automatic, as well as the presence in a desk drawer of the manufacturer's diagram of a Savage automatic pistol. In addition, the interest of the officers was aroused by an empty garage, which had room for two automobiles, and by two sets of tracks indicating that the garage had indeed sheltered two vehicles of different sizes. Boda, however, would admit to the existence of just one autombile, his 1914 Oakland, which was under repair at Johnson's garage here in West Bridgewater. An Oakland was no Buick and the extra set of tracks might be explained by an innocent coincidence, but, on the other hand, a smaller vehicle had been seen at South Braintree in action apparently connected with that of the Buick. Furthermore, an extra set of tracks was clearly evident near the Buick's resting place in Manley Woods. On the basis of all this, Stewart was tempted to arrest Boda, but he was on doubtful ground, since West Bridgewater was not in his Bridgewater jurisdiction and, also, since the man had done nothing overt. Forced by his logic to eliminate arrest, Stewart applied the best alternative, friendliness, as a means of damping Boda's possible fears. Frustrated, the officers left.

Stewart persisted on the dim trail. Boda had, for example, defined himself as a salesman; in truth, as Stewart discovered, he was a bootlegger's delivery man, and more interestingly, a former employee of the L. Q. White Company. When Stewart added these facts to another discovery—that Coacci had worked for both victim plants—he went back to revisit Boda two days after the initial acquaintance. But Boda was gone. Indeed, the furniture and all possessions had also disappeared.

Stewart was left to his thoughts. Two men had slipped through the law's fingers, but one of them, at least, had left an idea and a material object behind. The Oakland existed, as Stewart was able to confirm with a simple inquiry at the Johnson garage. He could reasonably trust that the owner would try to claim the vehicle, and Stewart impressed on Johnson his interest in the Oakland's owner and his desire to be informed upon that owner's expected reappearance. An Oakland was surely no Buick, but the Boda-Coacci garage was roomy, and the phantom satellite of the Buick was still to be hauled back into reality. It would be a vast satisfaction to tie the Bridgewater and South Braintree crimes into a single loop of arrest and conviction.

The events of May 5, less than two weeks after Stewart set his trap, resulted in new confusions. Boda had indeed reappeared at the Johnson garage on North Elm Street in West Bridgewater to claim his Oakland, but that little man had again showed his capacity for ricocheting against the law without getting caught in it. Stewart had been patient, and now he had to content himself with the strange fruit of his theory. For the police arrested two men on the evening of Wednesday, May 5, who were neither Coacci nor Boda.

Ruth Corinne Johnson, who was only twenty-one, must have been frightened by the knock on the door of her West Bridgewater home at 9:20 P.M. She opened the door to Boda, a larger, intimidating companion, and two other dim figures. She recognized Boda, who had been at the garage perhaps a dozen times since last summer, but a sum of four roughly clad men was a magnitude that made cooperating with the police an act of heroism. Boda, normally dressed with vain care and now uncharacteristically shabby, announced that he had come for the Oakland. According to plan, Ruth Johnson called her husband, indicating that he would handle this business matter, and Simon Johnson talked to the men, who remained grouped about the door. The Johnsons noticed a motorcycle with a sidecar, which doubtless had brought two of the men, but the transport facility of the other two was unexplained.

Johnson told Boda that it would be best not to take the vehicle because it had no license plates. Boda insisted, and a friendly debate spun out. Ruth Johnson, meanwhile, having taken a milk pail as an excuse, went out the front door past the group and walked toward the neighbor's house sixty feet up the street to telephone the police. Two of the men apparently did not believe that she was going to fetch milk and drifted along behind her, she testified at the trials. (She later remembered that she had heard the word, "telephone," in the pair's private Italian interchange.) At the neighbor's house Ruth Johnson carried out the plan and called the police while Simon Johnson was countering Boda's insistence by suggesting that the group wait until his wife returned. Boda finally said that it was too late and got into the sidecar, his companion swinging into the saddle and starting up the engine. By this time Ruth Johnson was approaching, the two men still behind her. The motorcycle drove off, leaving the two others to the devices that had brought them to the Johnson place. They walked away, Johnson following them at a distance and observing them board the Bridgewater-Brockton streetcar. Chief Stewart arrived to find all quarry gone, but he telephoned the Brockton police for help, and two policemen, Earl J. Vaughn and Michael J. Connolly, boarded the streetcar in the Campello section of Brockton. The looseness of events pulled tight about two strange Italians. Two dim figures in a sparsely occupied country streetcar at ten o'clock of a mild spring evening—the beginning, now in 1920, of the agony of Nicola Sacco and Bartolomeo Vanzetti.

5. Before Moore

THE period after the arrest remains dim. Out of it emerges, only half-formed, the figure of one of the two men. Bartolomeo Vanzetti will always take the lead over Nicola Sacco.

John Beffel's *New Republic* article, appearing at the end of the year, informed the intellectuals that "Mob temper was high. They were hooted and jeered." This report, however, had no basis in ascertainable fact. Actually, the local citizenry had received news of the arrest with indifference and failed to express opinions loud enough to be noted by any other observer. The local and Boston press reported the arrest with appropriate headlines as a criminal matter of some moment and then dropped it. While one Boston newspaper did make a casual reference to anarchist associates three days after the arrest, it did not go any further with the subject, nor did it attempt to connect the arrest to the current Red raids. The early period of the Sacco-Vanzetti case was accepted by newspaper readers on nonpolitical terms. If anarchism was an issue, only the anarchists seemed aware of it.

Looking back, Beffel had tried to infuse the arrest with political connotations. Against this, the arresting officers would put the prisoners in a light emphasizing possible criminality. At least, according to the police reports, Sacco and Vanzetti had acted like dangerous men. The officers testified that both men had made moves to pull out hidden armament. In the streetcar, the officers then discovered that Vanzetti was carrying a fully loaded .38 caliber revolver. In the police station they searched him and also found four twelve-gauge shotgun shells, which inspired new interest because of the shotgun observed at the holdups. Sacco, the officers said, had to be twice warned to keep his hands away from his coat, but they failed to search him until they got to the station. There they found a loaded .32 Colt automatic pistol tucked into his trouser waistband and, in his pocket, twenty-three loose pistol cartridges. We are not, however, obliged to believe the police against the explicit denials of both prisoners that they had tried to pull out their weapons. This is just one of many questions that must be left unresolved. There will be greater ones.

In any case the police had good grounds for holding the men. What were they doing with guns? What was their connection with the ambiguous Boda? All this need have nothing to do with subversive political ideas, but the matter insisted on breaking out of the narrow frame of payroll robbery. For the officers found in Sacco's pocket a notice, actually written by Vanzetti, which announced an anarchist protest meeting to be held in Brockton the following Sunday, May 9. When Police Chief Stewart arrived at the station that evening, he found himself faced with the question: Had he achieved the arrest of criminality or radicalism? The confusions were persistent.

The armament and the anarchist notice established the two major themes of the questions addressed to the prisoners. Indeed, their examiners tried to trip them by an artful reversal of emphasis, pretending more interest in anarchism than in weapons, but Sacco and Vanzetti responded to these subtle distinctions with a totality of denials that compounded a great many lies, as they later admitted. They began by denying that they were anarchists and that they knew Boda. Vanzetti, for his part, lied about the length of time he had known Sacco, the date he left his home before the arrest, the acquisition of his revolver, and his relation to the motorcycle that had borne Boda away from the Johnson garage. Sacco said he had not heard of the South Braintree crime and refused to admit that he possessed a pistol permit. What could you do with prisoners who denied a great many facts that were not only easily ascertainable but also innocent? What was the sense of it?

Stewart felt a little more secure after he called in the holdup witnesses. Enough of them placed Vanzetti at Bridgewater to support a prompt indictment in his case. For Sacco, however, the Bridgewater identifications were too few for court action. On the other hand, the more complex South Braintree crime produced more than a half-dozen witnesses against Sacco and only two or three doubtful ones against Vanzetti. It was not until October 1920—when Moore was arriving in Boston—that the District Attorney brought in indictments of both men for the greater crime. Meanwhile he could deal with Vanzetti.

Vanzetti was a meager residue of the four men who had descended on the Johnsons to pick up Boda's Oakland. Boda himself was gone. Later he would bob up in Italy, where in 1928 he told an adventurous story of dodging about New England, slipping into Providence, and embarking in the autumn of 1920 under a false name. The fourth man, however, was traced through his motorcycle registration and arrested late on May 6. He was Ricardo Orciani, a short, aggressive man, whom Chief Stewart defined as "not like Sacco or Vanzetti, a real tough." Although three witnesses put him in South Braintree, and Harding, the salesman bystander, identified him as a Bridgewater participant, he could show a factory time card punched for the Bridgewater date. The District Attorney thereupon decided that the total of the evidence was insufficient to withstand a court test. Orciani was released and Vanzetti, for the moment, faced his enemies alone.

There was no one of Fred Moore's caliber to help Vanzetti. His anarchist friends in Boston had organized the Sacco-Vanzetti

Defense Committee and engaged a respected but uninspired local lawyer, a district judge named John F. Vahey. There were the same needs—money, connections, and publicity—which Moore would fill so magically for the greater trial. The anarchists, however, could do little from their position in society, or rather, out of it. Yet they managed to raise enough money in the Italian colony to pay the defense costs, and they did their best to bring in friends to locate witnesses and build the case. One of the Boston anarchists was the typesetter Aldino Felicani, who has risen since that time to the ownership of a small printing shop. In 1958 Felicani told me how he had scrabbled about for help in early 1920, here and there getting support from middle-class persons but being rebuffed by the Communists, who saw no reason for solidarity at that moment. In North Plymouth, the headquarters of the defenders was the home of Vincenzo Brini, an anarchist with whom Vanzetti had boarded. His son, Beltrando Brini, remembered in 1958: "The house was like a hotel for some time. There was a steady coming in and going out of people who were interested, people we were getting to help." This kind of help had its uses, but it was not enough. Moreover, defense counsel Vahey, for his part, could not bring about a transforming fusion of the details of a nonpolitical crime and the great complex of radicalism. Vahey was only a lawyer.

Vanzetti's trial for the Bridgewater crime, which took place in Plymouth from June 22 to July 1, 1920, stirred little interest. Having avoided the subject of anarchism at the time of the arrest six weeks earlier, the newspapers evidently saw no reason to go into it now. Without that, the trial could not produce enough substance to fill out a news column. Thus the *Old Colony Memorial,* the Plymouth weekly, began its regular column on court events in the June 25 issue with a report of another case, which it regarded as much more important, and then gave a brief account of the opening of the trial of "Bartolomeo Vanzetti of this town." The Boston press was similarly cavalier, the *Boston Globe* limiting its first report on the trial to one and one-half inches on page five and the *Boston Herald* devoting to it four inches on page twelve. There was, it appeared, nothing to get excited about.

Fearful of the issue of radicalism, Vahey had seen to it that the subject would not be mentioned. By agreement of counsel, the trial was conducted without a word on Vanzetti's anarchism, and the courtroom settled down to a confrontation of prosecution eyewitnesses and defense alibi witnesses. Against Vanzetti the prosecution produced five persons characterizing him as the wielder of the shotgun: Benjamin F. Bowles, the policeman; Alfred E. Cox, Jr., the paymaster; Frank W. Harding, the salesman; Maynard F. Shaw, the newsboy; and Mrs. Georgina Brooks, the housewife. Their testimony was clear and resistant to cross-examination. Cox, for example, responded to defense counsel in this wise:

> Q. You are not sure that this was the man? A. I feel sure that he is the same man.
> Q. You are not positive that he is the same man? A. I can't say that I am positive that he is the same man.

Cox, in sum, gave the impression that he was reasonably sure that Vanzetti was the man but that he wanted to be scrupulously fair. This was the most qualified of the prosecution testimony. The other witnesses were confident Vanzetti was the man, Bowles saying: "I am positive." Under prosecution questions Mrs. Brooks reported how she saw Vanzetti on that winter morning:

> A. He was some kind of a foreigner.
> Q. Can you describe him? A. Well, he had his hat on. He had a dark moustache and a dark complexion.
> Q. How big a moustache was it? A. Medium size.
> . . . Q. What was he doing? A. He was sitting at the wheel watching me.
> . . . Q. How long did you continue to look at him?
> A. Well, as I walked over I kept turning around looking at him.

Q. Did you hear him speak? A. Yes.
Q. Whom did he speak to? A. The man right beside him.
Q. Do you know what language it was? A. It was foreign.

Failing to shake any of the prosecution witnesses, Vahey put his alibi witnesses on the stand.

The defense thesis was simple: Vanzetti, an occasional fish peddler during the past winter, had been engaged in selling eels on December 24. To support this argument Vahey had the formidable total of eleven alibi witnesses who testified on his sales operations. Thus Beltrando Brini, then thirteen years old, told in detail how he had assisted Vanzetti in selling eels, while his father, mother, and sister corroborated his account and other Italians identified themselves as customers. But the alibi witnesses had an important handicap. They were all friends and neighbors of Vanzetti, and the Brinis and others admitted having collected funds for the defense. Under cross-examination, these facts were placed in relief by the prosecutor, Frederick G. Katzmann, who got young Beltrando, for example, to admit rehearsing his testimony seven or eight times before the trial—"You learned it just like a piece at school?"—"Sure." Nor was it difficult for Katzmann to show that although the witnesses were unanimously certain of December 24—and not December 22 or 23—as the date in question, they were quite normally fallible and uncertain about other dates. The effect of the alibis was one of loyalty, not necessarily credibility, and this must be set in the context of criminal trials in general, where the alibi is distinguished for its frequent use.

In a trial with such a balance between incrimination and alibi, the testimony of the defendant would be exceedingly important. It had been expected that Vanzetti would take the stand, but then Vahey and his associate, James M. Graham, conferred intensely with him toward the close of the trial. They told him what he could expect in the form of a cross-examination but, as defense counsel does in such circumstances, they left the decision about testifying to him. A Boston newspaper reported: "There was great surprise when the defense counsel rested its case as the defendant was expected to testify." Of course, that failure was inevitably a vulnerable point in the defense, since the jury, however well instructed not to draw inferences from it, would nevertheless be left with the question: What did Vanzetti fear, if he was innocent?

There was also the unfilled blank concerning Vanzetti's actions on the evening of the arrest. What was an innocent man doing with a gun and doubtful companions? Although Katzmann did not press the point very hard, the jury could see that Vanzetti had no good explanation for his suspicious actions. This was the price that had to be paid for not encouraging the jury's prejudices. The defense had left too many questions unanswered.

In his summation Vahey eloquently emphasized the possibilities of an error in identification, the *Brockton Enterprise* reporting: "He received compliments . . . for his fine plea." The judge was Webster Thayer and now he told the jury: "The question is, did the witnesses take a true mental photograph of the defendant that morning?"

The jury spent five hours and twenty minutes trying to answer that question. At the word, "Guilty," Vanzetti made his only public expression of the trial, turning to his friends and saying firmly, as a leader speaks to his followers in a moment of peril, "Courage!" On the charge of assault with intent to rob, he was sentenced to twelve to fifteen years of imprisonment.

What can be added to the court record in seeking a better understanding of the Bridgewater crime and the Plymouth trial? While some aspects will be clearer in the light of subsequent events, we can ask questions of some of the people who had been engaged in the trial.

The surviving juror, Arthur S. Nickerson, had been the youngest member of the panel. In recent years a prosperous electrician with his own business and still a resident of North Plymouth, he told me that the jurors were chiefly concerned with the matter of identification. The radicalism issue, he insisted, was never discussed, no juror having the initiative or the knowledge to bring up a point not mentioned in the trial testimony: "I didn't know anything about all that until afterward. To me it was a trial about a holdup." Nickerson, a craftsman obviously content with his work and his world, has an undefensive willingness to discuss any point. The question, for example, of prejudice against foreigners? "I heard nothing said in the jury room that could be taken for that. All of us looked on the man there as a poor devil. It didn't make any difference what he was. The thing was—what did he do? If there was anything else I would have hollered." Nickerson said that he had lived among Italians, Portuguese, and Germans all his life and, he added, he was quite happy with his Italian brother-in-law: "A foreigner, I say, is someone who came over on the boat after you did." Yet Nickerson did have a doubt after the trial was over. At the time he had unhappily thought that in Vanzetti he was convicting a man he knew and liked, a mustached fellow employee at the Plymouth Cordage Company. When Nickerson returned to work he was pleasantly surprised to find the man still in the plant: "I said to myself that if I could be so mistaken, then you could not depend on identification. If I had known that Vanzetti wasn't Tony, knowing that they did look alike, then I would have had a doubt. I don't know how I would have decided."

If, thus, the juror accords Vanzetti this opportunity to escape the guilt of the Plymouth trial, what can his surviving friends, the Brinis, say in order to extend the area of doubt?

Like Nickerson, the Brinis are open to questions. Beltrando Brini, who had become principal of the Willard Elementary School in Quincy, the home of the Adams family, refused to retreat from Vanzetti's memory: "I want to see Sacco and Vanzetti really exonerated. They were scapegoats, Reds, condemned as such—victims of hysteria—in disfavor of the capitalist class that wanted to go on exploiting labor and attacked them for trying to spoil its game—idealists against crooked authorities—the case was a struggle between the different classes."

Married to an Episcopalian of native stock, Brini offers a summary of his own philosophy: "Of course I am not an anarchist, and I was too young in those days to know what it was about. I got a better grasp of civil responsibility in college."

Brini is reminded of the classic prosecution question: Can you be sure that the sales expedition had not occurred on another day, December 22, December 23?

Brini suggests: "But I would not have been out of school. I could look it up, the school records would show if there was school or not." And later: "If you have any evidence to the contrary—let me know. If I've made a mistake, it's a colossal mistake."

Brini muses: "Oh, there have been questions in my own mind. I've questioned my mother about it myself—hard. I admit I've had doubts, but I've settled them. It couldn't be!"

Brini appends another thought: "Whether he abetted a crime for a cause. . . . Vanzetti was a great idealist, that is the first thing about him. . . . To get money? Why, he wouldn't harm a cat!"

Can the defendant himself say something outside the formal confines of the court? Vanzetti treated the Plymouth trial exhaustively in the pamphlet, "Background of the Plymouth Trial," and a two-part article, "Awaiting the Hangman," the latter appearing in the *Sacco-Vanzetti Defense Committee Bulletin.* Both defenses, which were published in 1926, are not helpful. Vanzetti charges that $70,000 was applied to purchase his conviction, that he was betrayed by his lawyer and a treacherous anarchist associate named Doviglio Govoni, that "all the State witnesses . . . are perjurors," that the garage owner and his wife were "rabble," that the newsboy witness was a "mental defective whose lack of shame and consciousness [sic] proved him to be feeble-minded" and that, in short, "in the conduct of the judge, of the prosecutor, and even of my lawyer . . . ," the Plymouth trial was "a legal lynching." All these statements are unsubstantiated.

Yet, however incompetently the Brinis and Vanzetti himself defend his memory, the juror Nickerson, a man who helped convict him, does suggest a possible exoneration. Other arguments did militate against him, but the greater weight of the prosecution case lay in the identification, and Nickerson says he feels doubtful about it. In view of all the flawed human elements compounded in such a conviction, this is the best meaning we may derive today from the logic of the Bridgewater case studied in isolation: an irreducible uncertainty.

6. Dedham I: Moore

SACCO and Vanzetti went on trial for their lives almost a year after Vanzetti's conviction for the Bridgewater holdup. From the beginning Moore saw to it that the new trial would be nothing like the old one. He would not content himself with making a conscientious rebuttal to the prosecution case. Instead, he would take the initiative and shape the trial to the character of its defendants. He would make everyone see that Sacco and Vanzetti were not criminals and that crime was not the issue. They were radicals. The issue was radicalism.

It was, however, not enough for the issue to be made clear: people do not sympathize with an abstraction. Sacco and Vanzetti would come forward as men to be known in all their humanity. As a mute courtroom face Vanzetti had been a failure; Moore knew that the man must speak for himself. And if Sacco might not be so effective, his presence as a specific human being would be enough to second Vanzetti. Moreover, the courtroom would see Sacco's wife Rose, retiring and dumbly loyal, and a pretty woman with red hair besides, with their children, an eight-year-old son splendidly named Dante and the seven-month-old Ines, born after Sacco's arrest. Vanzetti would defend himself in his loneliness and Sacco in his family.

Moore had proved his skills as an investigator at the Lawrence trial. Securing a postponement to get all the time he needed, he used the same skills in preparing for this trial. His people talked or tried to talk with all the known witnesses and ranged throughout the area seeking anyone who had been missed. Whatever the prosecution might claim, Moore had put together a list of witnesses in whom he had great confidence. On May 31, 1921, when the trial opened in Dedham, Moore was ready for the enemies of Sacco and Vanzetti.

Again the judge was Webster Thayer. We have seen him at the sentencing, but he is worth studying more closely. He was not old, of course, not quite sixty-three, but he was already a cranky, elderly man. He was now on the plateau of a career that had lifted him above the status of his father, a small-town Yankee merchant. After leaving Dartmouth Thayer had settled in Worcester, some forty miles west of Boston, where he had a fair success as a lawyer while establishing himself as a leading personage. His success had satisfied neither his ambitions nor his vanity, and some of his remarks indicated that he hoped to gain valuable prestige from this trial.

Again the prosecutor was Frederick Gunn Katzmann, a small-town success of a magnitude comparable to Thayer's. Born of a German father and a Scotch mother, he had been a poor boy in Hyde Park, a mile or two to the east of Dedham, but had managed to matriculate at Harvard. Back at Hyde Park he had been unable to turn his B.A. to good account, subsisting with a humble position which did, however, permit him to get through night sessions of the Boston University Law School. Now in his prospering late forties, Katzmann had an almost square, determined skull and a middle-sized square body rounding slightly at the belly. At Plymouth he had been a fair but tough prosecutor, and there was no reason to expect any difference now.

Katzmann had three assistant district attorneys to help him. Chief among them for this case was Harold P. Williams, slim, nice-looking, and completely the portrait of the young attorney, as if selected by a film director. One of the juniors on the staff, he had been surprised at his assignment and assumed it was because Katzmann had thought it a lesser court concern of this session. But the district attorney doubtless saw the ability and character that later brought Williams to the bench of the Commonwealth's Supreme Judicial Court. When I spoke with him not long ago, Justice Williams was the portrait of the judge, as if selected by the same film director: the handsome features enriched by age, the serene dignity, and the beneficent courtesy.

For the defense, Moore also had three associates: William J. Callahan, a Brockton lawyer who had represented Sacco at a preliminary hearing, and the brothers Jeremiah J. and Thomas F. McAnarney. With their elder brother John, they practiced law in Quincy, home of the Adamses and the Beltrando Brinis, where they had become assimilated to the point of becoming Republicans despite their Irish ancestry. Actually, John, as the eldest, most successful, and best connected (he also maintained a Boston office), was more important to the defense, although he was not officially a member of it, than the ailing Thomas, who appeared in court as Jeremiah's silent assistant. Short, tense, red-faced and pince-nezed, Jeremiah had an uncertain grasp of syntax and an unerring instinct for the wrong word, but he was a thoroughly competent trial lawyer with a record of success. Moore, Callahan, and Jeremiah and Thomas McAnarney formed a unitary defense, although they were divided into pairs assigned to one of the defendants for the sake of courtroom maneuvers. In this way either pair could move for a separate trial. Officially, Moore and Callahan defended Sacco, while Jeremiah and Thomas McAnarney represented Vanzetti. There was no question, however, that Moore was in command.

The first chapter of the trial consisted of the jury selection, a more or less perfunctory matter usually, but here alive with a great many possibilities. Since the character of the jury is particularly important in trials that threaten to open a channel to prejudice in jurors, attorneys for accused radicals have learned the value of the open heart, and Moore viewed each prospective juror with scientific intensity. This was one matter in which he accorded himself absolute power. In fact, he enraged the McAnarneys by objecting to two candidates of their acquaintance. One was employed by a Boston broker, and Moore, with his long years of defending radicals, refused to believe that the Boston financial district was a good place for the nurture of proper jurors. He was not too tactful about overriding his colleagues, but he knew better.

If Moore was apprehensive about prejudiced jurors, the candidates gave no evidence that they wanted to apply their prejudices to Sacco and Vanzetti. There were two important reasons for this: the expectation of a long trial and a fear, encouraged by the less tactful of Moore's I.W.W. auxiliaries, that justice was a two-edged sword. The reluctance to serve was so general that Thayer took on the role of a judge militant, pressing a battalion of candidates to arrive at a squad of the inescapably fit. Many produced principled objections to capital punishment, evoking baffled expressions of doubt from Thayer, while others simulated deafness or produced doctors' prescriptions for the quiet life. On the other hand, Thayer himself showed such a ferocious regard for the character of the jury that nearly three-quarters of the first 160 persons called were put down without requiring the objections of the attorneys. At the end of the first day, only three jurors had been selected, despite the addition of a third session running from 7:30 until after ten in the evening.

The triple sessions continued for the succeeding days of jury selection. On the second day, Wednesday, only three more jurors were selected before Thayer adjourned court at 10:10 P.M. He rose to an even clearer dominance of the court scene on Thursday when the result of all labors was one juror. Harrying the recalcitrant citizens, directing the court staff, conferring with the attorneys, he performed the confident, articulate role of an active judicial conscience.

With seven men picked and the list of 500 veniremen exhausted, Thayer then ordered that 200 more prospective jurors be gathered "from the bystanders or from the county at large." Sheriff Samuel Capen and a dozen deputies launched themselves at Norfolk County on Thursday evening after court closed, but its citizens, warned of the hunt, fled from the streets. One deputy tried to capture the chief justice of Brookline Municipal Court. Another, dragging a groom from his wedding supper, expressed his regret, but insisted he was trapped by his orders. Still another deputy disrupted a band concert in Braintree, the audience of 300 vanishing as soon as his purpose became evident. On Friday, the fourth day of jury selection, Thayer had his stock of nearly 200 prospective jurors, but he knew that it would not be excessive; the county had been careless about the jury rolls. The judge was scathing in his comments on the great proportion of unqualified or missing. The names, qualified or not, were Anglo-Saxon in the great majority, but this was understandable, if unfortunate in relation to immigrant defendants. Many of the immigrants were still aliens or had not been so integrated into the community that they had got onto the jury rolls. There were a few Irish, no Italian names. The tension increased, occasionally relaxed when a new juror was at last plucked out of the new list.

Among those who observed the process was William G. Thompson, who would become chief defense counsel in 1924. Called unofficially to the case by Mrs. Elizabeth Evans and her friends, he contented himself now in taking notes and passing on informal counsel to the lay defenders. Moore felt no need for advice himself.

Thayer was determined to get a jury before the weekend recess, a purpose that seemed insensate as the evening session wore through to midnight. Spectators dropped away and the red-eyed attorneys repeated their objections as court officials maneuvered the jury candidates in and out of the courtroom. The judge's obduracy held and the last juror was snapped into place at 12:30 A.M.

With the jury staffed but not yet official, Thayer now ordered the sleeping jurors awakened and brought into the courtroom. At 1:30 A.M. the twelve men, coatless, and in those days of detachable collars, collarless, were assembled to be constituted as the jury in the trial of Sacco and Vanzetti. Opening at ten the previous morning, court had continued with two meal-time breaks for nearly sixteen hours. A reporter wrote: "Judge Thayer gave the most remarkable exhibition of perseverance and sheer strength through the four trying days of the examination of the jurors."

However unreceptive the tired jurors might have been, Thayer established them firmly in the context of their duties. He told them:

> Massachusetts guarantees protection to all citizens. It makes no odds where they were born; it makes no difference what their financial, social or religious standing may be. It is one of the boasts of the American law that the rich, the poor, the high, the low, the learned, the ignorant, all shall receive the same rights, the same privileges, and we must see to it that a trial of that kind is held according to American law and according to American justice and nothing must be done by anybody in any way whatsoever to mar or impair a fair, honest trial. The defendants are entitled to it. The Commonwealth is entitled to it, and as part of the government of this Commonwealth, it is a duty of this court to see that both parties have exactly that kind of trial.*

Moore could find no objection to this statement, although he might doubt the sincerity of the speaker. Nor could he object to the way the jury had been selected. He had had his chance to get the best possible jurors. There had been more than 650 jury candidates, compared with the 75 or 100 for an ordinary trial, and Moore remarked to a reporter: "Did you know that this jury is probably the most expensive that the Commonwealth ever got?" The jurors were no Boston Brahmins. They were small people from small towns: real estate dealer, shoe worker, photog-

* *Transcript*, vol. 1, p. 47.

rapher, farmer, machinist, grocer, mason, factory stockkeeper, and clothing salesman. However, they had names like Waugh, Ganley, Marden, and Dever, basic American and a cold distance from the Latin. It was the best you could do in Norfolk County.

The trial now took the form it would have through the weeks until July 14. Above Judge Thayer's head on the wall a marble-faced clock moved with the slow days. The courtroom, which could hold about 200 persons, had been designed with a thoughtful grace. Its white walls were suave with yellow lambeaux and a cream frieze, and the white ceiling was high enough to offer generous room to a cramped spirit. It was a pleasant chamber for dealing with murder.

The prisoners were established some twenty feet forward of the judge's high bench in a cage used until recently in capital cases. Actually, "cage" is a misnomer. It was a kind of pew with a latticework of metal strips. The prisoner could lean forward and rest his chin on the railing in front as he studied the other actors in the trial.

The court day always began with a brief prayer. The court clerk would poll the jurors and then say: "Nicola Sacco." Sacco jerks to his feet, his chin lifted: "Press-ent!" Vanzetti rises with Sacco and waits until his name is called: "Prez-ent."

With his clients silent in their cage, Moore resisted the formal structure of the trial, which would withhold the initiative from him until the defense presented its case. During the first set piece, the jury selection, he could not prevent Thayer's dominance, but his questions relating to prejudice and labor unions gave the first hints of the motif of radicalism. Now it was the prosecution's turn. This, too, could be countered. Moore's cross-examinations would not be defensive; he would carry the battle to the enemy. Any indications of weakness in the prosecution witnesses would be used to indict Massachusetts justice. More than that, Moore could act at will outside the courtroom. He intensified his efforts to reach public opinion.

Moore's effectiveness in the area of public relations was shown during the development of the prosecution case. Although Katzmann and Williams carefully avoided mention of radicalism, the *Boston Herald* of June 12 carried a long feature article which brought it up in terms sympathetic to the defense. A woman reporter who had been briefed by Moore's friends made his point: "Every so often in criminal history comes a case before the courts in which the real and vital issues seem to be completely obscured. . . ." The "real and vital issues," she emphasized at length, concerned radicalism. She continued with a comment on Thayer that combined faith in his fairness with encouragement for him to go on being fair: "Those of us who knew Judge Thayer in the Bessie May Sheels case in Lawrence, two years ago, know that these friends of liberals and radicals . . . can rest perfectly secure in the fact that every right of the defendant is being protected." Up to this point, moreover, Thayer had not disappointed her: "So alert is he in administering justice to the fullest degree that he protects the defendant when the defense is slow to move and hesitating to act." Then, having explored some of the implications of radicalism, the reporter made Moore's second point: the quality of the defendants as human beings. She found Sacco "an Italian who has to be sympathized with because of his fair faced wife who sits there uncomprehending" and Vanzetti "an older man, settled and serious . . . his forehead wrinkled with a concentrated frown." The other newspaper articles did not mention radicalism at that time, but at least they did not bring out any negative connotations. No Boston newspaper, for example, referred to the Coacci deportation or the anarchist manifesto found on Sacco, nor were there any attempts to connect the trial with the Wall Street bombing and the other events of the period of the Red raids, now a year in the past. In terms of newspaper coverage Moore was getting the best possible results: objectivity, sympathy, and silence.

Furthermore, in addition to the one well-timed *Herald* article, the *Boston Globe* was providing sympathetic coverage every day. This was probably due less to the defense persuasions than to the character of the *Globe* reporter, Frank P. Sibley. A six-foot four-inch nonconformist who wore a flowing Latin Quarter tie, Sibley was touched by the situation of the defendants and repelled by the expressions of Thayer. He would later sign an affidavit accusing the judge of prejudice. Meanwhile, Moore could have confidence in at least one major Boston newspaper besides the *Herald.*

The prosecution rolled out its witnesses, taking nearly two weeks to present witnesses who either identified the defendants or helped recount the chronicle of the crime. Its first effort, however, was a failure. Lewis Wade, the shoe worker who had been filling up his employer's car at the holdup time, had identified Sacco as the cap-losing killer when he saw him in the Brockton police station. Now he had a doubt. He explained that he had since seen another man who resembled Sacco: "Well, I ain't sure now. I have a little doubt. . . . Well, my best judgment is this: If I have a doubt, I don't think he is the man." Moore could take satisfaction from the *Globe* story under an eight-column, that is, a full-page headline: "Witness Fails to Identify Sacco," and the sub-headline: "Wade Has Changed His Opinion."

The prosecution tried again with Mrs. Lola Andrews, the confused woman who had asked directions of the crime automobile repairman. She was certain he was Sacco. The *Globe* reported: "This is the first time that Sacco has been at all startled out of his composure." Sacco rose to his feet when the woman pointed him out and almost shouted: "Take a good look. I am myself!" Moore attacked her ferociously but was unable to achieve any useful effect. Indeed, her testimony whipped back into his face when he mentioned his talks with her during the case preparation. He asked if he had used an inducement; she replied mildly that he had invited her to take a Maine vacation. When she had told him that she would lose her job, Moore promised her a job "as good or better," she testified. Moore then put her through a hard cross-examination about another matter. She turned white, closed her eyes and dropped. Katzmann, however, had started toward her and he caught her. The other identifications followed.

John W. Faulkner said that Vanzetti had been a fellow train passenger on the morning of April 15. Vanzetti had appeared to be anxious not to miss his stop, the East Braintree station, and had asked him each time the train approached the two previous stations if this were East Braintree. Faulkner assured the man that he would tell him when they got to the town. He did so and Vanzetti accordingly descended in East Braintree. It was the prosecution argument that Vanzetti had traveled by train from Plymouth to East Braintree, the closest connection to South Braintree, and that the gang had picked him up with the automobile at the East Braintree station.

Harry E. Dolbeare, the piano tuner who had seen "a tough-looking bunch" riding in an automobile in South Braintree during the morning, put Vanzetti among its passengers.

William S. Tracy, the real estate man who had seen a man leaning against his drug store property at 11:40 A.M., testified that Sacco was the man.

William J. Heron, the railroad police officer who had seen two nervous men, one of them smoking against the rules, in the South Braintree railroad station, testified that Sacco was one of them.

James Bostock, the millwright who had been so active at the crime scene and who had come to the aid of the dying Berardelli, was less effective as an observer. He could not identify the killers, contenting himself with the general observation: "I have seen Italian fruit peddlers, and as I saw them as I passed them I thought they was Italian fruit peddlers."

Louis Pelser, the Jewish shoecutter in the financially unscathed but operationally apropos Rice & Hutchins plant, identified Sacco as the killer who had stood over Berardelli, firing at him throughout the action that took the other killer across the road after Parmenter. Pelser raised an accusatory finger and a reporter noticed that Sacco winced. But Pelser allowed perhaps himself, perhaps Sacco, a small grace of uncertainty: "Well, I wouldn't say it was him, but he is a dead image of him." He turned his memory over again, described the killer in detail, dark hair and face, Army shirt, and remodulated: "I wouldn't say he is the man, but he is the dead image of the man I seen." Moore got him to admit lying to a defense investigator, but he could not damage the bulk of his testimony.

Michael Levangie, the gate tender in South Braintree, said that the gunman on the left side of the Buick was Vanzetti, but he embarrassed the prosecution by identifying Vanzetti as the driver. In his summation Katzmann tried to separate out the useful from the impossible in Levangie's testimony. The prosecution had never claimed that Vanzetti was the driver, having accepted the reports of various witnesses that the driver was a small, emaciated, yellow-faced man, and Katzmann was forced to make do with the contention that Levangie was right about Vanzetti and wrong about his function. Such a witness is poor support for any theory, but Katzmann could claim that Vanzetti, when Levangie had seen him, was in the act of moving forward from the rear to the front of the vehicle on the driver's side, and that confusing him with the driver was natural enough.

Mary Splaine, the strong-nerved bookkeeper who had continued working in the upper Slater & Morrill plant after the first shots sounded, identified Sacco as the man leaning out of the right side of the crime automobile as it crossed the tracks. Under cross-examination she admitted being less certain at the hearing in Quincy, where she had seen a resemblance between a convict's photograph and the gang member. Miss Splaine, however, insisted that she had been certain about Sacco when she first saw him but that the enormity of the crime had made her reluctant to be so absolute: "But still I hated to say right out and out, so I just put it that way." The point about the photograph was not important; a witness can always find one or two in a rogue's gallery that are similar to a remembered face.

Frances Devlin, Mary Splaine's bookkeeping colleague but now unemployed, testified that she saw Sacco intimidating Levangie from the back seat of the car.

Carlos E. Goodridge, the pool-playing salesman, testified that Sacco was the man who waved a pistol at him on Pearl Street just after the automobile crossed the tracks.

Another partial retraction embarrassed Katzmann when Louis De Beradinis, proprietor of a shoemaker's shop near the upper S. & M. plant, withdrew the statement he had made in Brockton jail. He had said then that a man resembling Sacco had pointed a gun at him. Now he retreated a few paces and stopped at: "I think it is, but am not sure."

A number of witnesses plotted the Buick's trip around the Brockton area, although only one claimed to be able to identify a defendant. He was Austin T. Reed, the crossing tender at Matfield Crossing and the last person who reported having seen the vehicle. He pointed out Vanzetti as the man who swore at him, while Vanzetti peered at him mildly from the prisoner's cage.

Against Sacco, thus, the prosecution was able to produce seven identifications as: amateur mechanic (Lola Andrews), lounger at the drug store (Tracy), the nervous man in the railroad station (Heron), gunman standing over the dying Berardelli (Pelser), and gunman on the right side of the departing Buick (Misses Splaine and Devlin; Goodridge). There were also two semiretractions (Wade and De Beradinis).

Against Vanzetti, Katzmann had four identifications as: train passenger descending at East Braintree (Faulkner), back-seat automobile passenger in the Buick during the morning of April 15 (Dolbeare), flourisher of a revolver at the South Braintree tracks (Levangie), and the profanely impatient Buick passenger at Matfield Crossing (Reed).

No criminal trial fails to throw up uncertainties. Human fallibility is encouraged by swift, disordered events, and this wretched amateur holdup invited a disorder of observation by its disorder of execution. Yet Moore was unable to break down the prosecution testimony despite his long preparation of the case and his occasionally cruel cross-examinations. He had launched sufficient bane at Lola Andrews to cause her collapse, but her testimony held, and his insistences only strengthened the memories of the other witnesses. Katzmann had also worked hard in preparing his case. Moreover, this was the prosecution's area of strength, as it set the early direction of the trial.

Dedham showed as little interest in the trial as it would later have in the sentencing. During the jury examination, a Boston reporter had written: "The procession of the defendants back and forth between the court house and the jail resembled a miniature police parade, with three blue uniformed men marching in front, three others behind and two on either side of the manacled men." The effect was wasted on Dedham: "Little interest in their passage was evinced by the Dedhamites, the streets being almost deserted." Enough of the curious had added themselves to the acutely concerned to fill the courtroom at first, but the press was commenting on sparse attendance by Friday, June 10, at the end of the first week of testimony, and it was not until near the end that the courtroom was completely full. Most of the regular trial spectators had some connection with the defendants, either as Italian friends or as sympathizers like Mrs. Elizabeth Evans, Mrs. Cerise Jack, who became Sacco's English teacher, and representatives of social work and church groups like Mrs. Lois Rantoul, a grandniece of President Lowell of Harvard. The Italian consul in Boston, Marquis Agostino Ferrante, also attended at a remove suggested by his monocle. But Dedham could not give its consistent attention to a six-and-one-half-week trial of two obscure Italians.

At last, Moore's chance came. Eleven prosecution witnesses had put the defendants at the crime; now Moore offered twelve witnesses who would put them elsewhere. Let the jury match credibility.

For Vanzetti, five persons testified that he was in Plymouth concerned with cloth and fish. Alfonsina Brini, supported by her fifteen-year-old daughter Lefevre, said she had counseled Vanzetti in the purchase of a piece of cloth for a suit in the course of his day of fish-peddling. She was followed by the cloth peddler, but he did not stand up well under cross-examination. In a corner he complained: "I am not a biographer!" Of the alibi witnesses relevant to the fish, one was a fisherman who said he sold fish to Vanzetti on occasion and who insisted he had seen Vanzetti around two o'clock that afternoon. The one fish customer, however, contributed a discrepancy that weakened the alibi. He placed the fish purchase at "about thirteen minutes past twelve or quarter past twelve," while Vanzetti would later testify he was in the Brini home between noon and one o'clock seeking Alfonsina Brini's advice and negotiating the purchase of the cloth. The alibi testimony did not give a completely convincing picture of Vanzetti as buyer and seller.

Sacco's alibi was more complex. He had seven witnesses, one represented by an affidavit, who put him in Boston on April 15. Sacco said he had taken a day off from work to apply for a passport in the Italian consulate. Six witnesses were Italian, two of them having worked with the defense in gathering evidence to help the Sacco case, and the one Anglo-Saxon was a left-wing Socialist, an advertising agent doing business with foreign language newspapers. Moreover, the two defense volunteers contradicted each other on a point that was meant to establish the alibi date. Both mentioned an Italian banquet on April 15 as the reason for remembering the sight of Sacco, but one put it during the evening and the other said he attended it at noon. At best, the total effect of alibi witnesses was confusion.

The alibis, as was also true in the Bridgewater trial, had the intrinsic difficulty of time placement to overcome. There was no reason for the witnesses to go through the process of trying to remember the events of April 15 until after May 5, that is, until after the arrest, when it became important to establish the activities of the defendants. Leafing through their memories, the witnesses had to be certain that they had seen Sacco or Vanzetti on April 15 and not April 13 or 14, or April 16 or 17. Each witness therefore was obliged to connect an ordinary meeting on April 15 with something not quite so ordinary in his own life, sufficiently distinctive to be marked as April 15. The difficulty was emphasized in Katzmann's cross-examination of the fish customer who had been so specific about the time of day:

Q. I take it, Mr. Guidobone, that the fact you were operated on on April 19th makes you remember you bought some fish on the 15th. Is that it?
A. Yes.
Q. And that is the only thing that makes you remember it?
A. Well, the operation and that, because I was very careful what I was eating.
Q. Do you think the codfish caused the appendicitis?
A. No, no, no.
Q. What is the connection between the operation on the 19th and your buying codfish on the 15th?
A. It had nothing to do with it with me.
Q. The codfish had?
A. Because I remember. The fish has nothing to do with the operation.
Q. How long were you troubled with the pain that resulted in the operation?
A. Over a year before. I did not have the courage to do it.
Q. Then you had the pain for quite some time, didn't you?
A. Yes. . . .
Q. Did you have a pain on the 15th?
A. No, sir. I did not. On the 17th I did.
Q. Did you have any—what was the last date before the 17th you had a pain?
A. Well, there were other days, different days, that I had pains, but I do not remember now what days.
Q. But you remember codfish on the 15th day, is that right?
A. Yes.

Again and again Katzmann emphasized the difficulties of date placement. Thus he won a victory over a witness who would have Sacco on a railroad platform on the morning of April 15 before he boarded a Boston train. Katzmann turned the man's certainty about the date against him by insisting on equal certainty about another date. When the witness obliged, saying he had been at work on that day, Katzmann offered a succession of dates, spaced a week apart, and the man swore to his consistent labors. Now, the courtroom became aware that Katzmann had got him to claim having worked on a succession of Sundays. It began tittering as the man persisted in response to Katzmann's singsong repetition of dates. Then, in Boston journalese, "when it dawned on the witness how he had been made ridiculous, the expression of his face was worth the trip to Dedham."

Moore realized that the alibis were a holding operation at best. Inevitably, the jurors would take account of the relations between the defendants and their witnesses. It would, however, be sufficient if their testimony gave the jury pause. His investigations had produced a mass of other evidence and now, in that part of the trial permitting a freer development, he would bring up his greatest force. He went over from defense to attack.

Against Pelser, the R. & H. shoe worker, Moore put forward three of the man's fellow workers to testify that he was not coolly observing the shooting. Rather, they told the jury, he was cowering under a bench at the time. Yet one of them, when asked which window he had looked through, said: "I looked out the window Pelser looked out." Furthermore, Pelser's accurate report on the license plates gave his testimony objective support. The other two workers had less trouble but they were not too clear.

Against the frailty of Lola Andrews, Moore launched her best friend. The woman, Mrs. Julia Campbell, had accompanied her on the job quest and now she insisted that Lola Andrews had spoken to a man near the automobile and not of it. The spatial transposition was weakened when Jeremiah J. McAnarney ineptly asked: "Are you blind?" Mrs. Campbell, who said she was sixty-eight, replied: "Well, I can't see as well as a great many, but I am not blind, sir." Under cross-examination she said she had cataracts, and Katzmann got her to agree that the man near the automobile could, when well considered, have been associated with the vehicle. This tour of approximations was not useful to the defense.

Against Goodridge, Moore first countered with the man's larcenous past, a moral relevancy which Thayer correctly disallowed as legally irrelevant. Moore then marched up four men to contradict Goodridge's testimony: Nicola Damato, proprietor of the barber shop near the poolroom; Harry Arrogni, a barber in his shop; Andrew Manganio, a musical instruments dealer and an unhappy former employer of Goodridge's, and Peter Magazu, the poolroom proprietor. The first three reported Goodridge as unable to identify any of the criminals, according to casual statements he had volunteered to them. Magazu, however, testified that the man had indeed marked the pistol-wielder well enough to describe him as a "young man with light hair, light complexion and wore an Army shirt." Again, the jury had to resolve the contradiction.

Then there were those, more than a dozen, who had been at the crime scene and who testified categorically that they had not seen Sacco or Vanzetti among the gang members. Most of them were Italians, and some were the laborers who had been seen by others taking shelter in the excavation they had been digging. The defense, perhaps because they were immigrant laborers, perhaps for the intrinsic weakness of their testimony, treated them almost peremptorily, drawing the negative and letting them go quickly. The prosecution waved them on casually.

Another negative witness was Moore's I.W.W. assistant, Frank J. Burke, who testified that the gunman had threatened him near the South Braintree crossing: " 'Get out of the way, you son of a b. . . .' " Burke described the man as very different from Sacco:

". . . very full face, broad, heavy jowl, a man that would be noticeable most in any place. . . ."

Objecting to the expression of opinion, Katzmann interjected: "I move that be stricken out, if Your Honor please. . . ."

Aware of the rules of permissibility of evidence, Burke tried to repair matters and broke in ". . . to me." Under cross-examination, Burke said he had been in Moore's office many times but he refused to admit that he had been working for the defense. One of the reporters who had covered the Dedham trial told me that "Katzmann tore him apart," driving him into evasions and hastily surrendered positions. Burke had claimed that the crime vehicle was a Hudson, but Katzmann, having noticed that he had been riding with Callahan in the defense lawyer's Super-Six Hudson, demanded that he identify the vehicle. Burke could not.

After the trial Moore would produce other witnesses who would add new impeachments to Lola Andrews, Pelser, and Goodridge. Moore would also draw on still more witnesses with additional testimony regarding identification. The curious episodes of the repudiations of testimony would also play across the case record. Moore's subsequent actions and the new evidence would form another valuable chapter of the Sacco-Vanzetti history.

The trial, which had begun on the last day of May, sprawled across June into July. The *Old Colony Memorial*, the Plymouth weekly, made its only reference to it in the edition of July 1; ignoring the home-town defendant, it angled its article around a ballistics expert who had been a Plymouth resident. With the heat holding high, people planning July vacations looked to the Fourth of July as the period to their labors. The defense witnesses, weaving the alibis of Sacco and Vanzetti, talked to weary attorneys and a reduced courtroom attendance, and a reporter, seeking more interesting news, learned that Mrs. Elizabeth Evans had already given $2,850 to the defense cause. The spectators awaited a better promise. At last Moore would put Vanzetti on the stand. Silent through the Plymouth trial and silent until now, he would have the opportunity to take on his full dimensions. He would be able to explain what others had explained so incompetently. Friday, July 1, was a particularly dragging day, and Vanzetti's attorney, Jeremiah McAnarney, accomplished his most apt action of the trial that evening. He collapsed presumably of heat and fatigue, actually as a defense strategic move to prevent Vanzetti's appearance now—facing the weekend interruption. Thayer accepted that as a legal judgment and adjourned until Tuesday, July 5.

The temperature reached ninety-five degrees on the Fourth, but the jurors, released from their imprisonment, had enjoyed an outing, and they returned to court on Tuesday red from the sun. McAnarney, a solicitous and innocent reporter noted, "seemed perfectly recovered after three days rest, and was as springily alert, as cheerfully tense, as he had been all through the long case." The court procedure, normally so efficient under Thayer's strict direction, seemed to take on the unexpended ease of the weekend. The prayer had been concluded and the attendance had seated itself, and the mysteries of the law whispered at the attorneys' desks. The spectators, more numerous today, shifted and peered. After a long wait McAnarney said, "The defendant, Vanzetti." Rising easily from the prisoners' cage, Vanzetti walked the few steps to the witness stand. He spread his finger tips on the shelf before him and looked gravely down at McAnarney.

7. Dedham II: Ecce Homo I

HIS heavy, drooping mustache marked him. Wearing a new dark suit, black bow tie, and stiff collar, Vanzetti offered himself as his primary defense. Articulate and assured, he rejected an interpreter. He spoke slowly, calmly, using his hands freely in gestures of plastic emphasis. Every thoughtful, gentle response put the question: could this man possibly be a murderer? Moore had been right about that, but he required more of Vanzetti. Vanzetti must also command the case events and their logic. This, too, was evident as he began.

Katzmann, leaning forward over his desk, studied him intently.

Vanzetti began with the story of his life, a slow recital that steadily built up his dimension as a person. As he told it, it had been a life passively subject to chance, another of the annals of the poor. Later, it took on new meaning. It became a life with a purpose, and every shabby detail would become progress toward that purpose. Right now, however, Vanzetti could not speak of that. There would be a proper time.

Vanzetti came from Villafalletto, a village in the Piedmont not far north of Nice. His schooling ended when he was thirteen, and his father sent him to a nearby town as apprentice to a pastry cook. Lonely and overworked, he endured the life for six years. He then returned home; he was there when his mother became sick. It was a fatal illness, lingering and painful, and the experience apparently left psychic scars in Vanzetti. Seeking a change, he emigrated to the United States, a typical act for a young Italian of that time. In fact, his father had spent three years in this country before returning to the home village to get married and settle down.

Vanzetti worked for two years as a kitchen helper in New York City, but the abominable conditions drove him, after a period of unemployment, to New England, where he worked on a number of jobs. Perhaps the kitchen heat and grease reinforced an earlier preference for the outdoors and the air of freedom, and now he took jobs as a railroad laborer, a bricklayer's helper, and an ice cutter. In 1913 he had gravitated to Plymouth, a good place for a man who liked open air, soon defining it as his home. First he spent a year or so working for the Plymouth Cordage Company, but then he took an outside construction job. Now he had the free air in which to work, a fixed abode and congenial friends, but his life never became routine.

More important to Vanzetti was his nonprofessional activity as an anarchist. Although he did not go into it at this moment—under Jeremiah McAnarney's direct questions—the next episode in his life was an excursion to Mexico in 1917 to avoid registering for the draft. Accompanied by Sacco, he had joined a group of anarchists in Monterey. The friends, however, found the conditions uninviting and left after three or four months, Sacco returning to his family but Vanzetti, ever the vagabond, spending more than a year wandering about the American midwest.

Back in Plymouth, Vanzetti engaged in a series of odd jobs and continued his spiritual adventures. For a brief time he flirted with Protestantism, a fugue that sat suspiciously with his anarchist friends. It was soon over, however, and Vanzetti was restored to his good standing. Professionally, he also added a new activity, taking up fish peddling in the fall of 1919, shortly before the Bridgewater holdup. It was only an intermittent concern, since

Vanzetti dropped it to dig clams and assist a contractor, resuming it only in March 1920. In his account, his last day of fish peddling was the April 15 of the second holdup. Thus his designation in the case literature as a fish peddler is correct enough as a specific but false as a generic title. Vanzetti was, more properly, a day laborer with somewhat more initiative or less consistency than most.

McAnarney led Vanzetti around the Bridgewater circumstances, which were excluded from the Dedham trial, into the events of April 15, the day he said he sold fish and bought the cloth. The next day, April 16, he said he dug clams and, the day after that, tried unsuccessfully to find work at a garage construction job. He went to Boston that evening, April 17, returning the following evening. Again he looked for work without results. On April 22, he testified, he met with friends who decided to send him to New York. The objective concerned the Red raids, and so carefully excluded from Vanzetti's trial history up to this point, the radical connotations now began to seep into articulation. For the moment, however, Vanzetti was not permitted to explain why he went to New York, because his trip was not yet connected in courtroom logic to the matters at issue.

Vanzetti said he left for New York on Sunday, April 22, remaining there until Thursday, April 29. He took the night boat to Providence and returned to Plymouth on April 30. He later explained that he had been sent by his friends to inquire into the fate of two anarchists named Andrea Salsedo and Roberto Elia, held on suspicion of bombing activities. It was after Vanzetti had returned to Plymouth that he heard what had happened to Salsedo. The man fell to his death in the early morning of May 3 from an upper floor of a Park Row building, where he was being questioned by Department of Justice agents. Vanzetti was arrested, we remind ourselves, on the evening of Wednesday, May 5.

Some persons have muttered that Salsedo might have been pushed, a theory that reflects and expands the hysterical atmosphere of the Red raid period. The accusation, however, is unsubstantiated. Elia, Salsedo's fellow prisoner, deposed that Salsedo had been in a morbid mood the night of his death. Moreover, the agents were hoping to get him to talk about the anarchist bombings. In point of fact they had lighted on Salsedo as the result of the bombing of Attorney General Palmer's home, some scraps of paper having been found there and traced to a Brooklyn printing plant where he had worked. Salsedo's death frustrated their hope of stopping future bombing attempts.

Vanzetti then told how he went to Sacco's home in Stoughton, a town some five or six miles south of Boston, where he remained for the few days until the arrest on May 5. During the afternoon Boda and the more mysterious Ricardo Orciani appeared at the Sacco home on a motorcycle. (Indeed, Orciani, still enwrapped in the tatters of mystery, was attending the trial and listening to Vanzetti; he was employed by the defense in its investigations, conducting his errands under Katzmann's helplessly baleful eye. While Vanzetti was testifying, however, he vanished. It is believed he went to Italy.) Vanzetti and Sacco left the house about seven that evening of May 5 to board the streetcar to Bridgewater, Boda and Orciani lingering briefly and then taking their leave with the motorcycle. The first pair was not pressed for time. First, the two friends went to a lunchroom, where Vanzetti composed the announcement for the anarchist meeting. He gave it to Sacco, who had it in his pocket when they were arrested. They then took the streetcar and eventually got to the Johnson place, Vanzetti recounted. Only now, when Vanzetti spoke of the events there, was the issue of radicalism expressed without inhibition in the courtroom:

Q. What were you going to get the automobile for?

A. For to take out literature, books and newspapers, from the house and the homes.

Q. What house and homes did you want to take the books and the literature from?

A. From any house and from any house in five or six places, five or six towns. Three, five or six people have plenty of literature, and we want, we intend to take that out and put that in the proper place.

Q. What do you mean by a "proper place?"

A. By a proper place I mean in a place not subject to policemen go in and call for, see the literature, see the papers, see the books, as in that time they went through in the house of many men who were active in the radical movement and socialist and labor movement, and go there and take letters and take books and take newspapers, and put men in jail and deported many.

Katzmann. I ask it be stricken out.

The Witness. I say that in that time—

Katzmann. Wait one moment.

The Witness. And deported many, many, many have been misused in jail, and so on.

This was the first moment of truth. Here was radicalism as an explanation for the events on the evening of the arrest and as an attack on conservative Massachusetts authority. Its uses for the first purpose were obvious enough, but Katzmann was also acutely aware of the second, as shown by his quick response—"I ask it be stricken out"—to Vanzetti's reference to the deportations. He did not want Vanzetti using the witness stand as a platform from which to denounce the deportations and police brutality. It was a vain effort. Katzmann had successfully objected, Thayer sustaining him, when Vanzetti was going to mention his radical activities in connection with the New York trip, but this had only postponed the subject. If Moore wanted his radicalism with its implications of official injustice, he was going to have it.

Recognizing its prime importance, Katzmann directed his cross-examination toward the story of the literature gathering. His strategy, however, was to soften up Vanzetti on other issues before getting to the literature. If he could catch the man in contradictions on any points at all, he would weaken Vanzetti's assurance when he arrived at the heart of the matter. Katzmann proceeded to test every part of his story.

Katzmann was hard. Some persons thought that he was, at best, an ambitious man who used his capacities to cruel advantage over men who had no training or education to fight back. Others have charged him with constructing a frame-up. From his bench on the Massachusetts Supreme Court Judge Harold Williams looks back on his old chief as a "fine man, splendid trial man," but he thinks the cross-examination of Vanzetti and particularly of Sacco was "hard, perhaps too hard." No one, however, has been able to prove that Katzmann was unfair. At one point, for example, he commented on his talk with Vanzetti the day after the arrest. At that time Vanzetti had apparently made a damaging admission, and referring to it now, Katzmann challenged him: "Don't you want me to ask you, sir?" Vanzetti replied with dignity: "I don't say that. You can ask me very well. That depends on you." Katzmann graciously gave way: "Well, if you put it up to my generosity, Mr. Vanzetti, I won't ask you." On other points, however, Katzmann did not let go.

One vulnerable area for the testing was the matter of dates. Katzmann attacked repeatedly: Why was Vanzetti so sure about some dates and so vague about others? He demanded: "But after waiting months and months and months you then remembered, did you?" Vanzetti returned the ball skilfully: "Not months and months and months but three or four weeks after I see that I have to be careful and to remember well if I want to save my life." Katzmann could do nothing with that answer, but he tried again: "You can't remember the day you called Connolly [the policeman] a liar but you say you can recall everything you did April 15, 1920." Vanzetti: "My head is involved—that is why I can remember the date." On the question of dates Vanzetti refused to be unsettled.

With the defendant countering the prosecutor so well, the cross-examination took on the character of a duel. At the time most observers did not feel strongly committed to either guilt or innocence. Giving up the effort to arrive at a hard decision, they retreated to marking off points for either side. Robert E. Riordan, city editor of the *Brockton Enterprise-Times,* who covered the trial for the old *Brockton Enterprise,* told me that the dozen reporters, with the exception of Sibley, shared that point of view: "Both prosecution and defense had a lot to offer and we had to go along, trying to measure out what this or that testimony or evidence could mean. It was a real contest." The attitude was illustrated by a series of front-page sketches appearing in the *Herald* of July 7. They had a Katzmann, caricatured into squatness, facing an unperturbed, operatic Vanzetti. The confrontation carried the comment: "Katzmann found it hard to feaze Vanzetti." So ended a full day's work for Vanzetti—four hours of telling his story to McAnarney's questions and four hours of cross-examination.

Vanzetti found the latter part of the cross-examination more difficult. The next morning Katzmann launched himself at the major target, to which he had been moving all the time: the literature story. Sibley observed: "Vanzetti spent the morning acknowledging freely and without anything in his voice except something like mild surprise at the question." But the *Herald* man saw him somewhat differently: "Vanzetti showed the effects of the strain of being on the stand all day yesterday. His calm, almost casual, air was gone. The biting cross-examination of the district attorney roused him to indignant, gesticulating retorts. At other times his voice was much less clear and strong." Katzmann drove hard at the events of the arrest day. He did not believe that Vanzetti had been intending to gather radical literature from the "three, five or six people" who, Vanzetti said, had "plenty of literature." Prisoner and prosecutor were agreed that this was the single most important part of the trial.

If Vanzetti could make the jury believe that he and his comrades had indeed intended to get the literature, he would have an explanation that would shelter him against the heaviest force of the prosecution's thesis. It would explain a great deal. It would explain why four men, two proven to have been heavily armed, wanted to acquire an automobile at 9:20 P.M. in a bucolic area that went to bed early. It would excuse the confused lies that Katzmann repeatedly snapped in Vanzetti's face. It would, in sum, explain all those actions of Sacco and Vanzetti upon their arrest which Katzmann wanted to define in legal idiom as evidence of "consciousness of guilt." Did their actions indicate a consciousness of the relevant guilt, guilt for murder committed?

Now, at Dedham, the explanation of radicalism contained all the pain and uncertainty about the Sacco-Vanzetti case. This was Moore's calculated risk. Vanzetti was addressing himself to a jury of average, small-town Americans during a time of back eddies from the Red raids. He was saying to them: "I am not a criminal. The proof is that I am a radical. In fact, I was engaged in radical activities the night when I was acting suspiciously." Each increment to the explanation of radicalism would be an increment to the reasons encouraging such a jury to dislike the man: if Vanzetti was innocent of murder, he was all the more guilty of attempted destruction of American society. Thayer might tell the jury to lay aside prejudice, accept the American ideal of justice and judge the case solely within its character as a criminal action. How much prejudice was in that jury?

Against Vanzetti's explanation, Katzmann began his attack by emphasizing the curious gap between cause and effect in the New York trip. There Vanzetti had been told, he testified, that he should hide the radical literature; there he had been warned about the Red raids of May 1. He was back in Plymouth on April 30 and yet no effort had been made to hide the material until May 5. One might reduce the time gap, however, if the spur to activity came from Salsedo's death, which occurred in the early hours of May 3 and which Vanzetti read about in the course of the day.

Nevertheless he and his friends acted very slowly for men afraid of drastic action by the authorities. Indeed, they went away from the Sacco house without attempting to hide the literature there.

On McAnarney's redirect examination after the cross-examination, Vanzetti was asked: "After you got back from New York, did you explain to your friends what you had learned?"

He replied: "A few days after, yes."

The details of that evening of May 5 remained vague. Vanzetti had been approximate under McAnarney's direct questions. He had first said simply that he was going to pick up the literature; he had then elucidated that he would first locate a Plymouth friend to act as a receiver for it. Against this, Katzmann was contending that Vanzetti had had no sense of urgency or fear about the Red raids. He emphasized Vanzetti's composition of the announcement that began: "Fellow workers. . . . Have you harvested the fruits of your labors?" The meeting was to take place publicly in Brockton on the following Sunday, May 9. Would a group of frightened radicals scurry about the countryside gathering up dumb pamphlets—while preparing to roar defiance at bourgeois society under the Sunday sun?

Despite his intense occupation with countering Katzmann's effects, Vanzetti could not forbear a lapse into the irritable pride of authorship. Of the announcement, he said: "I say I wrote that. It is not very well translated, but it is quite a good translation."

Katzmann inquired why the motorcycle could not have served to gather the literature. Under cross-examination fire Vanzetti had no good answer, but McAnarney later gave him another chance in the direct examination: "How much literature—what is your judgment—how much literature there was down in Plymouth, so far as you know?" Vanzetti: "It would be five hundred pounds, sure—four or five hundred pounds, sure."

Katzmann pressed the point about the objectives of May 5. Vanzetti had told the story in round terms in the first direct examination, and now Katzmann wanted specifics. Why May 5 and not immediately upon Vanzetti's return from New York? Just how did they propose to carry out their plan? What plan did they have? Vanzetti retreated in eloquent confusion and began talking about another objective. Forced to admit the curious failure to hide Sacco's literature, Vanzetti seemed to search for another ground firm enough to support the logic of the actions of that evening. He had wanted, he now amended, to locate a friend named Pappi in Bridgewater and charge him with announcing the Sunday meeting among the area's Italian community. But Vanzetti could tell little about his intercourse with Pappi since Pappi had moved from Plymouth to Bridgewater three or four years before. The disparity of objectives, hiding literature and locating Pappi, seemed even harder to explain. A stupid defendant would have held to his original testimony but Vanzetti was handicapped by his intelligence. Realizing that the business did not seem reasonable, he tried to shift about to the new position:

> Q. Was it your intention, then, not to take any literature on the night of May the 5th?
> A. No, I don't know when to bring that.
> Q. No. If you don't—
> A. Yes, yes, but it was not my intention.
> Q. I want you to be sure to understand my question. If you do not, you will do me a favor if you will say so.
> A. You asked me—
> Q. Wait a minute, please, and if you do not understand me, or if you are uncomfortable in talking with me other than through an interpreter, please say so now, and I will ask the interpreter to step forward.
> A. If I do not understand, I will tell you.
> (The question is repeated): Was it your intention then not to take any literature on the night of May 5th? The Witness: No.

At this point Vanzetti had failed himself and Moore utterly. He had permitted Katzmann to destroy their defense logic. The literature story was dead; Vanzetti had given up the best explanation for his activities of the arrest evening. Surely the story about Pappi was a feeble replacement. For the moment Vanzetti had rendered himself naked unto his enemies.

He was, however, given a second chance on redirect examination. Although it had suffered from the repudiation under pressure and lost its clarity, Vanzetti returned to the literature story on McAnarney's question:

> Q. Then what was your purpose and three others [sic], or two others besides Boda, in going down to West Bridgewater to get an automobile that was not to be used for that purpose that night?
>
> A. We want to take the automobile, and then my intention is to take the automobile with Boda, because I do not know how to drive the automobile, to go to Bridgewater and if we will be able to find the party, because I do not remember the address of the party. I do not know exactly where he lived. We will tell to Pappi about telling the Italian people of Bridgewater to come in Brockton next Sunday at the speech, and after I found Pappi, and speak to Pappi, go toward Plymouth and speak with my friends if I can find some friends who want to take responsibility of receiving such books in their house, in his house.

Let us suspend our awareness that Vanzetti faltered during the cross-examination and offered this modified explanation as response to his own counsel. After all, a skilful prosecutor can trip up innocence. Let us consider the Vanzetti account on its own merits. Who is Pappi? The first mention of that name actually occurred on the evening of the arrest. At that time the search for Pappi was Sacco's first explanation for their actions, but it was dropped in the course of the questioning. There is no Pappi to testify here in Dedham, but a Vittorio Papa did appear as a defense witness in the Plymouth trial. Papa said he had moved to East Bridgewater from Plymouth, where he used to see Vanzetti. He had invited Vanzetti to visit him in East Bridgewater, but, he testified, he had not given him his new address. Neither his testimony nor Vanzetti's indicate that Vanzetti ever found his way to Papa's house. Why had Vanzetti made such a point of involving Pappi with the meeting promotion—so late in the evening? Vanzetti did not even know precisely where or at what time the meeting would be held, and he could not have given him all the necessary information, his announcement having left the space for time and location blank. Of course it was idiotic, but we must emphasize: Vanzetti was not a logical person.

The next objective? Vanzetti would then look for a friend or friends in Plymouth, twenty miles from Bridgewater, to see if he or they would take the literature—"four or five hundred pounds, sure"—in the possession of "three, five or six people" in "five or six places, five or six towns." Would the four men not arouse unnecessary suspicion by searching about Plymouth so late at night? If they got the vehicle and found Pappi quickly enough, the complications of their Plymouth objective might continue to midnight or much later. It was idiotic.

It got worse when Vanzetti amended the location of the literature in a later direct examination: "There were some in Bridgewater, some in Brockton, some in Sacco house, some in Orciani house, there are some in Haverhill, some in Salem, and many other places that I don't know, but some other man knows the place and he will tell me." Haverhill and Salem are north of Boston, Haverhill by twenty miles. This was the only mention of an area north of Boston that touched on Vanzetti's activities, and it is an utter incongruity. Vanzetti had no concern with that district so distant from his normal meanderings: his Plymouth is twenty miles south of Boston. Can this madness be made credible?

Katzmann had a simple hypothesis: The group wanted the automobile to attempt a third holdup. That explained the late hour, the arms, the departure from the garage without the car—fear that Ruth Johnson was calling the police, ergo guilty consciousness—the alleged efforts to use arms on the arresting police, and the lies. Furthermore it explained Vanzetti's .38 caliber H. & R. revolver as booty from the second holdup—Berardelli's missing weapon. Katzmann's concept is as simple as the Copernican solar system. The Vanzetti explanation is Ptolemaic, requiring new epicycles to explain successive waves of irregularities.

When law students embarrass their seniors by demanding to know what constitutes reasonable doubt, they can be sent off with this statement of Judge Harold Medina: "If all the circumstances taken together are consistent with any reasonable explanation which includes the innocence of a defendant, the prosecution has not proved his guilt beyond a reasonable doubt. . . ." We can use the mechanics of the Medina formula in matching the Katzmann and Vanzetti theses. Katzmann's has the advantage of simplicity. But this is not the overriding factor, since a possibly complicated innocence must be protected against plain error. If a more complex explanation presents a chain of successively reasonable actions, then it is equally satisfactory. No part of it, however, is permitted outside the bounds of reason. Vanzetti offers two or three objectives—find Pappi, find a Plymouth receiver for the literature, perhaps actively gather the literature. We grant its complicated character but we know that Vanzetti was not a logical man. We might usefully seek enlightenment about the whole of the defendant as the trial continues.

8. Ecce Homo II

WE are observing the public Vanzetti. What is the quality of the private man?

At the sentencing Vanzetti spoke eloquently of his innocence and ideals. Perhaps a better expression, because less public, appeared in a letter written to Mrs. Elizabeth Evans a few days after the Plymouth trial:

> Thanks to you from the bottom of my heart for your confidence in my innocence. I did not spittel a drop of blood, or steal a cent in all my life. A little knowledge of the past; a sorrowful experience of the life itself had give to me some ideas very different from those of many other umane beings. But I wish to convince my felowmen that only with virtue and honesty is possible for us to find a little happiness in the world. I preached: I worked. I wished with all my faculties that the social wealth would belong to every umane creatures, so well as it was the fruit of the work of all. . . .*

It is a good letter; the man's ideals light it up for us today.

Like many idealists, Vanzetti had the feeling that he was chosen to do something of importance for his cause. He had a firm ego; he was willing to believe that he had the necessary ability. In a letter of April 3, 1927 he described himself as a

* Marion D. Frankfurter and Gardner Jackson (eds.), *The Letters of Sacco and Vanzetti* (New York: Viking, 1928), p. 81 (letter dated July 22, 1921).

"complete perambulating phylosopher of the main road,—crushing, burning a world within me and creating a new—better one." Later that month he wrote: "I am in a fit of self-boasting: Voltaire was brilliant and sharp, but I would be deeper in my petition." Perhaps such forthright "self-boasting" was not quite in earnest, but Vanzetti did find remarkable qualities in himself; with right.

His friends provide more details about the man. One gives an anarchist's view. It was Aldino Felicani who described him as a simple laborer—"simple, honest, good"—inspired by suffering to develop his powers to an extraordinary degree. Yet Vanzetti had been reading the anarchist press and such theorists as Proudhon, Reclus, and Bakunin before he went to prison, the meeting announcement he composed on the evening of the arrest documenting his acquaintance with the movement's thought and idiom. Perhaps Aldino Felicani has allowed his memory to be influenced by that tendency toward the legendary common among the dedicated. But then a nonanarchist like the prosperous lawyer William G. Thompson, who would succeed Fred Moore as chief defense counsel, might offer a less partisan evaluation. Thompson had the highest regard for both the character and the abilities of his client. At a memorial meeting for the prisoners, Thompson said:

> If Vanzetti had an education he would have been a professor in Harvard College. He is one of the most gifted men that I know of. I have heard him give a most enlightening talk on Ralph Waldo Emerson, he has discussed Shelley's poems with me, and I have heard him use words that I have had to go home to look for in the Century Dictionary to find the meaning of. He is a dreamer, and an idealist. . . . The Harvard graduate, the man of old American traditions, the established lawyer, is now quite ready to say that nowhere in his soul is there to be found the faith, the splendid gentility, which make the man, Bartolomeo Vanzetti.*

* Cited in Gardner Jackson, "The Power of Two Ghosts," *Nation*, Aug. 21, 1929, p. 191.

Thompson sketches a man of extraordinary parts, but we must not forget he was speaking to an audience that expected a eulogy. Besides, the lawyer's statements do not quite bring the man to life. Other people knew Vanzetti more intimately.

Although Beltrando Brini began with a string of commonplaces about official murder and proletarian martyrdom, he went on to recall affecting personal details of Vanzetti's years with the Brini family. When I spoke with Beltrando Brini he was principal of Willard Elementary School in Quincy and conductor of the Plymouth Philharmonic Orchestra, a station in life toward which Vanzetti had actively encouraged him. His father had not believed in a high school education, and it was Vanzetti who gave the boy the desire and the will to continue in school. When Beltrando showed talent with the violin, the family boarder, listening gravely as he practiced, urged him on. Once Vanzetti came upon him when he was playing conductor to the victrola; instead of laughing, he told the boy that he took the performance as a promise. It is a good story for the director of the Plymouth Philharmonic. Vanzetti's influence, moreover, extended to character building; he would take the boy into the woods for long, moralizing talks. Indeed, the last time Beltrando saw the free Vanzetti was the occasion for a lecture on right and wrong. Beltrando had been caught trespassing on a forbidden garden, and Brini recalled for me: "Vanzetti dropped down on his knee and lectured to me for fifteen minutes. He spoke quietly, something that I appreciated because my father would just get angry and shout." All this the boy's mother knew and approved.

Alfonsina Brini remembered Vanzetti as a good man and a good influence on her children. He did not drink, smoke, or consort with women, she specified. Furthermore, he had no interest in money, a noteworthy fact about a man accused of payroll robbery. She told me: Vanzetti had lost his pocketbook, but when police found one like it, he counted the money, decided there was too much in it and said it couldn't be his. When

Alfonsina Brini reminded him that he never knew how much money he had, he had said that he really doubted that the pocketbook belonged to him and that anyway somebody else needed the money more than he did. These are remarkable details but so intensely human that they are credible. After all, Vanzetti was an unusual man.

Yet they are all a catalogue of virtues. There was more to Vanzetti than goodness; he is not the faceless figure of a thousand parables. Vanzetti was surely better than an embodiment of idealism and martyrdom without distinguishing characteristics. To see him whole, however, we must save him from himself and his friends.

Fortunately for the real man, Vanzetti and his friends permitted themselves some human slips from the abstraction of goodness. We recall that Beltrando Brini asked: "Whether he abetted a crime for a cause . . . ?" In his letter to Mrs. Evans, Vanzetti, after his statement of anarchist principle, added: "But this do not mean robbery for a insurrection." Vanzetti dreamed of more things than a better world; he also dreamed of the methods to attain it, and the methods were necessarily affected by the injustices of the present one. In his denial he was taking cognizance of the accusations which the anarchists had brought upon themselves. Vanzetti consistently maintained his innocence of the Bridgewater and South Braintree holdups, but he never repudiated the Latin anarchist tradition that justified illegal action "for the cause." The Latin anarchists, making no distinction in principle between murder and theft, robbed banks and killed presidents, kings, and beggars in the latter part of the nineteenth and early in the twentieth century. Vanzetti's letters did not refer to anarchist robbery, but they indicated his approval of acts of violence in general. While this does not mean that he ever committed a crime, it is evidence of a harshness in his idealism.

Furthermore, Vanzetti reacted normally to the specifics of his situation. He could not look upon his own death with a saint's humility. His enemies were going to kill him; it was reasonable enough to hate them. Nor did Vanzetti hide his hate and his desire for revenge. Identifying himself with all oppressed, he wrote in early 1924: "I know the millions of youth that [the authorities] slandered, the virgins that they have torn in the breast; the millions of wives that they have widowed; the millions of bastards that they have let to miasma of the gutter. . . . I will ask for revenge—I will tell that I will die gladly by the hand of the hanger after having known to have been vindicated. I mean 'eye for an eye, ear for an ear,' and even more since to win it is necessary that 100 enemies fall to each of us." In the same letter he also said: "I abhor useless violence." He emphasized the point again, but went on: "I would my blood to prevent the sheading of blood, but neither the abyss nor the earth nor the heavens, have a law which condemns the self-defense."* In October 1926 he wrote: "I will make a list of honor of the perjurors who murdered us." Vanzetti was a real man and a real hater.

There is, also, another dimension of the man that must be considered, but considered with great caution. Undergoing a breakdown in the latter part of 1924, Vanzetti was diagnosed as "insane," "dangerous," and in a "hallucinatory and delusional state of mind" and spent the first five months of 1925 in the Bridgewater Hospital for the Criminally Insane. A psychiatrist named Ralph Colp, Jr., who studied the records in recent years, suggested that Vanzetti was never normal. Sympathetic to Vanzetti and convinced of his innocence, Colp nevertheless characterized his years of wandering in New York, New England, Mexico, and the Middle West as an indication of a profound disorder: ". . . paralysis of development, loneliness and nomadism." Such factors, Dr. Colp wrote in the *Nation* of December 27, 1958, are "hallmarks of a mental state of depression." In Van-

* Marion D. Frankfurter and Gardner Jackson (eds.), *The Letters of Sacco and Vanzetti* (New York: Viking, 1928), pp. 119–20.

zetti's account of the death of his mother, the psychiatrist thought he found the traumatic experience leading to the depression: an "unconscious guilt fantasy of having killed a parent." The sense of bereavement never left Vanzetti, who wrote in 1924: "My heart is a tabernacle in which my mother, and she was brave, lies." Now no one can claim that a depressed state, which too many respectable citizens endure, made a killer or outlaw of the man. It should, however, be put in context with our other views of him: the lonely wanderer taking human comfort from his relation to another man's son, the selfless man refusing money that might well have been his own. Vanzetti was a remarkable man.

If, however, we can see the extraordinary in his difficult virtues, we can find less evidence of the remarkable in Vanzetti's intelligence or articulation. Thompson, for example, cited none of the ideas that impressed him, while a search through the prisoner's writings shows nothing more than a simple rejection of the world and a faith in the anarchistic apocalypse. Vanzetti put it in one sentence: "To progress even a little, we have to destroy a world." When he attempted to think further, the result was embarrassing: "Indeed, I believe that nature is moral; that a real altruism is the same thing of a real egotism—and that the normal instinct of power is what we need." With his limited education and greater ambition, Vanzetti charged his untrained mind with impossible tasks and fell into deeper confusions. He did, however, have some traces of a literary talent, although this, too, was not on the level where sympathy would put it. In his letter to Mrs. Evans he used good phrases: "a little knowledge of the past; a sorrowful experience of the life itself. . . ." Or, in another letter: "I am a living hurricain of thoughts, feelings and sentiments." But Vanzetti the writer was unselective, illogical, and repetitious. He should not be taken seriously as a revolutionary intelligence or as a writer.

But Vanzetti was first-rate in the role thrust upon him. Arrest and imprisonment actually represented the best achievement of his life. Now his limited capacities could be used to maximum effect. His lack of coherence did not matter. As his letters show, he had a dramatic conception of himself, and he could use those letters and his engaging personality to communicate it. He was being heard for the first time. One day he reported having written "seven passable letters" and in a letter of September 21, 1926 he described his labors: "I am writing on the case: a book, maybe, if I will have time, will, and reason sufficiently. My long letter to Librado Rivera is ready to publication. It will be the first part of the book. After, 'The Journalistic Lynching' and 'A Journalistic Conspiracy of Quietness,' will follows. Then, a reproduction of the worst editorials against us and an answer to them. Then, a chapter on Katzmann, one on Thayer, one on the Massachusetts justices and one on Mr. Ranney*. . . ." The satisfaction he took from his situation is clear enough.

In his last letter, addressed to a literary friend, he made a final demand: "I hope you will lend your faculties in inserting our tragedy under its real aspect and being." In studying him coldly we have been trying to approach closer to the real man than sympathy would permit. The flaws we have found in him do not, however, justify any determinations on what he did or did not do in Bridgewater and South Braintree. Surely the real aspect and being of Vanzetti's tragedy can produce more important meanings.

* An assistant district attorney. See page 135.

9. Dedham III

VANZETTI had done well, despite his moment of weakness, and now, on the afternoon of July 6, Sacco succeeded him on the stand. Once again Moore put forward the person of the defendant and the issue of radicalism. Sacco also justified Moore's trust, responding to questions quickly and showing an awareness of the legal points behind them. Yet he lacked Vanzetti's ability to attract sympathy, and his bitterness went out against all the world.

Sacco's testimony was the last major effort of the defense. After him came judgment.

Like Vanzetti, Sacco began with the story of his life, boyhood in Torremaggiore, a small town inland from the Adriatic spur in Italy's boot, and apprenticeship to a mechanic. When he was seventeen, in 1908, he came to the United States with an older brother, who later returned to Italy. Sacco learned shoe edge-trimming and settled down in 1910 to seven years of steady employment with the Milford Shoe Company; Milford is another small town in the area southwest of Boston.

If the description of Vanzetti as a fish peddler is a strained *pars pro toto,* Sacco cannot accurately be called a shoemaker, as he was known in the case literature; he was a skilled shoe worker. Two years after he began his regular job, Sacco married his Rose, and their son Dante was born in 1913. Then came the flight to Mexico, where Sacco found no work and poor food. Back home, Sacco first had temporary jobs, including a week's work at the Rice & Hutchins plant, the observer, not the victim plant, of South Braintree. He then got a well-paying job at the Three-K shoe factory in Stoughton in November 1918 and was employed there until shortly before he was arrested in 1920. Except for the anarchist element, Sacco's life was almost the cliché of immigrant integration and modest well-being. Vanzetti was the purer proletarian.

Sibley reported for the *Globe* that Sacco "seems as sure of dates and hours as Vanzetti was." Vanzetti had begun to attract more people to the courtroom after the slackening in attendance, and now it was crowded in response to the lag effect, as people began to appreciate the attractions of a second defendant at bay. The heat continued high; palm leaf fans winked throughout the courtroom, and the walls and floor were slick with moisture. Fluent of purpose, if halting in words, Sacco then got into the story of the evening of the arrest. Unhindered by the characteristically careless Moore, who had other matters on his mind, Sacco blindly followed the Vanzetti rhythm of contradictory explanations. On the first day of his testimony, Sacco, like his comrade, defined the objective that evening of May 5 as simply the literature ingathering; the next day he added the amendment about seeking Pappi for the announcement of the anarchist meeting. It seemed a new proportion of idiocy, a recording of such fidelity that even the flatting was reproduced.

The subject of Sacco's second day on the stand, July 7, had greater effect than the detailing of the literature story. The subject was radicalism. It came out in the speech that Katzmann thought Moore had composed for Sacco. Whether Moore had actually written it or had merely reviewed Sacco's subject with him, the speech was the most explicit statement of radical principles during the trial, more aggressive than Vanzetti's remarks.

Passionately and at length Sacco described a capitalist existence that exploited workers and destroyed them in war. Anarchism would make a better world: "I want men to live like men. I like men to get everything that nature will give best, because they belong. . . . We no want fight by gun, and we don't want to destroy young men."

Katzmann counterattacked powerfully, but he was careful to avoid making an issue of radicalism itself. He did not want the court to be accused of prejudice. Nevertheless, Sacco's prizing of anarchist idealism left an opening for some heavy blows. Thus the prosecutor defined Sacco's refusal to register for the draft as the ingratitude of an immigrant who took his good wages and ran out when the country might have needed him. In the postwar period it was not an approach that would endear the defendant to the jury. Katzmann, however, was innocently unconscious of the distance between his civic values and Sacco's; he was defining as a failure in the performance of duty what Sacco's principles called an honest discharge of his duty. Yet Katzmann did not linger on the issue. The weight of his cross-examination, except for these few minutes, rested stolidly on the facts of the crime.

Sacco dealt with the other details confidently. He explained the pistol and ammunition: his wife was cleaning up preparatory to their trip to Italy, and he had been intending to shoot out the cartridges in the woods during the afternoon; he got into an argument and forgot his objective. The forgotten pistol, he said, remained tucked in his waistband through the afternoon and during most of the evening—until the arrest.

Sacco also handled the matter of the cap firmly. A cap lost by the killer who had stood over Berardelli had been found at the crime scene, and the prosecution claimed that it was Sacco's. Reporters saw the courtroom fitting differently. The *Herald* recorded: "It stuck on the top of his head and he turned with a satisfied air to let the jury see." Yet Sibley reported for the *Globe:* "Sacco . . . tugged it down on his head." One of the jury members told me he thought the cap had fitted Sacco, and the prosecution would emphasize the fact that the cap and another cap found in Sacco's home were both size 7⅛, while the defense would later make an appeal argument on the basis of the exhibit cap's trial prehistory. Yet the juror said it was not important in the jury's deliberations, and that casual piece of apparel, like many other of the case's material strays, would evoke more argument than it was worth.

Moore refused to be perturbed as Katzmann went on to attack various aspects of Sacco's account. Under Moore's guidance Sacco delivered his explanations through Wednesday and Thursday and, after an interruption caused by an indisposition of Vanzetti's, completed his labors on Saturday, July 9. A heavy storm during the night seemed to have swept away interest. Counting twenty-two spectators, Sibley recorded that the courtroom was "delightfully cool and delightfully depopulated."

The courtroom was crowded again on Wednesday, July 13, when Moore had his final chance. Making their summations, the attorneys explored the ultimates of hope and reason.

Four hours was allotted to the defense, Moore dividing the time equally with Jeremiah McAnarney. The defense strained to cover every point, McAnarney even addressing himself to the question of fairness:

> I want to say to you one of the pleasantest things that occurs in this case. . . . There is the patience of the Court and the District Attorney. . . . We had a funny experience here, Mr. Katzmann and I. He has been, as he always has been, a perfect gentleman. . . . They [the defendants] have had every opportunity here, they have had every patience, every consideration. I want them to know what we have done—that everything has been done as Massachusetts takes pride in doing, granting to every man, however lowly his station, the fullest right to our Massachusetts laws.

Moore, however, would not concede so much. Again he went over to the attack.

Having stressed the human in his case strategy, Moore now attempted to project it all the more through his own person. He began by referring to his own responsibility—"the responsibility for a human life"—and pointed to one possible outcome of the trial—"whether a woman shall be a widow and children fatherless. . . ."

Moore continued with the human element in attempting to reduce the whole trial to a matter of identification: "What is the issue in this case? The primary issue and the only issue here is the issue of identification." This would eliminate from serious consideration such matters as the ballistics evidence, which depended on a microscope, and also the question of the defendants' motivations at the time of the arrest—the whole complex about the literature gathering and "consciousness of guilt." Of course, Moore was not being strictly logical. He knew he would have to deal with the prosecution's use of the ballistics evidence. Furthermore, the literature story was too important to be discarded or even minimized. He would do the best he could with it, but first Moore wanted to explore all the possibilities of doubt in the matter of identification. Here was an element that was always vulnerable in its irreducibly human character.

Moore ran through the testimony of the prosecution eyewitnesses. About Lola Andrews, he asked the jury to agree with him that "she killed herself on the witness stand by her own personality" while other witnesses "finished her up." About other identifications, he emphasized the fact that the automobile was in motion when Mary Splaine, Frances Devlin, and Carlos Goodridge claimed to mark the man they identified as Sacco. He returned to Mary Splaine, arguing that the explicit nature of her description of the man made her testimony suspicious. He attacked the credibility of Louis Pelser because he had lied to a defense investigator. Against Pelser, also, he argued with massive irony that the man could not have seen what he claimed to have seen: ". . . he fastened his eyes down here on Sacco and fixed him in his mind forever. . . . Over here with his other eye he fixed it on the number of the car, and that number of the car remained fixed in his mind, bullets flying in all directions. . . ." Against all these witnesses, Moore demanded the jury consider the number of defense witnesses who had testified specifically that Sacco and Vanzetti were not members of the holdup gang. Furthermore, there were the alibi witnesses: "You have got to say that these men . . . have all stooped to the commission of perjury. . . ." And, returning once again to the fallibility of human witnesses, Moore ranged alibi against prosecution testimony: ". . . you have got to say that Mary Splaine, Lola Andrews, and Neal* and all of these people who never saw the defendant before—and when they did see him, saw him for a matter of seconds—that they are right and that the defendant (and the defense witnesses) are wrong."

Moore was weak on ballistics, having been badly assisted by the two defense experts. For its part, the prosecution got better support from its two experts, although one, State Police Captain William H. Proctor, made a bad impression when he was unable to dismantle a pistol on the stand. Proctor later gave an extraordinary interpretation of his trial testimony, but here he simply told the jurors that the fatal bullet taken from Berardelli's body was "consistent with being fired by that [Sacco's] pistol."

The other prosecution expert, Charles J. Van Amburgh, obviously knew his field, and he said, "I am inclined to believe that [the fatal bullet] was fired . . . from this [Sacco's] Colt automatic pistol." Van Amburgh pointed out to the jury a number of similarities, which could be seen either with the naked eye or with a magnifying glass.

* A slip of Moore's: Shelley Neal, the American Railway Express agent, did not identify either of the defendants.

Against this, Moore pointed to the defendants: "Gentlemen, when the time has come when a microscope must be used to determine whether a human life is going to continue to function or not and when users of the microscope themselves can't agree . . . then I take it that such ordinary men as you and I should hesitate to take a human life. . . ."

Moore then returned to the literature story, giving it the time its importance required. First he associated Pappi in the logic of it: "They did intend to see Pappi, but they did also intend to do something else, namely to get the . . . car." From this point, Moore went on to discuss at length the radical character of the literature and the fears of the men about deportation. But he did not attempt to organize the details of that evening, its problematic rationale remaining unresolved. Vanzetti's momentary weakening on the stand handicapped Moore here, and, for the last time, he could only seek to emphasize the challenge to the jury: Are you going to convict these men because they are radicals?

Moore, according to a reporter, had been "vehement, dramatic, forceful." He had been superbly persuasive in human terms, but he could not do everything himself. With all of his own strength he could not lift the whole case to that level where he wanted the jury to view it and feel it. It was too much to ask of one man or one lawyer.

Against Moore's force and McAnarney's competence—McAnarney had handled the case logic more effectively than Moore besides winning a better rapport with the jury—Katzmann spent four hours on the afternoon of July 13, rolling through the arguments one by one. First, the prosecutor attempted to reduce the radicalism out of the discussion. He told the jury that the issue was not radicalism; it was crime. With that precision, he struck hard at the literature story, showing how Vanzetti, and later Sacco, had shifted about on the details and the quest of Pappi. Katzmann thundered out the "consciousness of guilt" accusation: "Vanzetti had a loaded . . . .38 caliber revolver.

. . . This tender-hearted man. . . ." and "Nicola Sacco, another lover of peace, had with him . . . thirty-two death-dealing automatic cartridges, nine of them in a gun ready for action. . . ." The prosecutor's massive facts and logic crashed into the confusions and illogical character of the defendants.

Katzmann addressed himself directly to Vanzetti with another argument. He pointed out that Jeremiah McAnarney, although assigned to Vanzetti, had devoted most of his summation to Sacco. Why? Katzmann offered his explanation. The defense, he said, felt that Vanzetti's alibi was "hopeless"—in fact McAnarney had failed to promise an alibi in his opening statement—and now he was trying to win half a loaf by concentrating on Sacco's defense. If Vanzetti's person had been his best strength, his logic was his greatest weakness, and Katzmann the logician was merciless.

Against Sacco, Katzmann made one attack that did not affect Vanzetti directly. This was the ballistics argument, which Moore had tried to minimize. The prosecution's chief expert having given him useful testimony, he held Sacco to the guilt attributed to his pistol.

Katzmann would reduce the human element as much as he could. He was merciless.

Wednesday had belonged to the attorneys; Thursday, July 14, was Thayer's. He was to give the charge, an occasion celebrated with flowers in a custom of the area, and his bench was covered with gladioli from the sheriff's wife and pinks from the wives of the prosecution staff members. Sibley reported that the judge, who mounted the bench in the crowded courtroom at 10:38 A.M., had a "portentously thick, dark green folder." Sibley added, with an indication of asperity, that it was "noised about that Thayer's charge will be a legal document of great interest." Of course, Thayer had done the noising about; his vanity and ambitions were subsumed in the dark green folder.

Rose Sacco and Dante came to the cage, and the prisoners

teased the attractive eight-year-old boy and pulled his hair. "Vanzetti's eyes glowed, his smile seemed very merry," a reporter wrote.

Thayer spoke for nearly two hours,* telling the jury to clear away "the mist of sympathy or prejudice." He went on:

> Let me repeat to you what I said to another jury in a similar case: Let your eyes be blinded to every ray of sympathy or prejudice but let them ever be willing to receive the beautiful sunshine of truth, of reason, and sound judgment, and let your ears be deaf to every sound of public opinion or public clamor, if there be any, either in favor or against these defendants. Let them always be listening for the sweet voices of conscience and of sacred and solemn duty efficiently and fearlessly performed. The law grants to every person the same rights and privileges. . . .

Thayer moved to the principles of proof:

> The Commonwealth must prove beyond reasonable doubt every fact or element necessary to prove the crime of murder. If the Commonwealth should fail to establish every fact that is essential to prove the crime of murder, then crime alleged has not been established beyond reasonable doubt. If, again, you should find some fact to be true that is essential to establish the crime of murder and which fact is consistent with innocence and inconsistent with guilt, then the Commonwealth has failed to prove the crime of murder as alleged.

Thayer cautioned: "The law does not require proof so positive, so unerring and convincing that amounts to a mathematical or absolute certainty. You might obtain proof of that character in the exact sciences, but not in human investigations."

Thayer said it was for the jury to decide between the identifications and alibis; to make its own determinations on the ballistics testimony, the cap, and the defendants' actions of the arrest evening.

* *Transcript,* vol. 2, pp. 2239–64.

Thayer said: "I have tried to preside . . . in the spirit of absolute fairness and impartiality to both sides. If I have failed in any respect you must not, gentlemen, in any manner fail in yours. . . .

"Reflect long and well so that when you return, your verdict shall stand forth before the world as your judgment of truth and justice. Gentlemen, be just and fear not. Let all the end thou aimest at be thy country's, thy God's, and truth's."

The *Herald* reported: "Judge Thayer received the acknowledgement of the lawyers for the defense and prosecution for the fairness and impartiality in the able way he had tried the case."

The jury commenced collective thought at three that afternoon of July 14. It sent for a magnifying glass a short time later, interrupted its labors to sup for an hour and a half, and emerged at 8:15 P.M. The courtroom spectators, compressed down to a hard residue of the completely engaged, reacted sharply to the threat implicit in its comparatively brief time of deliberation. Judge John W. McAnarney, who had added his presence to that of his eloquent brother Jeremiah and silent brother Thomas, slacked into a gesture of despair; Vanzetti knit his brows in visible thought, and Sacco, pale and strained, searched face after face for explanation.

Thayer said to the clerk: "You will please take the verdict."

Worthington said: "Gentlemen of the jury, have you agreed upon a verdict?"

The jurors rose uncertainly to their feet; the foreman Ripley said: "We have."

Worthington said: "Nicola Sacco, hold up your right hand."

Sacco stood up. He said: "Press-ent."

Worthington continued: "Mr. Foreman, look you upon the prisoner. Prisoner, look upon the foreman. What say you, Mr. Foreman, is the prisoner at the bar guilty or not guilty?"

"Guilty."

The other jurors nodded assent. A guard motioned Vanzetti to stand. Sacco remained fixed, with his right hand still in the air, until the guard told him to put it down.

Worthington said: "Guilty of murder?"

"Murder."

"In the first degree?"

"In the first degree."

"Upon each indictment?"

"Yes, sir."

Worthington began again: "Bartolomeo Vanzetti, hold up your right hand. Look upon the foreman. Mr. Foreman, look upon the prisoner. What say you, Mr. Foreman, is Bartolomeo Vanzetti guilty or not guilty of murder?"

"Guilty."

"In the first degree, upon each indictment?"

"In the first degree."

Worthington said: "Hearken to your verdicts as the Court has recorded them. You, gentlemen, upon your oath, say that Nicola Sacco and Bartolomeo Vanzetti is each guilty of murder in the first degree upon each indictment. So say you, Mr. Foreman? So, gentlemen, you all say?"

The jury mumbled severally: "We do, we do, we do."

Like Sacco, Vanzetti remained stunned, holding his hand suspended as if he were waiting for a better verdict. A moment later he advanced to a new thought and leaned toward Sacco to whisper some words.

Thayer's face was a gray mask. He said to the jury: "I can add nothing to what I said this morning, gentlemen, except again to express to you the gratitude of the Commonwealth for the service that you have rendered. You may now go to your homes from which you have been absent for nearly seven weeks. The Court will now adjourn."

Sacco shouted, "Siamo innocente!" He repeated his insistences of innocence several times in English as the jurors filed out, some looking back in wonder at what they had done to this man. Sacco held up his arm again, two fingers waving in the extension of another thought. His wife rushed to him and they held each other against the decision. Sacco then disengaged himself partially to shout again: "Don't forget, they kill two innocent men!"

Rose Sacco echoed him with that idiom of the twenties: "You bet your life!"

She moaned: "Oh, they kill my man, what am I going to do, my two children?"

A guard tried to separate them but Rose Sacco became hysterical and Moore's wife comforted her. A *Herald* reporter noticed tears in the eyes of several guards. The prisoners were manacled and led out. Deputy Sheriff Oscar Capen motioned away the small crowd that had collected at the courthouse entrance, and the prisoners and guards walked down the street to Dedham jail.

In the courtroom friends and relatives of the men protested and wept, carrying their sounds into the corridors and, finally, into the streets. Riordan, the *Brockton Enterprise* man, found Assistant District Attorney Williams alone in a corner of the deserted courtroom. Riordan mentioned the victory. Williams was weeping. "Yes, because of that, two men have to go to the electric chair," he said.

Moore, stunned by the defeat, would not weep, would not admit the electric chair. At this moment he was overwhelmed, but he knew the moment would pass. He had given all of his heart and abilities to winning, and he had lost, and yet he had given so much that he had created forces which were still alive. With them he would continue to fight for his men. It was still his case and Sacco and Vanzetti were still his responsibility.

10. *Early Darkness: Moore's Motions*

> **". . . the hunchback plucked at the young man's sleeve and said, 'it's the appeal that counts, you know,' and Quentin said, 'Yes, I know. The appeal's everything.' "**
>
> —REBECCA WEST
> *The Meaning of Treason*

MOORE had failed in Dedham courthouse. Worse, he had failed outside. If we think of the effect of the sentencing six years later, we can measure the extent of the failure. With all the passion of the sympathizers in 1921, with all the front-page stories in the Boston newspapers, and with his conception of the injustice already active, Moore nevertheless had not been able to give the case national or international importance. For that, he needed the intellectuals and the Communists. In 1921 neither group had been ready.

We have seen how the Boston Communists turned Aldino Felicani away. With a few isolated exceptions, the intellectuals were not much more helpful. As a class they had not yet accepted the Sacco-Vanzetti case.

You could find little concern for it in their publications. In his *American Mercury*, H. L. Mencken never associated the case with all the injustices, bigotry, and provincialism he attacked. (Not even in 1927 did the magazine carry an article on it.) The *New Republic* failed to follow Beffel's early article in 1920 with consistent coverage. The *Nation* waited more than two months after the Dedham trial to publish any important comment, and then the comment was cool. In the issue of September 28, 1921, one of its editors, Arthur Warner, expressed the opinion that Thayer had been a fair judge and rejected the frame-up theory. While Warner thought there was still a "reasonable doubt" on guilt, he divided his skepticism into equal parts: "To me the whole mass of this [i.e., identification] evidence for or against the defendants is not worth a hill of beans." The intellectuals were standing aside.

In view of all that he lacked, Moore had done all that was possible in 1921.

Now he would build on his failure. The long trial had produced great amounts of evidence and testimony that could be worked over again, while the issue of radicalism could rise stronger than ever with proper management. The only rational way of overcoming the defeat was to call it a preliminary episode in a continuing battle. Moore would put the prosecution case to every test. He would appeal and appeal.

Moore would have to do much more than rebuild the legal elements of the defense. He would have to restore everything else, the money, connections, and publicity. For the defeat had reduced aid just when it was most needed. Since the trial had been exhaustive and well publicized, most persons were willing to accept the jury's verdict. Some friends of the defense lost their belief in the innocence of Sacco and Vanzetti; others lost their spirit. It was the period of Early Darkness, in the words of Eugene Lyons, who contrasted it with the era of Belated Chic in 1927, when the case attracted more distinguished sympathizers. In 1921, it seemed that the world and Boston had forgotten Sacco and Vanzetti.

Moore marshaled his allies among the few persons who would not forget the men. They were not only few; they were difficult. The anarchists remained at the core of the Sacco-Vanzetti Defense Committee, and their principles ran counter to organized action. While some of them, like the politic Aldino Felicani and the retiring Ermano Bianchini, who married the widow Sacco in

1929, recognized the need for discretion, others attempted to maintain their revolutionary purity. According to Eugene Lyons, the Boston anarchists were a "branch of the Galleani group, which advocated the use of bombs and printed booklets on dynamite bomb construction." In a talk with me in 1958 Lyons mentioned his suspicions of two men who held the post of Defense Committee secretary at various times. One was the stubborn Frank R. Lopez, a Spaniard with useful international connections who was deported in 1924. His successor, Emilio Coda, was a "little red-haired anarchist who liked to talk violence." (In 1927 Lyons published a book in passionate defense of the innocence of Sacco and Vanzetti, but he has since become somewhat doubtful of it as well as more critical of his associates.) In any case, anarchistic principles were useful neither in winning formal victories in the American courts nor in conditioning a favorable climate of public opinion.

The other allies were more practical. Good women like Mrs. Elizabeth Glendower Evans maintained their connections to Boston authority, and some conservative Brahmins found themselves aiding the Defense Committee at the urging of a maiden aunt or a social-worker niece. The women belonged to that reformist underworld so mordantly described by Henry James in his novel, *The Bostonians.* Years before the Sacco-Vanzetti case, James had studied the "great irregular army of nostrum-mongers" uniting Boston's "witches and wizards, mediums, and spirit-rappers, and roaring radicals." If this was at a fictional remove from the case, Mrs. Evans herself served as a model for the elderly heroine of Upton Sinclair's novel, *Boston.* Sinclair narrates the ideological prehistory: "Betty would drive Granny to anarchist or socialist or atheist or pacifist or pro-German meetings." James could find easy targets for his satire and Sinclair would reveal more family secrets than his naive sympathy was aware of. Nevertheless, the reformers were invaluable in bringing the future to Boston's attention and softening its chill reception of the Irish, Italian and other new residents. Reformist participation in the Sacco-Vanzetti case was another chapter in that tradition.

The relationship between middle-class respectables and anarchists had its entrancing aspects. In a 1948 magazine article Eugene Lyons recalled seeing the sinister Emilio Coda and "benign and soft-hearted" Mrs. Evans . . . mapping defense strategy together."

The composition of the Defense Committee was inevitably unstable. Lyons himself left Boston for good in 1922 to join the New York office of *Tass,* the Soviet Russian news agency. Now and then an anarchist like Lopez would be deported or disappear for other reasons known to himself. Now and then someone would gravitate to the Committee and stay. Along with Moore, Carlo Tresca had sent his mistress as another contribution to the Committee personnel. Also a veteran of the Lawrence strike, Elizabeth Gurley Flynn had grown fat and difficult in the service of good causes, a Committee member dismissing her as "that crazy woman" in a talk with me. The Committee attracted its share of eccentrics, including a poetess of free verse who disturbed several marriages and other private arrangements with her unrhymed morality. The surcharged atmosphere had an unsettling effect on persons sufficiently unorthodox to enter it in the first place, and the slim (in those hungry days), mellifluous Felicani was put to it to parry the distracting interest of emancipated females. Nevertheless, their overriding dedication to the cause was more useful than mere efficiency, and Moore, permitting the other drives to lunge about as they would, maintained command over the important currents of action.

Handicapped by the defeat, Moore did the best he could to get more money and publicity. He wrote hundreds more of begging letters. He had sent Lyons to Italy to persuade an Italian deputy to raise the Sacco-Vanzetti question in the Parliament (this was before Mussolini's capture of power), and he kept the publicity releases flowing to the labor press and any other publications that might still be hospitable. Unfortunately, at this time, the subject had become stale. Moore did his best to improve it by providing new elements in the appeals.

His efforts to reshape the case were epic. At the trial we have seen how he attempted to reduce the force of the prosecution's charges through countertestimony and repudiations. Of the latter, we recall that Lewis Wade and Louis De Beradinis partially withdrew from their original identifications of Sacco. Now with more time to master the material, Moore erected a massive and complex structure of new repudiations. His candidates for the roles of repudiators were three persons who had already undergone the weight of his heaviest attention in Dedham: Louis Pelser, Lola Andrews, and Carlos Goodridge.

On February 4, 1922, under questioning by Moore, Pelser made a statement repudiating his trial testimony. Two days later he wrote to Katzmann saying that he had made the statement under these circumstances: "Saturday afternoon a man called for me in regards the Sacco Case. . . . I was drinking pretty heavy . . . we went into some office in Pemberton Sq. he introduced me to Mr. Moore then he sat me down and locked the door Moore said to me you look like a white man. . . . He had 3 or 4 men in his office & a girl stenographer. He asked me one question & other and finally had my whole story contradicted what I had said at the Dedham Court. I am worried at the way they have framed me and got me in to trouble. . . ." On January 24, 1923, Pelser made a more detailed denial in the form of an affidavit, this time under questioning by Assistant District Attorney Williams. Insisting that his trial testimony was accurate and honest, Pelser deposed that Moore had got him drunk and had heaped threats and promises of money upon him. Judge Thayer, who heard the appeal, believed him.

On September 9, 1922, Lola Andrews filed an affidavit repudiating her trial testimony. She said she had been intimidated by Katzmann, Williams, Stewart, and another police officer, who had threatened her with publicity about her past. In a second affidavit, on January 29, 1923, however, she repudiated the repudiation. The first affidavit had been accompanied by the supporting statements of John Van Vaerenwyck, the Massachusetts A.F. of L. vice president, and Fred G. Biedenkapp, also a left-wing labor leader and a friend of Moore's, and now Lola Andrews swore that the two union men had aided Moore in intimidating her. She related:

Moore's associates had called her to Boston and confronted her with her nineteen-year-old son, Andrew John Hassam. Lola Darroch Moore had brought him down from Maine, where his perigrinating mother had long ago deposited him. (The boy was the product of Lola Andrews' marriage with a drunkard, whom she had left to embark on a life that made her vulnerable to investigation.) Whatever the unhappy details, Van Vaerenwyck and Biedenkapp told her that they had twelve or thirteen affidavits about her past in Maine, that they would blacken her life and ruin her son's future. The group attempted their persuasions from seven until midnight in the Essex Hotel in Boston and then in Moore's home for several hours longer. She was so tired and frightened that she did not know what she was signing.

Judge Thayer scolded Moore for unprofessional conduct.

The most energetic action was directed against Carlos Goodridge. In this case the witness's past was amply documented by court records: Goodridge was a thief. In fact he had first identified Sacco when his own difficulties with the law had, by chance, brought him into court at the same time. At that moment, in 1920, he had been arrested for robbing his employer; he escaped prison by promising restitution. Also he had been twice convicted for larceny several years previously, and a New York state indictment of 1911 had never been served, the authorities being, for unexplained reasons, no longer interested in prosecution. Moore attacked Goodridge through that indictment. Tracking his man to a farm in Maine, Moore told him he was wanted and deposited him in an Augusta jail on July 15, 1922. A deposition of Robert A. Cony, judge of the municipal court, said that Moore had persuaded him to issue an arrest warrant on the representation that the New York police wanted Goodridge. Cony said that Moore pretended to send a telegram to the New York authorities informing them of the arrest, that there was no response from New York, and that he accordingly released Goodridge two days later. Goodridge himself deposed that Moore had threatened him with arrest if he did not change his Dedham testimony. Goodridge said he refused; the arrest followed. In his final word, Goodridge reaffirmed his testimony at Dedham.

Judge Thayer called Moore's actions a "bold and cruel attempt to sandbag Goodridge. . . ."

Moore's efforts ranged well beyond the area of repudiation. Other motions attacked the prosecution case from various points. His first serious motion was directed against the jury foreman, Walter H. Ripley, who died before Thayer could question him on the point at issue. Jeremiah McAnarney deposed that Ripley had confessed to him that he had carried three .38 cartridges in his pocket during the trial. The motion argued that the presence of those bullets in the jury room compromised a fair verdict, although it was not clearly explained why they should have done so. In any case, the eleven surviving jurors signed affidavits saying that their judgment had not been affected.

Moore then sought to impeach Ripley with a second affidavit, this one dated September 30, 1923. According to William H. Daley, an acquaintance of Ripley's: ". . . the affiant said he did not believe that they were guilty; that it was not reasonable to suppose that a man would go and rob a factory where he had worked, was well known and in broad daylight, and thereupon the said Ripley said to the affiant, 'Damn them, they ought to hang them anyway.' " "Damn them, they ought to hang [them] anyway" became an ironical defense slogan heavily used at protest meetings later, a fine example of the publicity values Moore was seeking and creating. In the courts, however, it was useless under colder scrutiny, since it was, after all, unsubstantiated hearsay as reported by an aggressive defense partisan.

In another area of evidence, Moore produced still another witness who would deny that Sacco was the killer. The witness was Roy Gould, an itinerant salesman of a paste for sharpening razor blades. According to his affidavit of March 17, 1922, Gould had been on his way to sell his paste at the South Braintree factories when the holdup occurred. The gunman had fired at him from the car, Gould said, shooting a hole in his overcoat. He was definitely not Sacco for these reasons: Sacco's eyebrows were not as heavy, Sacco's eyes were not as piercing, Sacco's cheekbones were not so high, Sacco's features were not so sharp, and Sacco appeared to be older, heavier, and broader through the shoulders. The judgment on the quality of the gunman's eyes would indicate strong subjective factors, while the circumstances attending the affidavit also showed its highly interested character. Gould, himself an I.W.W. member, was an old friend of Burke, Moore's I.W.W. assistant. Indeed, Burke had located Gould for his chief, according to the affidavit material. Furthermore, Gould describes that moment of the shooting which had been Burke's subject for his testimony at the trial. It would be an extraordinary coincidence for two friends to experience the same part of the climactic action, each remaining unaware of the other's presence. Additionally, the date of the affidavit indicates that Gould took his time about reporting what he saw. He gives an explanation for the delay, but it contains a discrepancy which must be corrected in another affidavit a year later. If this were not enough, we can refer back to Burke's description of the killer and compare it with Gould's. Gould would have the gunman's features sharper than those of Sacco, while Burke described him with a "very full face . . . broad, heavy jowl. . . ." When we consider that several persons had testified at the trial that Sacco was not the killer (against the seven prosecution identifications), this one new negative can add little probative weight.

The case record throws up many traces of Moore's furious and imaginative energy. Besides his foray into Maine to seize Goodridge, a project that produced scores of pages for the case transcript, including court records and proof of the man's bigamous marriage, Moore went off as far as Georgia to develop another defense argument with information provided by two prisoners in the Atlanta penitentiary. His posttrial legal operations resolve down to six motions, the first a formal motion to set aside the verdict as against the weight of the evidence. Then he made five supplementary motions. These included the efforts to impeach three of the eleven identification witnesses (Pelser, Lola Andrews, Goodridge), introduction of the negative witness (Gould), the two affidavits attacking the jury foreman Ripley, and an affidavit of Captain Proctor, one of the two prosecution ballistics experts, which suggested a different meaning for his trial testimony. We shall study the ramifications of the latter in another chapter.

The appeals dragged through the years. Thayer quickly denied the formal motion, but illness and other factors delayed his decisions on the five supplementary motions until 1924. Meanwhile, Moore had to contend with office intrigues like those documented in a letter of October 21, 1922, from the Spanish anarchist Frank Lopez. Two women staff members were harassing a third woman, Lopez complained to Moore, and he added that less idealistic persons were going to the movies and claiming unearned overtime. Later in 1922 a letter from Moore urgently demands money from Mrs. Elizabeth Evans, as if it were a debt she was obligated to pay. Always conscious of the needs of publicity, Moore takes the time to write a letter of thanks to Upton Sinclair, who had sent a package of books to Vanzetti. Sinclair did lend his name to various demands for revision but his greatest effort, the novel *Boston,* was published a year after Sacco and Vanzetti were beyond assistance. In January 1924 Moore is impelled to "request the departure" of a Defense Committee employee because of "many unpleasant features in the office."

Opposition to Moore was rising in the Committee. He usually quarreled with his clients, long exposure to his temperament operating with exacerbating effect, and he was always unsettling in money matters. Speaking of Moore to me, Aldino Felicani paid his measured respects: "Moore did a good job. He penetrated the labor movement when we were completely out, when nobody would listen to us. I say this, he was sincere."

By early 1924 Moore's position in the Sacco-Vanzetti Defense Committee had become untenable. Attempting to establish a new base of action, he organized the New Trial League in April with support that included Mrs. Elizabeth Evans, John Van Vaerenwyck, John Codman of the New England Civil Liberties Committee and Professor Felice Guadagni, the latter one of Sacco's alibi witnesses. Lacking any coherence, however, the new group collected a little money, published a bulletin and a pamphlet—and faded away. Most of its people returned to the Defense Committee.

Meanwhile, in the last days of Moore's tenure, the anarchist members of the Defense Committee were permitting another leftist element to enter the inner circle of committee power. Suffering from personnel attrition through deportation and defection, the anarchists doubtless felt that the new people, as bona fide radicals although of an anomalous Irish character, would help them against such suspect allies as the labor union officers and the good Boston ladies. Organized as the James Connolly Literary Society, the Irish members were actually a defecting splinter of the Gaelic League distinguished for anticlerical views and a vague concern with Marxism. One of the group, John Barry, a stationary engineer with numerous children, became official chairman of the Defense Committee, filling his position with so much tact that he decided nothing and accomplished nothing. More important was the participation of Mary Donovan, an aggressive, slat-bodied, stringy-haired Commonwealth labor inspector. Curiously maternal, she adopted the anarchists of the committee and was soon important in their counsels. John Barry, Mary Donovan, and their friends added an odd striping to the committee coloration, but in this difficult period they brought saving strength.

To the anarchists of the Defense Committee, Moore's attempt to set up a rival organization was unforgivable. They easily won Sacco to their opinion. Like Vanzetti, Sacco had also undergone a psychotic episode, and a morbid sense of oppression and betrayal never left him. He turned his suspicions on Moore and told him bitterly to go, writing on August 18, 1924: "And I can see how clever and cynic you are, because after all my protest, you are still continuing the infamous speculation on the shoulder of Sacco-Vanzetti 'case'. . . . But, I would like to know who his this man that are abuse to take all the authority to do everything that does feel like without my responsibility, and carry my case always more long, against all my wish. . . . I am telling you that you goin to stop this dirty game!" In order to make his point with anarchist clarity, Sacco added: "Deluder . . . such sweet pay that has been come to you right long. . . . Let me tell you right now don't be illuse yourself because I would not be surprise if somebody will find you some morning hang on lamp-post. . . . Your implacable enemy, now and forever. . . . Nick Sacco."

The money situation had become worse as Moore waited for the decision on the pending motions. He was certainly no longer able to finance "theatre parties" and his worn clothes marked him as a poor credit risk. Yet success with just one of the five motions would change everything. It would mean a new trial, more opportunity to tear down the rest of the prosecution's case, and also new money sources, better connections, and more favorable publicity. Moore had moved many persons to many actions; he had thrown all of his weight against the masonry of the Commonwealth's justice; he had inspired hundreds of pages of testimony. Surely one flaw could be found in the prosecution case, and a retrial, as everyone knew, always gave the defense a better chance. Some prosecution witnesses might not be available, others might have begun to have doubts, and the new publicity and improved connections would give Moore more power to affect more people and create new situations. The possibilities were still rich. But, in spite of everything, Moore failed for the last time. Judge Thayer, whose duty it was to pass on the motions, denied every one on October 1, 1924. If prejudice had guided his judgment, the Defense Committee's first desperate study could find no clear indications of it in his very long opinion. Nevertheless, it was man-made and subject, upon reflection, to new attack. This was Moore's last contribution to the case. He would not, however, be the person to exploit the Thayer opinion. At the moment, identified with utter failure, he was completely used up as a force in the law and also in the larger conflict. The next month, in November, he left the Sacco-Vanzetti case.

Eugene Lyons remembers how he left. Buying an automobile with his last funds, Moore set out for the West Coast. Without any money to spare, he planned to finance the trip by selling an automobile attachment, a sign that read: "If you're close enough to read this, you're too damn' close." He was even without a wife at the time, Lola Darroch having left him, Lyons recalls. Also, according to Upton Sinclair, who drew upon him at length in 1927 for his novel, Moore had lost his belief in his clients' innocence.* When Moore had assumed the defense in 1920 he had stepped onto a rising development precisely at the time when his old employer, the I.W.W., was going down. By 1924 the I.W.W. had disintegrated and Moore had to seek a new field of action in a different era; the prosperity of the twenties had dissipated the initial burst of radicalism. Moore never again pleaded a great case. He died of cancer a decade later.

* Sinclair statement cited in Francis Russell, *Tragedy in Dedham* (New York: McGraw-Hill, 1962), pp. 256–57.

11. Moore and a Minor Applied Science

MOORE is always present in the Sacco-Vanzetti case by his works. When we go on from witnesses and arguments to the most scientific part of it, the ballistics identification, we shall continue to deal with Moore's contributions. This will take us to 1927—to the sentencing and beyond.

Let us first return briefly to the Dedham trial to examine its ballistics findings in more detail. We recall that after Proctor's limited testimony, Van Amburgh, then a firearms man with the Remington Arms Company of Bridgeport, said he was "inclined to believe" that the fatal bullet came from Sacco's pistol. He pointed out the markings on the fatal and test bullets: "There are irregularities evidently caused by similar scoring or irregular marks in rifling which appear on all bullets which I have examined. . . . I find on No. 3 bullet [the fatal bullet] such evidence of scoring in the barrel. It takes on the bullet the form of, well, a long streak bordering close on the narrow cut, the land [ridge] cut, on the bullet." Using a microscope, he pointed out to the jury a "rough track" alongside the land (ridge) in a part of the barrel of Sacco's pistol. He said this "rough track" was called a "pit" and was normally caused by allowing powder to remain in the barrel, permitting the development of rust. Van Amburgh showed the jury "quite a collection of pits." These tracks or pits, in turn, scratched the distinctive markings on test bullets fired in such a barrel. In Van Amburgh's opinion, the markings on No. 3 bullet, the bullet recovered from the body of Berardelli, were similar. Van Amburgh specified: "There seems to be one which has impressed me very much, one streak along each bullet fired through this exhibit gun—very pronounced." The jury looked at these markings through a microscope.

The defense fared badly in the cross-examination of Van Amburgh. The jurors could remember what they had seen in the microscope and compare it with Van Amburgh's explanations on the one hand, and the remarks of defense counsel, on the other. For their part, the defense experts further handicapped Moore by making impossible statements and contradicting each other. James E. Burns denied that the pitting marks, which Van Amburgh had shown the jury, could be of any value in identification. His colleague, J. Henry Fitzgerald, could not agree, since firearms identification is based on comparing just such markings. Fitzgerald advanced still another argument; he insisted that the pitting marks were different. In view of these confusions, Van Amburgh's simple statement easily withstood all the defense arguments.

The defense had also made ballistics tests, but its procedure was not helpful. Burns, who carried them out, had used U.S. bullets, which were smaller than the Winchester that had killed Berardelli. Of course the markings on the test bullets were less distinct, reducing the expert to the claim that his U.S. bullets were "close enough" to the Winchesters. Under cross-examination Burns turned balky. Katzmann asked: "Where my finger is do you see those pebbles, if I may so speak of them?"—he was speaking of the pitting—and Burns returned: "You might see mountains there, but I can't see them." Burns refused to answer a number of questions comprehensibly and finally burst out: "You hang right onto it. You fooled me yesterday, and I don't want you to do it again." He denied also that he could see a widening in a groove on the fatal bullet. Katzmann persisted: "Do you see such widening?" Burns retreated: "A slight, but not perceptible, only under the glass." Katzmann also got him to admit that his U.S. test bullet would be more lightly marked than the fatal Winchester, but Burns refused to be moved from his original position on the groove widening and simply refused to answer the question. The prosecutor drove hard at both Burns and Fitzgerald, but Thayer was particularly solicitous of their rights and held back some of Katzmann's force.

Katzmann had not completely mastered his ballistics, but he did handle it better than the defense attorneys. His summation dealt roundly with the defense experts, their contradictions and their obduracy. He repeated Burns' words: "I don't understand what you mean by widening." Also emphasizing the pitting, Katzmann then told the jury that it should decide on the basis of its own observation. The jurors, who had studied the bullets through a microscope during Van Amburgh's testimony, sent for a magnifying glass during their deliberations.

McAnarney was almost helpless in his final argument and we recall that Moore lapsed into eloquence: "Gentlemen, when the time has come when a microscope must be used to determine whether a human life is going to continue to function or not . . . then I take it that such ordinary men as you and I should hesitate to take a human life." It was a vain effort in view of the indisputable value of scientific evidence.

If Katzmann was clearly the superior on ballistics, he did miss two points that could have been damaging to the defense. He failed to say that the fatal bullet and some of the thirty-two cartridges found on Sacco were of an obsolete and rare type; hence Sacco's possession of such bullets would be an extraordinary coincidence. Indeed, the defense expert Burns had tried to excuse himself for having used different bullets in his tests by insisting that he had not been able to purchase any Winchesters of that type. Katzmann failed also to remark another coincidence: of the four shells (the so-called "Fraher" shells) found in South Braintree, two were Peters, one a Winchester, and one a Remington, and all three types, as well as a fourth, were represented among Sacco's thirty-two cartridges.

At Dedham Katzmann and his experts were more persuasive. Afterwards, Moore tried to repair the damage by placing more emphasis on the ballistics proof. His important effort, however, did not come until March of 1923. At that time he hired an expert named Albert H. Hamilton, who had been recommended to him by Frank Sibley, the *Globe* reporter. Unfortunately, Hamilton's capacities were more appropriate to desperation than to truth. A former druggist who once said he had testified in 229 murder trials, Hamilton offered himself as an expert in inks, firearms and bullets, and external and internal bullet wounds. Although his arguments, formalized in the fifth supplementary motion, were cast down in 1924, he would stay with the case into 1927, and Mrs. Elizabeth Evans noted in an article, "Mr. Hamilton's charges were high."

Hamilton was mentioned in *Convicting the Innocent*, published in 1932, a study of false convictions by a Yale law professor, Edwin M. Borchard. The expert had testified that the fatal bullets in a case of double murder had been fired from the revolver of an illiterate farm tenant. A former district attorney investigated, despite the fact that the defendant had confessed to the crime, and new ballistics tests showed that the bullets were completely dissimilar and, furthermore, that the man's rusty revolver had not been fired in years. The subnormal defendant had apparently confessed under suggestion or intimidation, the real culprits being later arrested and convicted. Borchard reported: "The experts . . . concluded that the trial testimony of Mr. Hamilton was clearly erroneous."

Using another skill, Hamilton testified on handwriting in a

New York City trial in 1934. The *Herald Tribune* of March 11 reported a curious change in Hamilton's expertise when he told the court that the handwriting of the defendant was different from the handwriting on certain kidnaping messages. Under cross-examination he admitted that he had previously expressed himself precisely in the contrary sense to the prosecutor, namely to the effect that the handwriting was indeed similar. A review court gave the opinion: "Three handwriting experts were sworn by the People. They expressed the opinion that the letters were written by the defendant. The force of the evidence of the handwriting expert [Hamilton] sworn on behalf of the defendant was entirely destroyed on cross-examination. He was confronted with a letter which he had written the district attorney wherein he expressed the opinion that the defendant wrote the ransom notes. His testimony to the contrary has little value."

In late 1923 Hamilton almost set Sacco and Vanzetti free. The episode, another of those almost unknown subchapters in the case history, occurred in the course of ballistics experiments that Hamilton was conducting. One day, bearing two similar pistols, Hamilton came to Thayer and requested permission to examine the Sacco pistol in the company of a defense lawyer. The expert was talking about the interchangeability of pistol parts as he dismantled and manipulated the three weapons. He then reassembled them, returned the Sacco pistol to Thayer, and prepared to leave. At this moment, Thayer, impelled by a suspicion he was not so garrulous as to articulate then, called Hamilton back. He ordered the expert to leave the two other pistols as well. Thayer impounded them without, however, pursuing the matter further.

Another expert came to borrow the Sacco pistol for a test a few weeks later. He discovered that the weapon had a new barrel which obviously did not belong to it. Thayer, justifiably marveling at his prescience, broke out the impounded Hamilton pistols and found that one of them bore the rusty Sacco pistol barrel. Hamilton thus had nearly walked away with that barrel attached to one of his own pistols. One is forced to ask if Hamilton's examination of the Sacco pistol had not been arranged precisely to that end. His demonstration of the interchangeability of pistol parts had no connection to any trial issues, and made no sense unless Hamilton was planning to take advantage of the confusion to cause the disappearance of an important piece of evidence. Had that pistol barrel vanished, subsequent tests demanded by the new appeals would have been impossible and a reasonable doubt could have been argued.

Hamilton's actions in the pistol barrel episode have nothing to do with the point at issue—whether Sacco's pistol did the killing. If we find the man and his activities suspect, we must not permit his shadow to fall on the helpless prisoner. Moore's expert did, however, get closer to the point with tests of the fatal bullet. Along with another man, Augustus H. Gill, Professor of Technical Chemical Analysis of Massachusetts Institute of Technology, he measured the markings—their length, width, and relative position—on the bullets. Both men concluded that the markings on the test bullets were different from those on the fatal bullet. Thus, they argued in support of the defense trial experts, the fatal bullet did not come from the Sacco weapon. Their statements, accompanied by lists of figures going to four decimal places, appear well taken at first view. Yet no ballistics expert would accept them today. According to an authoritative handbook, *Firearms Investigation, Identification, and Evidence* (1957) by Hatcher, Jury, and Weller: "Minute measurements of crime bullets and arms have been found to be of little practical significance." Thus the expert might make his measurements from either edge or the center of a given mark, while the figures themselves will change as bullets expand and contract with normal temperature changes. All of this was borne out in the Sacco-Vanzetti case.

Not one expert agreed with the others. Indeed, one of the experts disagreed with himself. This was Gill, who recorded three sets of figures, each set different. Furthermore, all of Gill's measurements differed from those of Hamilton. Van Amburgh also essayed measurements in rebuttal of the two defense experts, and *his* measurements supported his own opinion that Sacco's pistol was indeed guilty. At this point we must stop: the measurements are useless. After all, there is a better way.

At the trial Van Amburgh had placed the greater emphasis on simple recognition. You look at the bullets in question through a microscope and decide whether or not the markings are alike. This child's way of viewing ballistics evidence is still the best way, although an equally simple improvement, still based on the recognition principle, adds more probative weight. Every firearm will have markings in its barrel which are different from the markings on every other weapon—and these give the distinctive markings to the bullets. There are two reasons for the differences: the inner surface of the barrel is distinctively striated with tool scratches in the manufacturing; and rusting, pitting, and other accidents of use also leave their markings. All this concerns the bullet, but the shell, which stays in the chamber and is ejected after the bullet is fired, also has its unique markings. (Let us recall the four "Fraher" shells, which were found at the crime scene.) The shell is marked for two reasons. In the first place, it is jammed against the breechblock by the firing explosion, taking on a characteristic imprint. Also, the firing pin, which causes the initial explosion, leaves its distinctive mark at the point of impact in the base of the shell—this because the firing pin itself has its own peculiar scratches and, additionally, because it can be slightly off center. For all these reasons the bullet, which has been the subject of discussion until now, and the shell, which we shall also consider, can usually show a completely convincing similarity or dissimilarity by a simple test of recognition through a microscope.

There are, however, microscopes and microscopes, and this is where we arrive at the improvement on Van Amburgh's technique. He had used one type which is open to argument, at least in a courtroom. It was the compound microscope, a tandem arrangement of two instruments. In one of them, the viewer sees the bullet (or shell) in question; in the other he sees the test bullet (or shell). There is, thus, room for argument as the eye alternates between the two images. In 1925, however, the ballistics expert Colonel Calvin Goddard introduced an instrument that eliminated the gap between the images. Goddard was one of the three men who established firearms identification as a trustworthy element of forensic proof in this country and his instrument was the comparison microscope, originally developed in the textile industry. It functions with one eyepiece for the two microscope barrels, focusing on two objects but showing only one in the eyepiece. The image of this one object is actually a union of halves of the two objects being viewed—the left side of one bullet and the right side of the other, or top half of one and bottom half of the other. The observer can be sure that two bullets came from the same weapon if there is no break in the one object being viewed, if the markings are continuous and consistent. If that one object studied in the single eyepiece juxtaposes two different patterns of markings which stop abruptly at the invisible line of jointure, then the observer can be sure that the bullets had been fired from different weapons.

Until 1927, however, the ballistics questions had not been submitted to the comparison microscope. In 1924, when Thayer reviewed the fifth supplementary motion for a new trial, he had to deal with the conflicting reports referring to the findings of the *compound* microscope. In explaining his denial, Thayer noted the contradictory measurements, the admission by Gill of a "personal equation" in his figures and Hamilton's overeagerness to testify on numerous matters. Actually the sense of the denial went back to the recognition factor. The judge's discussion indicated he felt he could place more reliance on Van Amburgh's opinion as expressed at the trial, since the jurors had tested it by looking through the microscope themselves. In view of the undeveloped state of ballistics at the time, no one could quarrel with the principle guiding Thayer's denial.

Then, in 1927, Colonel Goddard entered the case. Reasoning that it would offer a splendid opportunity to demonstrate the value of his comparison microscope, he approached William G. Thompson, chief defense counsel at that time, but Thompson would have nothing to do with him. Persisting, Goddard then got the District Attorney's office to cooperate, and a test was held in Dedham courthouse on June 3, less than two months after the sentencing. Despite the defense's reluctance, it was represented by Herbert B. Ehrmann, associate defense counsel, and also by Professor Gill. Goddard gave as his findings: "(1) That the Fraher Shell No. 3 was fired in the Sacco pistol and could have been fired in no other, (2) That the so-called 'fatal' bullet, being one of four from the body of one Berardelli, was fired through the Sacco pistol and could have been fired from no other."*

* If Hamilton is suspect, the competence of both Van Amburgh and Goddard has been attacked.

About Van Amburgh: In a Connecticut murder case in 1924 he claimed that certain photographs he had taken proved the similarity between test and fatal bullets, but neither the state's attorney nor other experts saw that similarity. The disagreement was, however, never resolved by laboratory tests, and the case, the suspect having been released, never came to trial. Since it never got beyond a preliminary hearing, the circumstance was surrounded by so many unknowns and unsubstantiated opinions that it cannot be used to raise serious questions about Van Amburgh. Moreover, as far as we are concerned, his findings in the Sacco-Vanzetti case need not be accepted on his authority, since they were supported by other ballistics evidence and subsequent laboratory tests, as noted above. The Connecticut case was discussed in Homer S. Cummings, *The State of Connecticut vs. Harold Israel* (Washington, Government Printing Office, 1937) and Francis Russell, *Tragedy in Dedham* (New York: McGraw-Hill, 1962), pp. 249–51.

About Goddard: In the December 7, 1927 issue of the *Nation*, he was accused of a major error in a ballistics test. Goddard, then in a New York laboratory, had been asked to compare certain fatal and test bullets sent to him from Cleveland. He found that they had been fired from the same weapon, but the police later reported that the pistol of the arrested man had not been in his possession at the time of the murder and could not have fired the bullets in question. Thus there should not have been the similarity that Goddard claimed to have found. The *Nation* concluded that Goddard's expertise was not

The first public announcement of the experiment was made two months later by the *Boston Transcript* of August 8. According to the *Transcript,* Ehrmann had been unable to articulate any objection to Goddard's report, although he refused to sign it. The article continued: "The similarities were so marked that the defense expert [Professor Gill] said, 'Well, what do you know about that!' " Later, Gill quarreled with Thompson, broke off with the defense, and said he doubted the "present truth" of his earlier ballistics conclusions. James Burns, one of the two trial defense experts, also accepted the Goddard test findings. Seeking elucidation on the test, I questioned Ehrmann, who practices law in Boston and continues to defend the memory of Sacco and Vanzetti, but his long letters, following our talk in 1958, discussed everything except the point at issue.

A laboratory test by Hamilton himself supported the Goddard conclusions. He never announced the results but Professor Edmund M. Morgan referred to them in the *Harvard Law Review* of January 1934. The expert had taken photographs of the Fraher shells and test shells fired in Sacco's pistol. The markings, according to Morgan, a law faculty associate of Felix Frankfurter, were completely similar. This was further confirmed by Professor Charles O. Gunther of Stevens Institute of Technology, who enlarged the photographs and superimposed the one set on the other—finding a complete duplication of the markings. Curiously, Gunther failed to mention that experiment in his book on firearms identification, in which he discussed the Sacco-Vanzetti case and argued for innocence. In his article, Morgan concluded: "If the comparison microscope shows . . . what Colonel Goddard insists that it does . . . then the balance of probability that

---

to be trusted in the Sacco-Vanzetti case. It failed, however, to credit the fact that Goddard was at the mercy of the identification tags on the bullets he received, since the bullets might have been incorrectly tagged. In any case the matter was never tested, since the indictment was dropped and no one actually disproved Goddard's results.

they were fired from the same pistol is so heavy as to leave no room for a reasonable doubt. . . ."

Hamilton, however, persisted in defending the validity of his original experiments. In July of 1927, a month after the Goddard test, he again argued his case. In this last effort, on the occasion of the final review of the case, we once again find a vital product of the initiative of Fred Moore as incorporated by the man he hired in 1923. Once again it was a failure. But, as we know from Upton Sinclair, Fred Moore had given up believing in his own case.

Yet one question must be raised. Could the exhibits have been switched in the course of the years? To this, any answer but a negative would suggest an action by the authorities that would have been as monstrous as it would have been difficult. The bullets and shells had been scratched with identifying marks immediately after the South Braintree murders, and these marks as well as the other characteristics appear in all the photographs. Although Thompson brought up the matter during the final review in 1927, it was clearly a last-minute argument of desperation when all else seemed to be failing and no responsible friend of the defense took it seriously.

The Goddard test was repeated in our time by two of the authors of the firearms identification text cited earlier: Jac Weller, honorary curator of the West Point Museum, and Colonel Frank Jury, once chief of the New Jersey State Police Firearms Laboratory. Using a comparison microscope, they matched the fatal bullet and a Fraher shell with bullets and shells they themselves fired in Sacco's pistol. They also checked the bullets and shells from the Goddard test. The new test, which took place in the laboratory of the Massachusetts State Police on October 11, 1961, confirmed the Goddard conclusions in every detail. All three sets of bullets and shells had identical markings.

For anyone who would derive his own understanding independent of other men's interpretations, the best, the densest, the grittiest truth of the vast rubbish of the Sacco-Vanzetti case lies buried in the Harvard Law Library. Showing both bullets and shells, it is a series of enlarged photographs of the Goddard test made with a comparison microscope. In one plate, Goddard reproduces the bullet enlarged to about four by one and one-half inches; this is actually a composite of the nose of the fatal bullet and the base of a test bullet. Like the others, this photograph had been taken through the single eyepiece of a comparison microscope, with the two projectiles being viewed by the two microscope barrels, the eyepiece splitting the images and joining the halves to form the one image that appears in the photograph. It is impossible to distinguish the two halves; one would think one were looking at an ordinary bullet in magnification if the photographer had not sketched in a broken line to indicate the invisible line of jointure.

The various markings are very distinctive; they look like tracks on a muddy road. Imagine photographs of two *different* muddy roads and imagine trying to join halves of those two photographs: there would be an abrupt line where the tracks—differing in width, depth, and darkness—of the one half would begin and those of the other half would end. You have no better chance of matching photographs of bullets fired in two different weapons than of matching pictures of any two different rutted roads. The Goddard photography is clear and precise; the viewer's recognition of the similarity is absolute.

All the responsible tests are unequivocal: Sacco's pistol killed Berardelli. Despite his imagination and power Fred Moore had to fail on the ballistics issue.

12. Confessions

THEIR defenders have always argued that Sacco and Vanzetti, whatever idiocies they professed, were illogical candidates for the roles of payroll holdup men. The perpetrators of such bald crimes, one would think, should be professional criminals. Fred Moore had been acutely aware of this possibility. Through his connections with the underworld, moreover, he had been able to pursue the theory to the point of acquiring a convict's confession to the Bridgewater job. According to the man's detailed account, he had joined three friends in the effort to stop the L. Q. White payroll truck. Shortly after Moore left the case, another confession implicated another professional gang in the South Braintree holdup. On the face of it these confessions of criminals to both holdups should offer satisfactory solutions.

One must, however, begin with the proper proportions. False confessions are exceedingly common in the history of crime. The reasonable man assumes that a person will not confess to a crime he has not committed because he thereby seeks punishment gratuitously. But confessions can mean important advantages for the confessors. Aside from the mentally disturbed seeking catharsis, criminals have often tried to offer a confession to a minor crime that would eliminate them from suspicion for a greater one. Indeed, confessions have been questionable since the Amelekite countered the story of Saul's suicide with his version of an obliging murder. Many major crimes inspire numerous confessions, the police reporting at least 205 in the Lindbergh kidnaping. On the basis of wearying experience, law enforcement officials are as suspicious of confessions as they are of denials.

Nevertheless, Moore had originally been hopeful enough about the Bridgewater confession to travel to Atlanta on the vague promise of it. Even if it left the South Braintree crime unexplained, he doubtless thought that it would cast useful doubt on his clients' conviction at Dedham. In the end, however, he let the matter drop. Yet we know he was in Atlanta penitentiary for the interview, since the visit was noted down by the prison's record clerk. The story itself, furthermore, although it is told by people with little claim on our trust, might contain, if not a solution, at least a suggestion of one. It is enough to merit our attention; surely, Sacco and Vanzetti deserve as much.

The story goes back to April 1922. At that time the convicts, Frank Silva (also known as Paul Martini) and Jacob Luban received the visit of a treacherous friend. When they had been arrested for the mail robbery that put them in prison, their accomplice, Adolph Witner, had turned state's evidence and got off with a light sentence. Now he was in Atlanta with a mollifying suggestion, and he was accompanied by two men to give it authority—Fred Moore and another of Moore's helpers, an ex-convict named John Jocomo. Witner offered to confess that his testimony against Silva and Luban had been perjured. In return for that, Silva would have to confess to the Bridgewater job, naming three men whom Witner specified. (When it had done its work, Silva would then, of course, repudiate the confession.) For his part, Luban would be required to sign a corroborating affidavit. Moore and Jocomo eloquently seconded the Witner proposal, Moore confiding that leading officials in Washington and Boston were anxious to clear Sacco and Vanzetti. They wanted, he said, to avoid trouble with American labor unions and foreign radicals bent on bombing our ambassadors. Impressively, Moore added that he had just come from an interview with the United States Attorney General. Silva and Luban were overwhelmed; they accepted the proposal and money in earnest of it. (Silva got only $5, against $20 for Luban, a remarkable inequity, since it was Silva who would make the actual confession.) And then nothing happened.

Before Silva would sign his confession, he naturally insisted on seeing Witner's repudiation of the testimony that had incriminated him. The repudiation never came. Finally, Luban sent his two sisters to talk to Witner, and now Witner said that he was afraid to go through with the plan, that he had been told he would go to prison for life if he did. Feebly, he promised that he would indeed sign the repudiation—but later. The moment never arrived and the disenchanted Luban put the details in a letter to W. J. Burns, Director of the Federal Bureau of Investigation. Burns thereupon informed the Commonwealth authorities, and in December 1922, Assistant Attorney General Albert Hurwitz of Massachusetts interviewed Silva and Luban in Atlanta. The result of his talk was a double statement, signed by the two convicts, with the account as above.*

That ended Moore's efforts to obtain a confession. Had he got it, the Sacco-Vanzetti case might have taken a different course, but the difference probably would not have saved his clients. Frank Silva was a slender reed on which to build an important argument for a new trial—and Moore's lack of initiative following his Atlanta visit would indicate that he knew better than to attempt it.

Yet the Silva confession did not end there. After Moore, wretchedly, after Sacco and Vanzetti, Silva came forward with the story once more. This time it was told in the October 31 and November 7, 1928, issues of the *Outlook & Independent*, a topical

* Statement of Frank Silva, alias Paul Martini, and Jacob Luban. Massachusetts Documents; also Boston *Herald*, January 13, 1929.

magazine now long deceased. The editors, in their introductory note, remarked that Silva had refused to sign his new confession until they had paid him. If the circumstances were not sufficiently doubtful, the 1922 and the 1928 confessions, besides containing many errors of fact, also contradicted each other—to the point of naming different men as members of the Bridgewater gang. No one, on close view, has been able to do much with the Silva story.

The story, however, has still one more twist in it, acutely relevant to the efforts to save Sacco and Vanzetti in 1927. In the spring, about the time of the sentencing, William G. Thompson, Moore's successor as chief defense counsel, mined his heritage again and found the Silva material. When he got in touch with James Mede, an ex-convict named by Silva as one of his Bridgewater companions, Mede was willing enough to make a confession of sorts. His story was that he had planned the job but that he had not actually participated in the action. In any case, this is what he told the Governor on July 12 in the course of the final review. The Governor, who had been hearing innumerable testimonies of various kinds, asked Mede to repeat his story to a captain of the State Police, but the proposal frightened Mede and he refused. On August 3, Mede, inexplicably heartened, sought out the same officer, but this time the captain refused to see him. Since the Mede version adds new contradictions and more incredible elements to the Silva stories, it is impossible to regret the treatment it received.

Much more important was another confession, this one for the South Braintree holdup. Directly concerned with the absolute Dedham verdict, it was also more credible and more aptly timed. To Thompson, the Silva story had been one more marginal argument of many, but the new confession appeared at just the right moment. It came after Moore, who can claim no credit for it. Yet the confessor in question, according to prison officials, had displayed an intensive interest in the Sacco-Vanzetti Defense Committee financial report before putting it to paper, and Moore was responsible for the encouraging magnitude of the finances reported. Furthermore, he had kept Sacco and Vanzetti alive up to the point when the new confession would be available. In fact, the man who made it had been moved, he said, by the tragedy of Sacco, after he had become his fellow prisoner in Dedham jail—and this was in early November of 1924, within days of Moore's departure from the case. Whether it was inspired by honest sympathy or self-interest, the confession became one of Thompson's two major arguments—the other was Thayer's prejudice—when he took over from Moore.

William G. Thompson had been an excellent choice. If anyone could make something out of Moore's defeat, it was this eminently successful Boston lawyer. A hawk-nosed, hard-driving advocate, Thompson owed part of his success to a sense of moral indignation and a resolute belief in his clients' innocence. An associate remarked of him: "He always got emotionally involved and he always believed the other fellow was a crook." A friend of the Sacco-Vanzetti defense since the Dedham trial, he had actively joined it to a limited extent in 1923, and had helped Moore argue the supplementary motions for a new trial. On succeeding Moore, his first project was to appeal from Thayer's denial of the supplementary motions. Thompson worked conscientiously on this already exhausted material all through 1925 and spent three hard days in January 1926 arguing before the Supreme Judicial Court. But he had nothing new to say, and it was no surprise when, on May 12, the Court rejected his appeal. At that moment nothing stood between Sacco and Vanzetti and the sentencing, but meanwhile the new confession had appeared. Its timing was perfect; Thompson swung his massive attention to it.

The confession was provided by Celestino F. Medeiros, an epileptic in his early twenties, who had added a holdup murder to a wretched career of precocious delinquency and adolescent fraud. At the time he spoke with Sacco, in the summer of 1925, he was facing a prospect that Sacco and Vanzetti had been trying so desperately to achieve—a new trial. Here another irony played through their trial history. Idealists defended by the sympathy of so many good people, they were unable to gain a consummation that was presented so undeservedly to this unequivocal murderer. On November 1, 1924, Medeiros had shot and killed the eighty-year-old cashier of the Wrentham National Bank—Wrentham is fifteen miles southwest of Boston—during an ordinary bank holdup. Arrested on the eleventh by Providence police, Medeiros admitted it readily enough: "I lost my head." He was convicted of first degree murder in a brief trial in May 1925.

It would have been a simple matter of a mandatory death sentence. Like the South Braintree holdup, the crime at issue was murder committed in the course of a felony, ineluctably defined as first degree murder. Medeiros, however, was presented with an odd hope by a technical lapse, a question of law. It was precisely the kind of question which the Supreme Judicial Court had to review; Sacco and Vanzetti, whatever forceful arguments they could make about judicial prejudice, were never able to produce that terrible triviality. The judge, a fat, bearded original named Henry Lummus, had developed the theory that there was no presumption of innocence, one of the premises of Anglo-Saxon law. In the Medeiros trial he tested the theory by simply leaving out the stock phrase. The Boston area produces a remarkable variety of philosophers, but the Supreme Judicial Court, possessing no sympathy for this kind of imaginative legal thought, ordered a new trial.

It was at this time, just before the Supreme Court had ruled on his appeal from the trial, that Medeiros first spoke to Sacco, suggesting he knew who did the South Braintree job. In point of fact the suspicious Sacco had ignored this approach and several more. Then, on November 18, 1925, a half hour after having studied the Defense Committee financial report, Medeiros sent this note to him: "I hear-by confess to being in the south Braintree shoe company crime and Sacco and Vanzetti was not in said crime." Sacco passed the note on to Thompson, who promptly came to Dedham to interview Medeiros.

The exciting part of the confession was the fact that it led to an unquestionably existent gang of thieves, the Morellis, who had robbed both the victim Slater & Morrill and the observer Rice & Hutchins plants. Here were both reality and relevancy. If, beyond this point, the confession had its flaws, Thompson nevertheless wagered heavily on it.

Affidavits and corroborative statements fluttered into the record. First, James P. Weeks, one of the accomplices of Medeiros, gave a version of what he said Medeiros had told him. Next, under questioning by Thompson, Medeiros gave a detailed account of the South Braintree holdup. He then signed a confession affidavit on May 29. Following that, he submitted to more questions, this time by Assistant District Attorney Dudley P. Ranney, as well as Thompson, on June 28.

Medeiros told Thompson that the holdup gang had invited him to join as a sixth member. Eighteen at the time but already an established criminal, he had been promised $5,000. He said he had remained in the automobile back seat, slack with fright, while the holdup was carried out. He added a number of circumstantial details about the route of the vehicle. He said however, that he had been cheated of his share and had unsuccessfully sought the gang members in New York and Chicago "hoping to find them in cabarets spending the money." Some of the details of this account were in order, but many others were not, and Medeiros refused to answer a number of Thompson's questions.

Under Ranney's questioning, moreover, Medeiros was sullen and infertile. He refused to say what had happened to the money. Furthermore, he did not seem to be acquainted with the crime scene. Ranney told me he gave Medeiros paper and pencil and bade him, if he felt inarticulate, to draw the scene. Medeiros made no effort. The area was dominated then by a huge water tower, but the man made no mention of it. There were other discrepancies. The Medeiros account contradicted the version of his friend Weeks in many important details, and other parts of his confession were not in accord with the known facts. Thus he put the day at April 5 and not the correct April 15; he said the Buick was abandoned immediately, while we know that several witnesses testified on its circling of the Brockton area; he said the money was in a black bag, while it was in two metal boxes; he said that .38 caliber weapons were used, and Berardelli and Parmenter were killed with .32 caliber bullets. Most important, however, was the fact that Medeiros himself did not name the Morelli gang in his confession. Although his friend Weeks mentioned the Morellis, it was only after Thompson's assistant, Herbert B. Ehrmann, had made some investigations of that possibility. Ehrmann himself arrived at the Morellis when he learned about their robberies of shoe shipments from the South Braintree plants. If it was easy to credit the Morellis with the payroll holdup, Medeiros himself refused to accord them the honor. In fact, he refused to give a single name of his accomplices. Thus the best part of the Medeiros story does not even belong to his confession. If, furthermore, there is no question about the gang's incrimination in the robberies, these actions were far different from holdups and but tenuously related to South Braintree. Actually, the Morellis had broken into freight car shipments in the Providence railroad yards, victimizing a number of companies that happened to include Slater & Morrill and Rice & Hutchins. The connection between Medeiros and the Morellis is not very firm.

The timing of the confession, moreover, suggests another reason for caution. Although he had tried to communicate with Sacco while his case was pending, Medeiros did not make any official statement until after his second trial on May 17, 1926, when he was quickly convicted for the second time. It was only on May 29, twelve days later, that he signed the confession affidavit.

Inasmuch as he was facing the electric chair, he had nothing to lose and a life to gain. The conviction meant death; a confession to another crime committed under extenuating circumstances meant adding a feather of guilt to the already unbearable guilt burden of the Wrentham murder. Moreover, if Medeiros could get the courts to believe his confession or, at least, take it seriously, he would gain time while the matter was being investigated, and time is always an ally in the law. A new legal error might save him again.

The Morelli gang, however, gave the defense another reality to pursue, and the young, Harvard-Law-trained Ehrmann attacked it brilliantly. With the energy and skill that have since made him a prominent member of the Boston bar, Ehrmann launched himself at the Morelli gang members who were in jail in 1926. To help him, he won another ally, a Providence lawyer and former U.S. marshal named John J. Richards who was acquainted with the history of the Morelli gang. On June 1, 1926, Ehrmann and Richards interviewed Joe Morelli, the senior of the gang, in the federal prison in Leavenworth, Kansas. According to their affidavit,* Morelli was recalcitrant. As they put it: "Morelli's manner was defiant and sneery." Richards had begun the interview by referring to the "accusation" that the Morelli gang had participated in the South Braintree holdup. To this, "Morelli then said he had never worked with the others, but always alone." Then, when Richards persisted with the charge, Morelli accused the lawyer of attempting a frame-up. Ehrmann later wrote a book on the case and there** the scene is presented more dramatically than in the joint affidavit: "'You are trying to spoil my record with the warden!' cried Joe over and over again in a voice that whined and wept. . . ." Upon the failure of Richards to get any admission from Morelli, Ehrmann essayed a series of questions.

* *Transcript*, vol. 5, pp. 4452–55.

** Herbert B. Ehrmann, *The Untried Case* (New York: Vanguard, 1933), p. 110.

According to the affidavit Morelli, however, was moved to suggest that "there was a just God who knew of the wrongs done against him and who would judge him."

Morelli continued his denials. Ehrmann made an eloquent statement to the convict, pointing to "hundreds of thousands of people who believe Sacco and Vanzetti innocent." Morelli replied first with silence and then "said he had nothing to say and would have nothing to say the next day. Thereupon the interview was closed."

Morelli himself composed an affidavit on June 20, giving this account: "John J. Richards took a letter out of his pocket stating that he had evidence against me and that I done this killing and wanted me to sign a confession to it. I told him I wouldn't do it because I didn't know anything about it. He says it is best for you to sign it; it will make it easier for you. I told him I would not do it; well he says the Boston Police is going to indict you for that murder next week. I says thanks and then he tried to bulldoze with the warden telling the warden what a bad fellow I was and so on and so forth."*

This is the best that Ehrmann could do with the Morelli story. He went one step further, however. One of the names mentioned to Joe Morelli was that of an Antonio Mancini. Morelli had denied knowing him, but Ehrmann found another possible link in Mancini to the South Braintree murders. On February 10, 1921, Mancini had killed a man in New York with a pistol that might—at least by its caliber—have been used in South Braintree. Yet the caliber is too common to be significant, and the chain of incrimination Medeiros-Morelli-Mancini appears, when closely studied, to have no links.

The Medeiros-Morelli matter has continued to react closer to our time. Another student of the case has produced a possible addition to our knowledge of it. According to *Tragedy in Dedham,* by Francis Russell, Joe Morelli did have a connection with

* *Transcript,* vol. 5, p. 4604.

Sacco and Vanzetti, actually filling some 600 manuscript pages with his story. Russell writes that Morelli's granddaughter had the manuscript and he tells of her refusal to let him see it. Later, however, Russell did "manage to learn the contents of Joe Morelli's document." Russell goes on to recount Joe Morelli's claim that he had helped plan the South Braintree robbery. However, the actual perpetrators, according to Morelli-Russell, double-crossed Morelli by carrying it out a week ahead of schedule and without his physical participation. The men were, again according to Morelli-Russell: Sacco, Vanzetti, Coacci, Boda, and Orciani. Of course, this finding is of no great value in providing a foundation for any opinion on the question of guilt or innocence. Indeed, Russell himself discounts it, since his book, published in 1962, arrives at still another conclusion. Furthermore, a reporter who helped Russell in his investigations, but disagreed with his conclusions, took issue with him in an article in the *New Republic* of July 13, 1963. The reporter, Ben H. Bagdikian, emphasized the fact that Morelli had owned an exhaustive book on the case written by Osmond K. Fraenkel, general counsel of the American Civil Liberties Union. Bagdikian suggests that Morelli got his facts from Fraenkel and added rumors or private conclusions—all in an attempt to make money out of the case with a literary confession. But this is a far way from the Medeiros confession, which in 1926 and 1927 was a powerful force in keeping Sacco and Vanzetti alive.

For five days in September 1926 Thompson and Assistant District Attorney Ranney argued over the Medeiros affidavit before Judge Thayer. Although Thompson had another subject, it was of minor importance, and with Felix Frankfurter observing in Dedham courthouse, Thompson applied his most eloquent conviction to the story of a professional holdup. For his part, Thayer listened good-naturedly and then worked more than a month on an opinion that totaled 25,000 words. Handed down on October 23, the opinion, pointing out the discrepancies and inaccurate facts in the confession, concluded with a denial. Brutal as this new defeat was, it opened up for Thompson the opportunity to make his second great argument—Thayer's prejudice.

The first courtroom attack on Thayer's prejudice was launched before the Supreme Judicial Court on January 27 and 28, 1927. Thompson based part of his charges on a comment by Thayer in which the judge had permitted himself the use of irony. Referring in his opinion to Thompson's aggressive suspicions, Thayer suggested:

> . . . a new type of disease would seem to have developed. It might be called "legopsychic neurosis" or "hysteria" which means: "a belief in the existence of something which in fact and truth has no such existence." This disease would seem to have reached a very dangerous condition . . . when [Thompson] charges Mr. Sargent, Attorney General of the United States and his subordinates, and subordinates of former Attorney General of the United States Mr. Palmer and Mr. Katzmann and the District Attorney of Norfolk County, with being in a conspiracy to send these two defendants to the electric chair, not because they are murderers but because they are radicals. . . .*

Against this suggestion of irrationality in Thompson, the lawyer countercharged that Thayer himself had become so upset by the case that he could no longer reason "with a calm mind free from impartiality." From the courtroom, with the help of Felix Frankfurter and the awakening intellectuals, the argument would go out into the world with swiftly increasing force. The Supreme Court judges themselves were not impressed. On April 5 they handed down their decision, supporting Thayer on every point. It was this decision that cleared the way for the sentencing of Sacco and Vanzetti on April 9. Now, with the world aroused, the Medeiros confession would take on new life. Always one would come back to the question: Isn't it more reasonable to suppose that professional criminals committed the South Braintree killings?

* *Transcript*, vol. 5, p. 4748.

13. Conclusions

WITH the ballistics material and the confessions we have reviewed all the meaningful evidence and arguments. Let us summarize the facts. Against Sacco and Vanzetti, these can be listed:

The two holdups were obviously amateur efforts and remarkably similar in terms of personnel—four or five foreign-appearing men, one with a prominent mustache—and means of transportation—a seven-passenger touring Buick.

The idealists Sacco and Vanzetti had associates—Boda, Orciani, and Coacci—of nonidealistic, surely doubtful, and possibly criminal character; these five are a much more logical staffing for the holdup gang than the distant Morellis. Boda had admitted to a defense partisan that he was a bootlegger; association with criminals is an important feature of the history of anarchists, and the accused believed in violence and justified it to destroy the state. Their character shows no inclination to rob for self, but similarly no disinclination against robbing for the cause; and the cause needed money at the time, particularly for legal fees to defend men arrested in the Red raids.

Sacco and Vanzetti were armed when they were arrested. Both men told many lies to account for their suspicious actions, many of the lies unrelated to the question of radicalism. Their story about gathering literature was partially broken down during cross-examination.

Sacco was identified by seven persons at the South Braintree crime scene. Two others tried to retreat from prior identifications but they did did not withdraw the statements completely.

Sacco's alibis were furnished by friends and associates.

Empty pistol shells of three different manufactures were found at South Braintree. Among the thirty-two bullets found in Sacco's pistol and pockets were all three of those varieties.

The ballistics evidence demonstrated by Van Amburgh and Goddard and supported by Weller and Jury in 1961 shows a complete duplication of identifying characteristics: test bullets fired from Sacco's pistol are similar to the fatal bullet in Berardelli's body; test shells ejected from Sacco's pistol are similar to the empty Fraher shells found at the crime scene. Photographs made in a comparison microscope document that similarity.

Sacco was not at his place of work on April 15, 1920, the date of the South Braintree killings, although he was a steady worker. His work records for the period of the Bridgewater crime are missing.

The Berardelli killer wore a cap and lost it during the action. That cap was a 7⅛, Sacco's size, and appeared to fit him at the trial. It was similar to a cap found in Sacco's home.

Sacco had worked at the Rice & Hutchins plant, neighbor to the victim Slater & Morrill plant. Boda had worked at the plant of the L. Q. White Company, whose payroll was the objective of the Bridgewater holdup. According to Chief Stewart, Coacci had worked at both of the victim plants and up to the same date relative to the holdups, that is, until the Monday before each attack.

Early in April 1920 Boda was seen by one witness and Vanzetti by another witness in a Buick similar to the crime vehicle.

Vanzetti, of striking physiognomy and expressive mustache, was identified by five witnesses at the first and four at the second holdup.

Vanzetti's alibis were furnished by friends and associates.

In addition to the loaded revolver, Vanzetti had four shotgun shells in his pocket when he was arrested. A shotgun or rifle was seen at both crimes, and South Braintree witnesses said they saw a shotgun or rifle barrel protruding through the broken-out rear window of the crime vehicle. Also, the dead guard normally carried a .38 H. & R. revolver; Vanzetti had a .38 H. & R. revolver when arrested, but no extra ammunition. His claim of having purchased it was not supported by all of the buyers and sellers he named, and he told different stories about how much he had paid, the price ranging from five to nineteen dollars.

The desperate nature of the defense case is suggested by the unscrupulous acts of Moore: intimidation of witnesses, use of such charlatans as Hamilton, etc.

In their defense the friends of Sacco and Vanzetti put forward these arguments:

Sacco had seven alibi witnesses for the South Braintree crime; Vanzetti had five for that holdup and eleven for the Bridgewater attempt.

More than a dozen South Braintree crime witnesses said that Sacco and Vanzetti were not among the gang members.

Defense witnesses said that certain prosecution witnesses (Goodridge, Lola Andrews) had privately told them stories differing from their trial testimony.

The actions of Sacco and Vanzetti on the evening of the arrest can be explained by their fear of arrest for radicalism.

The accused may have professed an acceptance of the theory of anarchist violence, but that is no useful proof about the actual commission of crime. In any case, the point is to prove that they did it, not that they had a possibly appropriate mental attitude for doing it.

Sacco was a stable family man with one child and a pregnant wife at the time of the holdups; Vanzetti's idealism and hopes for a better world are uncontested.

Five ballistics experts, two at the Dedham trial and three during the appeals, denied the similarity in markings seen by

Van Amburgh, Goddard, Jury, and Weller. Additionally, one of the prosecution experts at the trial altered his testimony in a post-trial affidavit.

No one can prove that the bullet exhibits were not switched by the police or prosecution.

What can be done with these arguments and counterarguments? In the area of public opinion, the thesis of innocence betrayed has been dominant until recently. Under continuing study, however, the negative indications have been forcing a reinterpretation. At this point in time the thesis is in the process of breaking down, at least partially. The new concept suggests that Sacco might indeed be guilty but that Vanzetti can be retained among the innocent.

The view was apparently encouraged by the revival of a rumor that had been current in 1927 but had never been pursued any great distance. More recently, in the October 21, 1961 issue of the *National Review,* Max Eastman, a leading radical of the twenties, elaborated on it, offering no new evidence but citing the anarchist Carlo Tresca as an authority. Actually, Eastman had been brooding on it for many years, since Tresca had been dead since 1943. A few months after the Eastman article, the January 1962 issue of *Commentary Magazine* carried a law professor's discussion of the theory based on a study of the court record. Next, Francis Russell, who had begun his researches with the assumption of innocence, retired to the half-and-half position. Yet all the new interpreters have little more than one negative fact to go on: Vanzetti escapes the ballistics evidence pointing at Sacco. Beyond that, the Tresca-Eastman theory offers anarchist rumors but no substantiation, the law professor puts forward legal argumentation and Vanzetti's idealistic character, and Russell depends essentially on that character and the Beltrando Brini alibi. Nothing new has been added.

Furthermore, the known facts do not fit into the thesis. In the first place, it ignores Vanzetti's calls to violence in his letters and assumes he was too idealistic to kill. Whatever the truth, no one can say with confidence that this theorist of violence was incapable of carrying it out. Moreover, the new exegetes cannot explain away all the points of incrimination raised against Vanzetti: the eyewitnesses at the two crimes, indications of consciousness of guilt, and the rest. Also, if Sacco is to be written off as guilty, how can we disentangle Vanzetti from his activities? The men were close friends and saw each other almost daily around the time of the South Braintree crime; indeed, Vanzetti had spent the night before the arrest in Sacco's home. Of the two men, referring once more to the argument of character, we know that while Sacco was the passive follower type, a family man and only an after-hours revolutionary, Vanzetti, unhampered by family and intermittent at work, was a much more serious anarchist; that, if we accept his account of participation in a strike in 1916, he was a leader of men. Are we to assume that the passive Sacco plunged into the adventure and left the man-of-initiative Vanzetti behind? If, moreover, we accept the guilt of Sacco, then we might well believe that the prosecution witnesses had been telling the truth about him. Can we then assume that the betrayal of justice—mistaken or lying witnesses and prejudice-ridden court—affected only Vanzetti? On the basis of the known facts and simple reasoning, the student of the case is forced to conclude that the guilt-innocence division creates many new problems and leaves the old ones unresolved.

Do I think Sacco and Vanzetti were guilty? I found I liked the men more, the more I knew about them. They were real men, and brave, and not stock figures from any martyrology. I am glad I was not on the Dedham jury. Assistant District Attorney Williams, whose competence helped bring it about, wept at the verdict of guilty.

14. The Law and Prejudice

WHEN, in January of 1927, Thompson accused Thayer of prejudice, he opened the gate to broad charges against almost everyone concerned with the case. Although he was referring only to an opinion of Thayer's written in 1926, his attack was followed by accusations going back to the trials and directed also against jury, prosecutor, and community, then, by extension, against Boston and Massachusetts, and finally, from the vantage point of Europe, against the whole of the United States as a nation of Philistines. Inevitably, in the passionate struggle to save the men, the charges lost precision and grew with exaggerations. Yet one would expect to find some truth in them.

The question of prejudice and possible judicial murder is larger than that of the prisoners' complicity in the crime of South Braintree. If Sacco and Vanzetti helped kill Parmenter and Berardelli, then their small figures must bear a heavy burden of guilt. Yet, even so, if they were not fairly tried and heard, Boston and the nation must be even guiltier. Did Sacco and Vanzetti have a fair trial? Were their appeals fairly heard?

The friends of the men have always argued that their case never had a fair chance. Of the friends, the ablest was Felix Frankfurter and the most compelling statement for the defense was his long article in the *Atlantic Monthly* of March 1927. (It was later that year expanded into the book, *The Case of Sacco and Vanzetti.*) The article was a powerful factor in preparing public opinion in the United States and throughout the world for the sentencing speeches of Sacco and Vanzetti. Accordingly, we must consider the Frankfurter arguments closely while paying measured regard to other defense statements. What do they say?

In sum, the friends of Sacco and Vanzetti make these charges: the trial judge was prejudiced and guided the trials in a manner harmful to the defendants; prejudice and hysteria were so great in the community that they could not be kept out of the courtroom; the jury was prejudiced; the prosecutor took unfair advantage of the defendants under the license given him by the prejudiced judge; prosecution witnesses lied or gave incorrect statements because of their prejudice; and the Supreme Judicial Court, the Governor, and his advisers were either prejudiced or felt obliged to support the trial verdict regardless of the facts. In short, the charge is prejudice.

While the charges affect everyone, their sharpest point is raised against Judge Thayer. We recall Vanzetti's reference to the remarks Thayer made to the Dartmouth professor and the Boston city treasurer. (It is curious, however, that neither statement was formalized as a signed affidavit.) There is no doubt that the judge thought Sacco and Vanzetti were guilty and announced his opinion to other persons. Clearly, also, he felt strongly about it. But one must show how that opinion affected the trial and the appeals. Robert E. Riordan, who covered the Dedham trial for the old *Brockton Enterprise,* told me: "I am inclined to believe that he said—off the bench—all they claimed he said. But he was a different man on the bench." Before considering that possible difference, we might hear the testimony of another reporter. In July 1927 Frank P. Sibley of the Boston *Globe* testified at the final review: "His [Thayer's] manner was anything but dignified, especially when counsel for the defense were presenting their case; he would sit forward in his chair with a prejudiced expression on his face. His method of conducting a case was something I had never seen before. The rulings against the defendants were done with an air of prejudice, and scorn." But this attempt to connect Thayer's thoughts to his overt trial conduct rests on one man's interpretation of his expression and posture. None of the other reporters covering the trial supported Sibley's testimony. Furthermore, unable to produce anything stronger than that, Sibley made a feeble showing under cross-examination. We must seek further.

It was at this final review in the summer of 1927 that the memory of Fred Moore was called upon again—this time as another substantiation for the existence of Thayer's prejudice. Thomas McAnarney, the silent assistant to his brother Jeremiah at the trial, now became articulate and blamed Moore for causing ill feeling in Thayer and also in the jury.* Moore's conduct, he said, had the effect of "waving the red flag in the face of a wolf." He specified: "I think Judge Thayer . . . couldn't conduct a trial fairly with Attorney Moore on the other side. I have the highest respect for his character [and] ability, but this man Moore got under his skin as I said before to such an extent and so irritated him, so that people around could see his reaction on the jury. . . ." McAnarney was asked: "Was he [Moore] a disagreeable person?" His reply was not strictly relevant: "I will tell you now. At the trial, the jury there, there would be friend Moore offering his best interests . . . on hand with coat and vest off and his shoes off." McAnarney was also asked: "Did the judge treat you fair?" He replied: "Yes, that was one of the things that made it embarrassing. He would say to Moore, 'Why don't you do the same as Mr. McAnarney does?' and Moore was chief counsel." This is the sum of McAnarney's accusation. Against this Moore would have little difficulty winning an acquittal for himself, and Thayer as well. In effect, McAnarney says he observed

* *Transcript,* vol. 5, pp. 5047–48.

Thayer's irritation; beyond this, he draws the conclusion that the irritation was strong enough to affect justice. As a private conclusion it cannot be put forward as evidence that Moore aroused or Thayer possessed a killing prejudice. Furthermore, Thompson, actively present at the final review, never accused Thayer of prejudice at the trial—although he had opened up the prejudice issue in reference to the judge's denial of the Medeiros motion in 1926. We must seek still further.

If Sibley and McAnarney were unequal to the task of finding judicial prejudice at the Dedham trial, and if Thompson made no apparent effort in that direction, Felix Frankfurter believed he found it in Thayer's charge to the jury. In the final chapter on the trial I quote Thayer's lengthy admonition on fairness: "Reflect long and well so that . . . your verdict shall stand . . . as your judgment of truth and justice." But, one may ask, did Thayer slip an element of distortion into his charge under cover of the noble statement? Frankfurter says he did just that in his discussion of the ballistics question. Specifically, he accuses Thayer of emphasizing and strengthening the statements of the prosecution experts while ignoring the testimony of the defense experts. It appears, however, that Frankfurter derived his argument from a defense appeal, which is couched in just such terms. Actually, the case transcript shows that Thayer reviewed both sides of the ballistics testimony at equal length and carefully left the judgment to the jury. Yet this instance is the only specific citation which Frankfurter makes to prove his general accusation that Thayer's charge "directs the emotions only too clearly." Moreover, Frankfurter brings forward no fact about the judge's other actions and expressions in a trial that lasted six and one-half weeks, a duration that inevitably opened up many opportunities for harmful influence. We recall that the *Herald* reported the defense lawyers' acknowledgment of "fairness and impartiality in the able way Thayer tried the case." The jurors, for what their statements may be worth, all said they never knew what Thayer thought about the defendants, and one said flatly: "The judge tried to help the defendants." Riordan also thought that Thayer favored the defense—the transcript shows that he ruled for the defense more often than for the prosecution—and he told me he had asked the judge about it. He recalls the reply: " 'I've never been overruled by the Supreme Court. I don't want it to happen now.' " This could be a reasonable enough motive to inspire fairness in an ambitious judge, assuming he was not guided by integrity. Riordan concludes: "It was a fair trial conducted by a fair judge. . . . It was a trial by the book."

In strict fact, not even the most damning report of Thayer's opinions provides a scintilla of evidence, as a lawyer might put it, that Thayer was prejudiced. The accusations against him refer to statements made well after the trial began. By that time Thayer had had the opportunity to study the evidence at length. Thus one cannot claim that he had made a prejudgment before the trial. It may have been a stupid, cruel or even completely wrong judgment, but it was not necessarily the result of prejudice.

Going beyond the trial, Frankfurter takes up an argument that Thompson had used against Thayer's denial of the Medeiros motion. In effect, Frankfurter says the opinion proved Thayer to be so unfair that he could not be considered an instrument of justice. His discussion goes on to call the opinion a "self-justification" by a judge who gave himself "meretricious authority" falsely derived from the Supreme Judicial Court. According to Frankfurter, Thayer claimed the Court had approved the Dedham verdict, when it had done nothing of the kind. The point refers to the difference in appeal jurisdictions of the various state supreme courts, some reviewing both the facts and the law, and others reviewing only the law. Now, Massachusetts at that time reviewed only the law, intervening only when legal procedures had been violated, viz., the Medeiros mistrial because the judge had failed to instruct the jury about the presumption of innocence. If it finds nothing wrong legally, the state supreme court does not "approve" a verdict; it merely "affirms" it. The Massachusetts Supreme Judicial Court had not inquired if the Sacco-Vanzetti verdict was just, and if Thayer said that his judicial superiors had "approved" the verdict, he had indeed made a false statement.

Frankfurter is right: Thayer had indeed used the word "approved" in mentioning the Supreme Judicial Court's opinion. We must, however, stop right here. In his own overlong, overconscientious opinion, Thayer referred to the Supreme Judicial Court eight or nine times. He used the correct word—"affirmed"—five times, paraphrases of its meaning two or three times, and he used the wrong word—"approved"—just once. The broad sense of the opinion is clear; Thayer was discussing an "affirmation." Since every Massachusetts lawyer knew that the Court could only "affirm" the verdict, it would have been senseless to have pretended otherwise, and Thayer's one-word slip did not alter the meaning. Surely the error cannot support the Frankfurter conclusion that Thayer's denial was a "farrago of misquotations, misrepresentations, suppressions, and mutilations." Surely it cannot disqualify the judge.

Beyond the question of judicial prejudice, the defenders of Sacco and Vanzetti argue that the general prejudice in the community made a fair trial impossible. More specifically, they point to the Red raids, which were occurring at the time of the arrest and Vanzetti's first trial. (Indeed, the arrest was an accidental by-product of the raids.) Thus Frankfurter mentions the raids and cites John F. Moors, a Boston broker and one of the few people of his class to support the defense, as authority for this statement: "Boston was one of the worst centres of this lawlessness and hysteria." Yet Moors was hardly an impartial authority as a member of the Sacco-Vanzetti Defense Committee, and the Red raids, as we have seen, were ordered from Washington to stop the sufficiently real anarchist bomb attacks. As an official action, whatever injustices they caused, the raids were neither lawless nor hysterical, and Boston showed no enthusiasm for them. Indeed, Judge George W. Anderson of the Boston Federal Court produced a 30,000-word opinion acutely criticizing Attorney General Palmer: "We have sufficient confidence in [our institutions'] endurance not to be frightened into intolerance and hysterical lawlessness by the dominating spectre of Marxian Socialism." Furthermore, no one has been able to establish a connection between the raids and the Sacco-Vanzetti case in terms of expressions of prejudice loud enough to be heard and reported. In the Boston press during the trial period there was not a single report of a demonstration, not the vaguest suggestion in an editorial, of strong feeling directed against radicals in general or Sacco and Vanzetti as radicals in particular. The press uniformly treated them as defendants in an ordinary crime (except for the sympathetic *Boston Herald* article cited earlier) until the defense introduced the radical literature story, and then no newspaper made a negative issue of radicalism. Moreover, Sibley's *Boston Globe* was consistently favorable to the defense. Of course, Boston had its prejudices like every other community, but the charge of an *active* antiradical prejudice in the community remains unproven.

Within the courtroom, we know that prejudice never expressed itself overtly. William Thompson, who had attended the Dedham trial as a friend of the defense, never broadened his argument of prejudice beyond the specific target of Thayer's 1926 opinion. Nevertheless, the friends of the prisoners argue that there was enough prejudice around, however inarticulate, to have affected the jury's judgment. Accordingly, let us narrow our focus to the jury.

The only specific charge against the Dedham jury was raised in an affidavit, we recall, which attributed this statement to Walter Ripley, the foreman: "Damn them, they ought to hang them anyway." Yet the man filing the statement brought out the alleged remark when he accosted Ripley and launched into an energetic defense of Sacco and Vanzetti. Surely a defense partisan's untested affidavit—the foreman had died before it was submitted—deserves little trust.

We can ask the jurors about the general charges. We might recall the juror Nickerson of the Plymouth trial and his statement that radicalism was never mentioned in the jury deliberations. Concerning Dedham, where radicalism was introduced, there is much more dispute. Of course, the jurors defend their integrity, but we can listen for a note of apology and compare the factual elements of their protestations with the trial transcript and the newspaper reports. If they attempted to conceal something, they would too easily give themselves away. What do the Dedham jurors say?

In 1950 Edward B. Simmons, a reporter for the New Bedford *Standard-Times,* interviewed seven of the eight jurors then alive and also children of the four who had died. According to Simmons, who told me he had no objective other than an interesting feature story,* all the jurors denied having been influenced by the anarchism or foreign origins of the accused. Of the jurors the most articulate was John F. Dever, now dead, who became a lawyer some time after his service in the trial, and who discussed the case in the light of his knowledge of the law. About radicalism he told Simmons: "I can repeat it over and over again. The talk of radicalism was absurd. Radicalism had nothing whatsoever to do with it." About the character of the accused as aliens, Dever said flatly: "It is nonsense to say that we were prejudiced against Sacco and Vanzetti because they were Italian immigrants." The verdict, he said, resulted from a study of all the hard evidence: "Various pieces fitted into chains of evidence, which to my mind, not having a weak link, were pretty strong. . . ." Dever did admit to bias: "Funny thing, too, I was a defendants' man. . . . I was a defendants' man all the way through the trial. I don't mean I was determined to vote for their innocence regardless, but

* Published November 12, 1950 in the *Standard-Times,* p. 6.

I was going to find them not guilty until the facts proved otherwise, to my definite satisfaction." The quest of his definite satisfaction, according to Dever, led him to voting against conviction in the first balloting. His story, if we find it credible, can illuminate the jury's deliberations for us.

Dever said that he got the impression that "most everybody felt Sacco and Vanzetti were guilty." Wanting to "give them every opportunity," he suggested an informal ballot at the beginning "to get a sample of opinion." In this ballot Dever voted against his judgment on guilt—with the objective of inspiring "a thorough review of what we had heard and seen." (The vote was 10–2 for conviction, with one other reflective juror joining Dever in the "nay" position.) Precisely that thorough review occurred, Dever said, and he was satisfied that the defendants got their due in terms of jury thought. Accordingly, he could vote for conviction in the final ballot with a clear conscience.

The other jurors interviewed by Simmons supported the Dever commentary in every significant detail. Denying prejudice, all emphasized various elements of the evidence and identification, citing the ballistics findings and the credibility of prosecution witnesses. In my own pursuit of the jury question I spoke with Harry E. King, a welfare agent in a town near Boston, whose comments to me accorded with what he told Simmons. A keen-minded man with a no-nonsense New England incisiveness, King faced the prejudice issue squarely: "I know there was a lot of talk about it afterward, radicalism and all that. The jury didn't consider it, didn't mention it when we discussed the evidence. We were asked about everything twice since then—by the Governor and the Advisory Committee. I didn't change my opinion—the other jurors didn't. I've got a clear conscience on that. . . . I'm a church member. I was a deacon then. I wouldn't make a decision on a man's life unless I was sure I was doing right. The Lord giveth and the Lord taketh away. Well, I have no regrets about the decision—only that I was picked to make it." If King,

Dever, and the other jurors nurtured a malevolent prejudice, it is impossible to find any trace of it in the confident and unashamed way they discussed the trial. Furthermore, everything they said about the details of the trial—elements of evidence and testimony of witnesses—is confirmed by the record.

If the judge, community, and jury defend themselves ably, we must also consider the charges against the prosecutor. His assistant at the Dedham trial, Associate Justice Harold P. Williams of the Supreme Judicial Court, told me he thought Katzmann had been "hard, perhaps too hard" in his cross-examination of Sacco and Vanzetti. This is an admission of some weight, but surely not enough to call the prosecution's conduct into question. More importantly, Frankfurter accuses Katzmann—and, necessarily, Williams as well—of chicanery in manipulating the ballistics testimony. His attack is based on an affidavit filed on October 20, 1923, by State Police Captain William H. Proctor, who claimed, in effect, that his trial testimony had been prearranged with Katzmann and Williams in such a way as to mislead the jury. This is a serious charge by a prosecution witness. The point at issue was Proctor's original testimony that the fatal bullet was "consistent with being fired by that [Sacco's] pistol." To that, his affidavit adds that he had actually found no "affirmative evidence" for the consistency and that he would have answered in the negative, had he been asked the question. For Frankfurter, who writes that Proctor "was offered by the Commonwealth with elaborate reliance as a most important expert," the man's statement is damning evidence that the prosecution conspired with a witness to falsify his expert testimony.

On closer study, however, the accusation in the affidavit seems to vanish. In effect, Proctor confesses he perjured himself legally—in a manner for which he could not be prosecuted—but which was nonetheless criminal in intent. Yet there is little difference between his trial testimony and his affidavit statement. If Proctor had no "affirmative evidence" at the trial, the affidavit can offer no negative evidence: the man simply lacked the ballistics knowledge to testify to more than he did. Van Amburgh carried the weight of the prosecution ballistics case, Katzmann referring to him at length and ignoring Proctor in his summation. This can help explain the "prearrangement" of Proctor's testimony. Justice Williams admits that the question put to Proctor had been agreed upon in advance, but he points out that this is a normal enough courtroom practice. First, he explains why the prosecution used Proctor: "We felt we had to put Proctor on to identify the exhibits and because he was head of the State Police." Beyond that, Williams explains why Proctor testified as he did at Dedham: "He knew very little about bullets and he used the word 'consistent' because he wasn't competent to testify to more than that—he wasn't saying that this particular bullet came from that particular—Sacco's—pistol. He hadn't made the actual test—didn't know how." Even accepting the fact that Williams would defend his own conduct, one must conclude that the Proctor affidavit was a hair-splitting exercise by a man who gives no evidence he knew his subject. As the statement of a man who claimed he was a perjurer—and produces no evidence that he was—it lacks the force to discredit the prosecution.

What motive could have led Proctor to his extraordinary statement? At the review in 1927, Katzmann suggested two reasons. He said he had removed Proctor from the South Braintree crime investigation, which he had originally headed, and replaced him with Chief Stewart. Furthermore, the prosecutor said that Proctor had demanded a fee of $500 for this trial testimony. Katzmann, after consulting with a judge, refused to pay him for doing his duty as a police officer. After that, Proctor would not speak to him, Katzmann said. It might be added that Proctor was inspired to produce his affidavit after a talk with Fred Moore's ballistics expert Hamilton. But whatever its motives or origins the affidavit offers too little substance for serious regard.

The above, then, is a summary of the charges of unfairness by reason of judicial prejudice, community prejudice, jury prejudice, and prejudicial cheating by the prosecution.

Other charges allege false or incorrect testimony by prosecution eyewitnesses under the influence of prejudice. We note that Pelser and Lola Andrews canceled out their affidavit-repudiations with new affidavits claiming defense intimidation. Frankfurter also attacks the testimony of Carlos Goodridge and the Misses Splaine and Devlin by arguing that the crime automobile was going too fast—"the murderers . . . were driven away at high speed"—for trustworthy identification. Uncontradicted testimony, however, put the speed at the moment of sighting at less than twenty miles an hour. As yet, no one has been able to prove that any element of the prosecution testimony was misleading or wrong in any significant way.

Still other charges allege that the new evidence was not properly considered during the appeals. Of the post-trial evidence, the Medeiros confession was the most important. Frankfurter discusses it at length in his book, but we have seen how badly it withstood a serious testing. Frankfurter also places emphasis on the affidavit of Gould, the I.W.W. razor-paste salesman, who deposed that the killer looked different from Sacco. Yet another new argument revolved around the cap which Sacco may or may not have owned, a sartorial issue impossible to take seriously. In sum, the new evidence was less than significant. Nevertheless, the case transcript shows that it was exhaustively considered.

Beginning with the question of prejudice and arriving at the matter of the new evidence, we have reviewed all the important legal discussion by the best defenders. In view of their inability to produce anything stronger, the Supreme Judicial Court and the Governor had no alternative but to uphold the verdict. Nevertheless, the defense arguments, presented with great skill and sincerity, shaped the view of the case generally held today. Many other legal experts, however, had other opinions and they deserve some attention. Thus, in an article in *Current History* of March 1928, William R. Riddell, justice of the Court of Appeals of Ontario, concluded that: ". . . neither Judge nor Prosecuting Counsel was guilty of misconduct before the jury . . . there was nothing except subsequent declamation and vituperation to suggest prejudice or failure to perform their duty on the part of the jury . . . the refusal of the motions to hold a new trial cannot be held erroneous . . . there was a fair trial." A lecturer at Yale and Columbia, Riddell knew the American courts well and his article shows a close study of the case record. Another judge took direct issue with Frankfurter. In a letter to the magazine *Outlook* of September 7, 1927, Samuel R. Stern, formerly a justice of the State of Washington Superior Court, argued that Frankfurter "has done what any technical, or theoretical lawyer can do—find the weakness or flaws in any trial, and yet overlook the main facts and the main controversy." Stern added: "Any lawyer of average ability can . . . point out discrepancies and even possible errors, but they will not necessarily destroy all other testimony . . . nor will they bring out an unfair or illegal trial." The layman, if he likes his argument from authority, has his choice of authorities.

It is interesting to note, furthermore, that Frankfurter's writings, ignoring both the man's triumphs and his embarrassments, virtually eliminate Fred Moore as a figure of any importance in the case. The book mentions Moore in only one passage and then as a "factor of irritation and not appeasement." Compared with this, it discusses Thompson's participation in great detail. In sum, Frankfurter gives the impression that Moore botched the job which Thompson's competence was trying to repair.

In the spring of 1927 a lawyer friend* chanced to meet Frankfurter in Boston's genteel subway and essayed a pleasantry: "That was a wonderful brief you had in the *Atlantic*, Felix."

* Richard C. Evarts, who gave me this account in an interview in his Boston law offices, May 28, 1958.

Frankfurter reacted sharply: "Brief! No! It was a precise statement of the facts." The response, indicating that Frankfurter would brook no jest on the subject, destroyed the mood for an easy fraternal exchange and the men parted unhappily on the ruins of their meeting. Sitting in his offices more than a generation later, the lawyer reiterates the statement of his good will, but insists: "I still say it was a damn fine brief!"

He is strictly accurate. Frankfurter's book uses as its authority (the magazine article does not refer to sources directly) not the official case record, although it was available to him, but the *Defendants' Exceptions in the Commonwealth of Massachusetts versus Nicola Sacco and Bartolomeo Vanzetti,* their *Amended Bill of Exceptions,* and other defense briefs. More than eighty of the book's direct citations are drawn from the *Defendants' Exceptions . . . ,* their *Amended Bill of Exceptions,* their *Supplementary Bill of Exceptions,* or the *Brief for Defendants on First Appeal before Supreme Judicial Court;* the book does not mention the official case record. In effect, Frankfurter's arguments refer back to defense documents. This explains, for example, why his review of the ballistics points in Thayer's jury charge gives an inaccurate impression of what Thayer had actually said, Frankfurter having simply repeated the argument as given in the *Defendants' Exceptions.* . . . A number of other statements in his book similarly echo defense documents in a way that defeats objectivity. Thus he refers to Sacco as "in continuous employment" when Sacco was not at work on the South Braintree crime day and lacked the pay records (they had disappeared) to prove he had worked on the day of the Bridgewater holdup. It would be wearying to review other instances of this partiality. Frankfurter had indeed written a fine brief.

This is not to criticize Frankfurter's efforts for Sacco and Vanzetti. Under our adversary system of justice, a legal brief anticipates the exaggerations of opposing counsel by its own one-sided arguments. Obviously Frankfurter was convinced that the prosecution had not proved its case, and he argued as persuasively—and professionally—as he could to save the men. Heroic measures were needed at the time. If we refuse to accept the Frankfurter arguments as the most impartial available, this need not affect our commending him for the generosity of heart and the great ability he contributed to a cause he found just.

Repeated examination has not been able to substantiate the charge that Sacco and Vanzetti were betrayed in the courts.

15. The Time of the Intellectuals

TIME was Fred Moore's greatest gift to the defense of Sacco and Vanzetti. He had not been able to win the world's attention in 1921; the event was too immediate and its facts too disorderly. The defense needed distance that would transform the merely human into the legendary. Now, but only now, the Communists and the intellectuals could bring their powers into the case.

We have been moving from 1919—the Bridgewater crime—through 1920—the South Braintree holdup, the arrest and the Plymouth trial—through 1921—the Dedham trial; and on through the twenties to 1927.

It was a time when F. Scott Fitzgerald was hearing a steady golden roar. Later, he would think back to the period through the sharp, broken insights of his breakdown and feel the pain he had missed. Accepting their defeats, the other intellectuals experienced that pain in its immediacy. In 1922 T. S. Eliot published *The Waste Land*, which found "agony in stony places," and the Railway Labor Board cut wages, causing an unsuccessful strike of 400,000 railroad shopmen. The board's action had innocently carried out the conservative economic thinking which dominated the twenties so absolutely that few liberals thought to protest rationally. The theory was that wages must be kept down to a point where profits would encourage expansion. There was, however, no corrective on the other side of the equation: corporate profits, spilling back dangerously into the stock market, rose 62 per cent from 1923 to 1929, against an 11 per cent increase in workers' incomes. During the decade, meanwhile, the American labor unions lost more than one and one-half million of the five million members they had in 1920. In England, the deflationary policy was more obviously disastrous, causing unemployment throughout all those years. The British workers, who knew they were being cheated, went out on general strike in 1926, but the middle classes, Winston Churchill exhorting them in the name of sound economics, thrashed them in eight days of volunteer strike-breaking. John Maynard Keynes, helpless against the suicidal drive of orthodoxy, found himself and his fellow liberals "at the dead season of our fortunes."

In Washington, the intellectuals saw the mindless nonentity Harding succeeded by Coolidge, who believed in exercising the presidency as little as possible. The national leadership was not merely hostile to their beliefs; it was nonexistent. There was, however, a disorderly undercurrent of progressivism—the Progressive Party of Senator Robert M. La Follette won nearly five million votes in the 1924 election—but the intellectuals were far removed from both its labor and its agrarian elements. The intellectuals had nothing to do with the little that was being done in their sense.

In 1925 a Tennessee trial confirmed their unhappy judgments on American provincialism. With the revived Ku Klux Klan able to attract 200,000 persons to a meeting in Indiana, it was not extraordinary that the fundamentalists could insist on prohibiting the teaching of evolution. When a high school teacher violated the state law, he was found guilty with the assistance of William Jennings Bryan, a former presidential candidate and Secretary of State, as prosecutor. For H. L. Mencken, the period's loudest critic, the Tennessee monkey trial was more important than the

Sacco-Vanzetti case. Other intellectuals made the connection between the two.

It was a time that evaded thought. The economy was pouring out a stream of things, and the nonwealthy were buying automobiles, refrigerators, silk stockings, furs, and trips to Europe. At Walter Lippmann's invitation a pioneer American psychoanalyst explained Freud in the lower Fifth Avenue salon of Mabel Dodge in 1913, and sex became public property after the war. Film titles were: *Up in Mabel's Room, The Blue Flame* with the vamp Theda Bara, *A Shocking Night,* and *Male and Female,* which had been James Barrie's innocent *The Admirable Crichton.* To all that, a pitch of frenzy was contributed by the prohibition phenomenon, which included Al Capone's business empire, liquor that killed, blinded, and caused internal bleeding, and a pervasive corruption. If you refused to take it seriously, you could, like Mencken, enjoy the spectacle, but even he gave evidence of internal bleeding.

It was the Sacco-Vanzetti case that permitted the intellectuals to crystallize their general protest around a hard, definable issue. Nevertheless, although the protest was an expression of defiance and alienation, it became an important stage in their progress back into American society. They had been absent a long time.

At the time of the American Revolution men of culture and self-conscious intellectuality had been the leaders of the country. Benjamin Franklin, Thomas Jefferson, Alexander Hamilton, James Madison, John Adams, and their associates had belonged to the European world of the Enlightenment. They thought with the concepts formulated by Locke and Hume, by Montesquieu, Voltaire, and Rousseau. They used those concepts in the Declaration of Independence and the Constitution. But America turned away from Europe upon the success of the Revolution. Americans had little use for European ideas in the work of killing Indians, clearing forests, and building railroads. The American mind had little time for thought.

The character of American culture a generation later was reported by Alexis de Tocqueville, the great liberal historian and political scientist. In his *De la Démocratie en Amérique,* written after more than a year of observation in 1831 and 1832, he found an intellectual desert: "I think there is no country in the civilized world where the people are less concerned with philosophy. . . ." As a result of the frontier necessities, the useful had become a tyranny over the wise and the beautiful; the nation was producing nothing first-rate in thought, art, literature, or science. It was a period of an unsatisfying materialism: "It is a strange thing to see with what feverish passion the Americans pursue well-being, and how eternally tormented they are by the vague fear that they have not chosen the shortest route to it." A half-century later the British historian Lord James Bryce also found "a want of serious and sustained thinking." In his *American Commonwealth,* published in 1888, he listed among the important intellectual characteristics: a fondness for bold effects, a love of intellectual novelties, intellectual impatience, and an overvaluing of the multitude's judgment.

As the philosopher George Santayana saw it, the nation was enduring "that separation which is so characteristic of America between things intellectual, which remain wrapped in a feminine veil and, as it were, under glass, and the rough business and passions of life."* The nation preferred Henry Wadsworth Longfellow and William Cullen Bryant over Melville and Whitman, and Melville recognized: "I am an exile here."

One man who had first accepted his role as a tame writer was shocked by a forerunner of the Sacco-Vanzetti case into a bitter review of his situation and the nation's. William Dean Howells had achieved an extraordinary eminence for an Ohio farm boy when he became editor of the *Atlantic Monthly.* Yet he felt an unease, which he first palliated by a move from Boston and the *Atlantic* to New York and *Harper's.* In 1886, during the Hay-

* *Character and Opinion in the United States* (New York, Macmillan, 1920), p. 44.

market strike in Chicago, someone threw a bomb at a group of policemen and killed seven of them. Anarchists had been active in the strike; several were arrested. One of them anticipated justice by exploding a dynamite fuse in his mouth, and four of his comrades were executed after a trial held in an atmosphere of high emotion. Howells defended the anarchists, writing to a Chicago friend that the case had not been out of his waking thoughts for an hour: "It is the last thing when I lie down, and the first when I wake up; it blackens my life." According to Van Wyck Brooks, "Howells was to see the writer and artist as a working man, economically like a mechanic, a day-laborer, a farmer. . . ." Permanently affected, Howells went on to write *Annie Kilburn,* which was almost a proletarian novel, and then the utopian *A Traveler from Altruria,* which imagined an anarcho-socialist commonwealth of equality and brotherhood. Howells never got over the Haymarket case, but he never communicated the full force of his protest to the American public. In a letter to Henry James in 1888 he wrote, "after 50 years of optimistic content with 'civilisation' . . . I now abhor it, and feel that it is coming out all wrong in the end, unless it bases itself anew on real equality. Meanwhile, I wear a fur-lined overcoat, and live in all the luxury money can buy."*

Howells' sense of alienation and futility before injustice almost immediately became a continually repeated pattern. A new generation of intellectuals found new reasons for protest: the Homestead strike in 1892, broken after a pitched battle between workers and a battalion of Pinkerton operatives; the Pullman strike of 1894, broken with the help of federal troops; and a series of I.W.W. strikes in the first two decades of the new century. "After about 1890 American writers and other intellectuals became a more cohesive class than they had been, became restless with the restraints of gentility and conservatism, and took

* Van Wyck Brooks, *Howells: His Life and World* (New York: Dutton, 1959), pp. 180, 181.

up arms against American society," Professor Richard Hofstadter of Columbia University wrote in his *Anti-Intellectualism in American Life*. "In the struggle for new freedoms in expression and criticism that occupied them from about 1890 to the 1930's, the idea of their own alienation became a kind of rallying point, a part of their esthetic or political protest. . . . after 1890 it became possible for the first time to speak of the intellectuals as a class."

Individually and collectively the intellectuals needed a philosophic base, and this was provided by William James and John Dewey. More or less uncomfortable themselves in the American business society, the philosophers had formulated a rationale for dealing with it. They had accepted its practicality and transvaluated it into pragmatism or instrumentalism. Eliminating external standards, both taught Americans to refer to experience as they found it. James wrote: "The truth of an idea is not a stagnant property inherent in it. Truth happens to an idea." George Santayana objected, "the continual substitution of human psychology—normal madness, in my view—for the universe, in which man is but one distracted and befuddled animal, seemed to me a confused remnant of idealism, and not serious." Earlier, Tocqueville had pointed out the effect on Americans of a lack of training in philosophy, a situation James and Dewey were rationalizing more than correcting. The Americans, Tocqueville wrote, "do not go any further in their study, and, without examining in detail how the various factors are similar or dissimilar, they hasten to line them up under the same formula, in order to get on with something else." All that would be seen in the Sacco-Vanzetti case.

Although it was a compromise with American society, the philosophy of James and Dewey did not alter the intellectuals' sense of alienation. Remaining estranged, the intellectuals made practical use of the practical philosophy to express their protest more effectively. Meanwhile, other thinkers were encouraging their defiance. Thorstein Veblen, an angry and original spirit, taught that the economy was a dishonest game run by businessmen who contributed nothing to society and took too much for themselves. The historian Charles Beard showed that the founding fathers were moved by economic interest as well as by patriotism in his *An Economic Interpretation of the Constitution,* published in 1913. Beard himself warned against making too much of his idea, but the intellectuals translated the sense of the book into the accusation that the Constitution was an instrument of economic exploitation. Referring to the thirties Arthur Schlesinger, Jr., wrote in his *Age of Roosevelt,* "very little of what [the intellectuals] had learned from Dewey, Beard, and Veblen equipped them to resist the Soviet Union." For "Soviet Union" in the thirties one might substitute "Sacco-Vanzetti case" in the twenties.

Just before the first World War many of the intellectuals were heartened by the promise of Woodrow Wilson's New Freedom. At about this time a few of the more radical or Bohemian among them were gathering in Greenwich Village. With a physical community in being they began to have a small effect on the society around them. Some of them, John Reed and Mary Heaton Vorse, for example, could reach the general public through articles in conventional magazines. Their friends, meanwhile, were founding magazines devoted to social or esthetic protest. In December 1912 Max Eastman took over *The Masses,* announcing his purpose by a masthead that read "a revolutionary and not a reform magazine." Its contributors included Sherwood Anderson, Mabel Dodge, Vachel Lindsay, William Carlos Williams, and Amy Lowell, who was A. Lawrence Lowell's sister. Eastman believed *The Masses* was an important connection between the intellectuals and the working class. In a book published in 1948 he remembered, "the militant leaders of the working class without a single exception took the magazine into their hearts. Bill Haywood [the I.W.W. leader], Carlo Tresca, Elizabeth Gurley

Flynn, Ettor and Giovannitti [leaders of the 1912 Lawrence strike] . . . William Z. Foster [a union leader and later an important Communist] . . . every agitator who really intended to overthrow capitalism . . . felt he had a body of friends and colleagues in the writers and artists of *The Masses*."* Whatever the quality of the association, the intellectuals were still alienated from American society in general.

With the effects of the war and rising prosperity the intellectuals despaired. In 1922 the Greenwich Village inhabitant Harold E. Stearns published his *Civilization in the United States: An Inquiry by Thirty Americans*. The thirty, who included Van Wyck Brooks, H. L. Mencken, Robert Morss Lovett, Lewis Mumford, and George Jean Nathan, surveyed various aspects of the American culture from art to philosophy and called them all bad. Hypocrisy and emotional and esthetic starvation, they said, were the main themes of the American civilization. Stearns wrote the book's preface on a ship bound for France, where he remained until the depression and illness drove him back. None of the contributors mentioned Sacco and Vanzetti.

By 1925 the Sacco-Vanzetti case had become a new case.

Time had been permitting the American Communist Party to come into existence, build a minimum of strength, and finally—in 1925—recognize the case. Back in 1919, a few months before Bridgewater, two quarreling Communist parties were organized, a schism that continued until 1922. When Aldino Felicani tried to enlist the Boston Communists in 1920, it was neither surprising nor important that he was turned away. Too weak to be of any great use then, the American Communists, moreover, were not inclined to help anarchists at a time when Soviet Russia was beginning to liquidate its own anarchists. This small error of omission was followed by an active error typical of the Communist world organization. In October 1921, three months after the Dedham trial and at the most inappropriate time, the Third International stirred up demonstrations in France, Switzerland,

* *Enjoyment of Living* (New York, Harper, 1948), p. 409.

Spain, Portugal, Sweden, and Norway. (One enthusiast sent a well-packaged grenade to the American ambassador in Paris, Myron T. Herrick, but his valet opened the package and managed to throw it far enough away to escape with minor injuries.) The European protests lost themselves in futility, and the Communists turned their attention elsewhere.

In 1925, however, the Communists were ready to deal with the case more effectively. In June the Workers (Communist) Party of America, as it was then called, organized a front group called the International Labor Defense to penetrate the labor movement. Labor was virtually impenetrable at the time, but the Communists could use the I.L.D. for other objectives and they launched it at the Sacco-Vanzetti case. The I.L.D. began by collecting money for the cause. It then doled out small sums to the Defense Committee—Aldino Felicani said he got no more than $6,000 in all—and tried to purchase command with the rest. The anarchists resisted, and the Communists hurled a few insults and retired to reconsider strategy. A year later they tried again. This time they were not so tactless as to demand surrender; they merely asked to share the leadership equally with the Defense Committee. Of course, they would settle for nothing less than their original objective, but they were willing to get there in two steps instead of one. Some of the more trusting Defense Committee members were persuaded, since the Committee was desperate for money, but Frankfurter and Felicani knew better and got their associates to agree on a second rejection. This resulted in more Communist denunciations of the Committee's bourgeois betrayers and deviate radicals, but the issue was too good to be given up now. At worst, the Communists were making money and friends for themselves.

The Communists in Europe, less concerned with the details of control or cooperation, found the cause a superb vehicle for their purposes. Was this not a perfect example of oppression in the most capitalistic of nations?

Beginning in 1926 the European Communists mounted their

campaign. Unlike the American Communists, they had real strength to contribute. In France the Communist Party controlled the Confédération Générale du Travail Unitaire, a large labor federation. In Germany, where it had been blooded in the Revolution of 1918, the party also had a substantial membership and extensive support in the labor unions. With active parties in most of the other countries of Europe as well, the Communists were able to order armies of shouting followers into the streets of the great capitals. Moreover, they could support any campaign with their widely distributed newspapers and other publications. And finally, they had created a great range of front organizations to maintain innocent contact with non-Communist segments of society. With all these resources, the European Communists proceeded to mobilize most of Europe, middle-class as well as proletarian, for the cause.

The most conservative of Europeans found it easy to believe that the authorities had conspired to murder two innocents. In the first place, such phenomena were not unknown in the history of Europe. In the second place, the Europeans have the greatest difficulty with the simplest events. Thus many of them instinctively assumed that President Kennedy's assassin was a minor figure in a ramified plot: a murder resulting from one man's psychosis was too plain an explanation. Presently, the Communist demands were being supported by scores of internationally distinguished names, including John Galsworthy and H. G. Wells (Bernard Shaw typically refused his sympathy while condemning American justice); Romain Rolland, Henri Barbusse, and fourteen other leading French writers, the Comtesse Anna de Noailles and former Premier Joseph Caillaux; Thomas Mann, Fritz Kreisler, Albert Einstein, and Paul Loebe, president of the German Reichstag—and Benito Mussolini. Ramsay MacDonald, the Labor Party leader and past and future prime minister, commented: "The whole affair is too terrible." Besides these individuals, many non-Communist organizations joined the defense effort. In France, the Ligue des Droits de l'Homme, which had fought for Alfred Dreyfus among its other great causes, began turning out Sacco-and-Vanzetti pamphlets, although Dreyfus himself avoided any expressions of solidarity. This activity in Europe, as well as direct communication from American sympathizers, also aroused Latin America, which had its energetic anarchist groups, and the rest of the world. Sacco-Vanzetti committees were organized from Stockholm and Moscow to Montevideo and Johannesburg.

The Communists had preceded the intellectuals into the case both at home and abroad.

As we have seen, however, there was one important exception to this timing. In the United States a few pioneer intellectuals, Felix Frankfurter and his associates of the American Civil Liberties Union among them, had actually taken over the leadership of the defense. Beginning when their fellow intellectuals were still indifferent, they had kept the case alive during the slack period after Fred Moore's departure. Now they were in a position to profit hugely from the activities of the Communists. They happily accepted delivery of the support of the foreign intellectuals and middle classes. They continued skilfully to avoid Communist control.

The international concern made the most of the talents of the American intellectuals. By right of function they dominated the channels of communication to the outside world. The world had never heard of Thayer, Katzmann, and the leaders of Massachusetts authority, but it knew Frankfurter, John Dos Passos, and Upton Sinclair. Naturally it was prepared to listen to the latter and pass on their arguments. The *Atlantic* article of Frankfurter (or his book) and the pamphlet of John Dos Passos (who got his material from Frankfurter) were reworked by the Europeans to build up more passion. A law professor's article in the Belgian *Revue de Droit Pénal et de Criminologie* began: "What is the truth? To find it the learned professor of Harvard University

Felix Frankfurter made an extensive study of the very voluminous dossier of this case. . . . here is a résumé of the Frankfurter book. . . ." H. G. Wells made Frankfurter's points without his qualifications in an article for a major London newspaper.* The headlines began the arguments forthrightly: "Outrages in Defense of Order: The Proposed Murder of Two Americans." Wells went on to say that the "evidence for the presence of the accused upon the scene of the murder . . . is contemptible" while the "evidence that [they] were elsewhere is sound and convincing." He added: "On the evidence of the alibi alone, the active complicity of the two men in the Braintree crime would have been laughed out of court in an unimpassioned trying of the case." However one-sided, these statements were in the area of reason, but the effects in the world went beyond reason. Through their international leverage the American intellectuals were able to exercise real power.

By midsummer of 1927 Americans were being urged to save the men not because they were necessarily innocent, but because their case was harming the United States. A Boston man on vacation in Europe wrote to the *Herald* from Lausanne: "By reason of the unexampled notoriety of the case and the propaganda connected with it, millions of earnest and intelligent people all over Europe seriously believe that these men are being railroaded to death on shaky evidence for social and political reasons. . . . This is a capital international calamity, and whatever its history I should consider the execution of the men, in the presence of such widespread conviction, a cardinal calamity. . . ."

Meanwhile, throughout 1926 and into 1927, the Thompson appeals were producing new material at regular intervals for discussion and anger. The succession was: argument before the Supreme Judicial Court appealing Thayer's denial of Moore's five

* Reprinted in H. G. Wells, *The Way the World Is Going* (London: Ernest Benn, 1928), pp. 240–51.

supplementary motions, January 1926; the Court's rejection of Thompson's arguments, May; argument on the Medeiros motion again before Thayer, September; Thayer's denial, October; appeal of Thayer's denial again before the Supreme Judicial Court, January 1927; and the court's rejection, April. Meanwhile, also, Frankfurter was beginning to reach more influential people in Boston.

Thompson's Medeiros motion and Frankfurter's persuasions combined to achieve the first great public relations feat of the new efforts. Three days after Thayer denied the motion, on October 26, 1926, the *Herald* carried an editorial backing the defense on every point. The editorial demanded a review of the case and summarized all the major Frankfurter arguments which would appear a few months later in the *Atlantic*. Written by F. Lauriston Bullard, the *Herald's* chief editorial writer, it was a striking indication of the new power and respectability of the cause. All Boston, which had refused to take the case seriously until now, was being informed by a major newspaper that Thayer was prejudiced, that the prosecutor had conspired with Captain Proctor to falsify his testimony, and that a professional criminal had confessed to the South Braintree killings. Bullard had been convinced of an injustice when Frankfurter showed him the Proctor affidavit. His employer, Robert L. O'Brien, editor-publisher of the *Herald* and also the *Traveller*, was never persuaded of that, but the excesses of the Red raid period had left him with a profound disgust; here was an opportunity to counter those phenomena with an instructive defense of radicals. Later, according to a privately printed account, O'Brien decided that the convictions had been just, chiefly because "not one of the 63 persons officially connected with the case had doubts of guilt."* Meanwhile, O'Brien was willing to affront conservative Boston with his conservative newspapers. The intellectuals took heart.

* Cited in G. Louis Joughin and Edmund M. Morgan, *The Legacy of Sacco and Vanzetti* (New York: Harcourt, Brace, 1948), p. 335.

The Bullard editorial went on to win a Pulitzer prize, another proof of the powers of the intellectuals, while the Frankfurter article itself would attract more support on its own. Originally planned for the *New Republic,* where it would have had limited effect, it was promoted to the *Atlantic* as a result of the cause's new respectability. When the *Atlantic's* editor, Ellery Sedgwick, had heard about the article, he overrode Frankfurter's desire-whetting arguments about the commitment to the *New Republic.* It was a negotiation comedy Frankfurter happily remembered; there had been no commitment, the *New Republic,* with which he was associated anyway, having been the best available platform until Sedgwick's interest was aroused. Now, under the aegis of so hallowed a Boston institution as the *Atlantic,* the defense was gaining all the more respectability. Following these signals, newspapers and magazines throughout the nation intensified their coverage of the case. The *New Republic* and the *Nation,* making up for past intermittence or indifference, began printing running accounts. In Boston and the nation at large the power of the intellectuals increased daily.

Taking the Bullard editorial and the Frankfurter article as points of departure, the intellectuals organized one of the greatest public relations campaigns in American history. In the summer of 1926 the Sacco-Vanzetti Defense Committee hired a director of public relations in recognition of that function's prime importance. He was Gardner Jackson, a Boston Brahmin on his mother's side, who had quit business and become a *Globe* reporter out of vaguely liberal and nonconformist leanings. In the city room one day he made a shy remark of sympathy for the accused to Frank Sibley and, as he remembered it, "Sibley fell into my arms." It was Sibley who recommended him to the Defense Committee, and Gardner Jackson justified that trust by putting the Committee's publicity operations on a regular and more rational basis. One of his innovations was the publishing of the

Defense Committee *Bulletin* every month, but he would have been effective had he restricted his contribution to running the mimeograph machine. Gardner Jackson had priceless allies.

The American Civil Liberties Union, the first and most enduring of the Committee's friends, could now act with much greater effect. The situation was brilliantly different from the days when the A.C.L.U. was unable to reach the intellectuals outside its own circle or to get them to act because of the case's earlier limitations. With its connections, it provided another administrative machine for the defense, and one of much greater force than the Defense Committee's incorrigibly sectarian operation. The extent of its assistance was described in a letter of Roger Baldwin, the A.C.L.U. executive director, which was quoted by G. Louis Joughin in his *Legacy of Sacco and Vanzetti:* "The Civil Liberties Union has been connected with the Sacco and Vanzetti matter, but has hidden its participation under various false fronts. We are at present instigating a nation-wide movement among lawyers in the various university faculties to join as signatories . . . for a review of the case *de novo.* This work is being done behind the name of a group of lawyers at Columbia. Karl Llewellyn is the chief promoter."

Now able to make good use of them, the defense had a number of great advantages in the area of public relations. This might seem strange at first view. After all, the nation was dominated by reactionary or conservative business, and publishers were businessmen. Yet the efficiencies of capitalist organization depend on specialization, among other things, and businessmen, denigrating a faculty that earned little money, were content to let others do the thinking and writing. These others were nearly all liberals. Lionel Trilling has written: "In the United States liberalism is not only the dominant but even the sole intellectual tradition." The liberal intellectuals were strong even in the conservative newspaper press, the *New York Times,* for example, while they were welcomed by book publishing in general and some magazines in particular because they were, at least, alive, and because readers would pay money to read them. Private soldiers of the communications field, the despised intellectuals had more authority than they themselves or their chiefs realized; the story of a martyrdom-in-process made the most of it. Some conservative newspapers continued to point to the doubtful parts of the story, but they were defensive about it. Even the Hearst columnist Arthur Brisbane, a skilled rationalizer of reaction, wondered: "Is it absolutely essential to the dignity of this country that Sacco and Vanzetti be executed?" It would have been impossible to use the conservative press to support labor legislation of the type passed in the thirties, but a matter of two men's lives, upsetting no economic arrangements, could find tolerance among publishers who were too busy to study the facts of the case.

With most of the press neutralized, the defense got unequivocal support from one of the nation's leading newspapers. On August 27, 1926, one day after Bullard's editorial appeared, Vanzetti wrote to one of his lady correspondents: "I met a representant of the 'New York World.' He came to interview me, since the journal will launch a campaign on the case." Walter Lippmann, the editor of the *New York Evening World*, had worked with Frankfurter as early as 1914, when the two men had joined in the founding of the *New Republic*, for which Frankfurter acted as legal advisor. In an interview in 1958, Lippmann told me that Frankfurter was his "chief contact" on the case. They got "full cooperation," as Lippmann put it, from the publisher, Ralph Pulitzer. Lippmann proceeded to write a series of important editorials on the case, and the *World* became the clearest, most widely heard newspaper voice during the last desperate summer of Sacco and Vanzetti.

The *World* sounded another, less solemn note through the columns of Heywood Broun. Writing on its famous opposite-editorial page, a popular feature section, Broun celebrated the persons of the defendants lyrically:* "The men in Charlestown prison are shining spirits, and Vanzetti has spoken with an eloquence not known elsewhere within our time. They are too bright, we shield our eyes and kill them." In attack, Broun could use his skills with great finesse: "Already too much has been made of the personality of Webster Thayer. To sympathizers of Sacco and Vanzetti he has seemed a man with a cloven hoof. But in no usual sense of the terms is this man a villain. Although probably not a great jurist, he is without doubt as capable and conscientious as the average Massachusetts Judge, and if that's enough to warm him in wet weather, by all means let us stick that compliment against his ribs. . . ." If the irony escaped the reader, Broun found another way to communicate his meaning: "When at last Judge Thayer in a tiny voice passed sentence on Sacco and Vanzetti, a woman in the courtroom said with terror: 'It is death condemning life.' " Broun did not stop there. He was experiencing that profound emotion reported by his son in his specific case and by Malcolm Cowley in the case of the intellectuals in general. Retrospectively, Broun also described it, more acutely than the son: "For years [Broun] had complained with some reason of an inability to work up a satisfactory amount of hate. And now he had it. . . ."** With it, Broun went on to write: "It is not every prisoner who has a President of Harvard University throw on the switch for him. . . . If this is a lynching, at least the fish peddler and his friend the factory hand may take unction to their souls that they will die at the hands of men in dinner coats or academic gowns, according to the conventionalities required by the hour of execution." Broun tried to go even further, but the *World*, finding that an intellectual's catharsis of this extreme nature was harming the cause, felt obliged to stop his columns.

* These articles were reprinted in Heywood Broun, *Collected Edition.* (New York: Harcourt, Brace, 1941), pp. 197–199.

** Also reprinted in *Collected Edition,* this citation is from an article entitled "The Rabbit That Bit the Bulldog," pp. 210–213, which originally appeared in the *New Yorker.*

Besides the running editorials of Lippmann and the columns of Broun, the *World* made one more contribution of great value to the publicity campaign. This was in encouraging and printing a special interview with the prisoners. The interview was actually undertaken not by a *World* reporter but by a feature writer for the North American Newspaper Alliance, a small feature press service; the newspaper was one of its most important clients. Appearing in the May 12, 1927 issue of the *World*, the article was also syndicated widely in the United States and abroad. The N.A.N.A. man, Phil Stong, had brought with him a ready sympathy—he was then living in Greenwich Village among intellectuals committed to the cause—as well as the skills that would extend beyond his occupation of the time to that of a successful minor novelist. (His *State Fair* would be a best-seller of the thirties.) Stong's interview was so effective that a citation from it won thousands more to the cause and later entered literary anthologies as an example of distinguished expression. The citation is the most famous Vanzetti statement:

> If it had not been for these thing, I might have live out my life talking at street corners to scorning men. I might have die, unmarked, unknown, a failure. Now we are not a failure. This is our career and our triumph. Never in our full life can we hope to do such work for tolerance, for joostice, for man's onderstanding of man, as we do now by an accident.
>
> Our words—our lives—our pains—nothing! The taking of our lives—lives of a good shoemaker and a poor fish-peddler—all! That last moment belong to us—that agony is our triumph!

Euripides gives Hecuba a simpler expression in *The Trojan Women* as she laments the destruction of Troy: "And yet—had God not bowed us down,/ not laid us low in dust,/ none would have sung of us or told our wrongs/ in stories men listen to forever."

Stong reported that Vanzetti had made the statement casually, in the course of the interview—"not declaimed, just said simply."

Of himself, Stong later said he had jotted down the sense of it in a personal shorthand after leaving Dedham jail.* If this admits error and editing, and if the circumstances indicate a less than objective approach, the character of the citation opens its real authority to question. The statement makes its point with great economy; it has a conceptual beginning, middle, and end, arching into a stirring general declaration—"such work for tolerance, for joostice . . ."—from the specifics of "these thing." Its phrasing, furthermore, is precise, rich in images, and dramatically cumulative in effect. Nothing that Vanzetti ever wrote or said exhibited those qualities. Consistent with his intelligence and background, Vanzetti was wordy, irrelevant, approximate, and unordered. His forty-two-minute sentencing speech, a 7,000-word petition, and ten-page letters were typical of his expression. Thus we can recall his excursion on the well-poisoning at the sentencing.** Contrasting with the density of the citation, most Vanzetti

* Letter published in the *Lantern*, August 1929. Sacco-Vanzetti Collection, Harvard Law Library.

** Following is an excerpt from the Vanzetti sentencing speech: "I remember that Mr. Katzmann has introduced a witness against us, a certain Ricci. Well, I have heard that witness. It seems that he has nothing to say. It seemed that it was foolishness to produce a witness that had nothing to say. And it seemed as if he were called by the Commonwealth to tell to the jury that he was the foreman of that laborer that was near the scene of the crime and who claimed, as it was testified in our behalf, that we were not the men and that this man, the witness Ricci, was his foreman, and he has tried to keep the man on the job instead of going to see what was happening so as to give the impression that it was not true that the man went towards the street to see what happened. But that was not very important. The real importance is that the man say that it was not true. That a certain witness that was the water boy of the gang of laborers testified that he take the pail and go to a certain spring, a water spring, and therefore it was not true that he see the bandit, and therefore it was not true that he can tell that neither I nor Sacco were the men. But it was introduced to show that it was not true that the men go to that spring, because they know that the Germans has poisoned the water in that spring. That is what he say on the stand over there. Now, in the world chronicle of the time there is not a single happening of that nature. Nobody in America—we have read plenty things but that the Germans have die in Europe during the war, but nobody can prove and nobody will say that the Germans are bad enough to poison the spring water in this country during the war."

statements can be cut to a half or quarter without loss of substance. Its style is not the man.

More important than style, the sense of the citation is also a denial of the man. Whenever Vanzetti discusses his conviction in his letters, he is naturally angry and full of hate. He was not prepared, as the citation would have it, to present his death as a gift to an improving humanity; rather, he would use it to kill: "Ah: to see the world drown itself in drowning us. . . ." Or, once again, in a letter written to Roger Baldwin less than two weeks after the interview was published: "I will try to see Thayer death. . . . We will ask for revenge and rivendication. . . . I will put fire in to the human breaths." Vanzetti never showed the desire to compose his own elegy.

Although his own writings abounded in faults, one might prefer them to the famous statement. One can appreciate their rhythmical quality, dreamlike imaginings, and dramatic conception of revenge. As communicated by Stong, Vanzetti loses the natural and the original.

One might apply similar questions to another citation in the same article, the words attributed to Sacco:

> First they give me basket to weave, like children. Better than nothing, but not much. Then I set alone—seven years—thousands of days—and all for say man's nature can be perfect—day after day—nothing do—breathe, eat, sit up, lie down—because I think man innerly noble—not beast—

Now Sacco was an inarticulate man and these words are even less typical of his normal expression. One can only say that it was extraordinarily fortuitous for Stong to have captured this diptych of the best statements—in terms of public relations—of either man.

Whatever its origins, the Vanzetti citation was a superb instrument for the purposes of the defense. Since men are still creatures of the emotions, its emotional force was immensely more effective than mere reason. It added the last features to the portrait of Vanzetti the martyr. And this was the most perfect of the intellectuals' triumphs.

Caught up in their act of faith, believing in their own publicity, the intellectuals became more and more impassioned for the cause. They gave testimony for Sacco and Vanzetti at their cocktail parties, they wrote articles and letters to the editor, they signed petitions. With the help of the A.C.L.U., they organized demonstrations at hundreds of universities, where faculty and student liberals made angry speeches and collected more signatures. In May 1927, for example, the work of the A.C.L.U. and Professor Llewellyn produced petitions from more than sixty law faculties, including Columbia, Cornell, and Yale, and even the Universities of Alabama and Texas. In June the Defense Committee would hand the Governor of Massachusetts a huge petition signed by a half-million persons. Nor was this all the intellectuals would contribute. During the earlier years an occasional sympathizer had gone to Boston to help the Defense Committee. Now in 1927 a number of intellectuals would gather there prepared to do more. They would stand on street corners facing scorning men and the Boston police. When their time came the intellectuals laid siege to Boston.

16. Solstice

EXCERPTED and broadcast by the intellectuals, the sentencing speeches of Sacco and Vanzetti served as texts for the demonstrations that broke out throughout the world, and, with the help of natives, in the Boston area itself. In Union Square in New York the Vanzetti words, "I never spilled blood," were bannered over a meeting of 10,000 protestants. (The anarchist leader Carlo Tresca, still helping his comrades, found himself the only anarchist among a company of Communist and left-wing speakers that included James P. Cannon, head of the International Labor Defense, still trying to capture the cause.) In Massachusetts the demonstrations were not nearly so large or aggressive. A rally of Smith College girls listened to Professor James M. Landis, then a Harvard Law School colleague of Frankfurter's, who called for their signatures on one of the petitions the defense was circulating. The meeting ended unpleasantly, however, when some Northampton townspeople attacked the Landis arguments with enough anger to frighten the girls. At the case's point of departure, in South Braintree, Edward Holton James, an eccentric nephew of William and Henry James, personally carried out a demonstration of another kind. He reenacted the escape of the holdup gang's automobile, an experiment that attracted two carloads of reporters as well as spectators from the same factory windows that had looked down on the murders. James' objective was to prove that the prosecution witnesses could not have had time to identify Sacco and Vanzetti. He assisted his conclusions by driving his automobile at twice the speed of the gang's Buick. The pressure on Boston increased.

The intellectuals' siege of the city got more substantial help from the actions of some of its well-placed inhabitants. Bullard's editorial had done more than give the best defense arguments; it had also made a demand that was part of the defense strategy. It had asked the Governor to appoint a committee to restudy the whole case with his active participation: beyond the courts one could always fall back on executive clemency. The sentencing, which would have the prisoners die on July 10—in three months—gave the needed urgency to the demand.

The defense leaders, however, were necessarily less than candid about their real objective. They would not be satisfied with clemency. The first objective, of course, was to preserve the men, but once Sacco and Vanzetti were safe from execution, they could strive for a real vindication following the precedent of Tom Mooney, the great labor martyr of the period. Convicted with another man, Mooney had been sentenced to death for his alleged part in a bomb explosion that killed nine and wounded forty persons during the San Francisco Preparedness Day parade in 1916. The Governor of California had commuted the sentence to life imprisonment in 1918, and the Mooney campaign continued until his pardon in 1939. The pattern had been set.

The defense strategists put the demand in the form of a negotiable reality—a petition. But the most convincing petition, even with the tremendous world support behind it, was not enough. This was Boston, and Boston would resist both logic and foreign force: the petition needed the weight of good Boston names. By now, however, the defenders had another group of allies of a more acceptable character than the radicals and academic people. These were the middle-class sympathizers, who formed what Gardner Jackson called the "middle-brow committee." Their leader, the State Street broker John F. Moors, spoke to Bishop William Lawrence, Episcopal Bishop of Massachusetts and one of the Commonwealth's most influential personalities. A man who enjoyed fund-raising and the company of millionaires, Lawrence retained a noblesse oblige that included sympathy for the downtrodden. Prepared to put his name before all others on it, Lawrence let the Governor know that he would carry the petition himself, after informing the press, if that were necessary to get his attention. It is doubtful if the threat of an active Canossa staged on Beacon Hill frightened the Governor, who was willing enough to act under the proper conditions. He could not justify reopening the case simply because radicals and eccentrics found unfairness in it, but Lawrence gave him the absolute rebuttal to reactionary objections: if there were a fatal weakness in him, then all Boston was lost. The bearer of the temporal power accordingly communicated, also unofficially, with the lord spiritual and indicated he would receive the petition with due earnest.

Lawrence consulted with Charles P. Curtis, a young, well-connected lawyer and member of the Harvard Corporation, about other signers. A Brahmin as well as a friend of Frankfurter's, Curtis was respected for his soundness by his class and for his liberalism by the liberals (he later became a defender of Robert Oppenheimer), and he helped put together a series of sound names. Curtis told me he had been inclined to believe Sacco and Vanzetti guilty and fairly tried, even advising his mother against joining her reformist friends in the defense effort, but like Bishop Lawrence, he thought a review was a proper way of making sure that justice was done. Besides Lawrence and Curtis, the signers were: Professor Frank W. Taussig, Harvard's conservative economist, Heman W. Burr, a lawyer and wealthy banker, and Roland W. Boyden, an erudite and unprovincial lawyer who had been the American representative on the Allied Reparations

Commission. Curtis took the petition on Sunday, April 17, to Joseph Wiggin, the Governor's private counsel. Two weeks later, as the law required, a petition from the prisoners was also delivered to the State House. The prisoners, however, made some difficulties by refusing to play the game. Sacco, sinking into morbidity, refused to sign at all, while Vanzetti, imposing his own meanings, demanded justice and not mercy. This was impossible, as his lawyers must have told him, since justice belonged wholly to the courts, leaving only clemency to the executive. The Governor's mercy, however, extended to the point of ignoring the technical flaws in the prisoners' petition. He commenced brooding sympathetically but indistinctly over the essential demand in both petitions.

The Lawrence petition was documentary proof that Brahmin Boston was no monolith of denial in the Sacco-Vanzetti case. Many respectable citizens supported it. Within less than two months of the sentencing, the Governor received 17,000 letters, most of them demanding a review or outright clemency.* One of the letters,** which put a series of questions formulated in a way that would call up sections of the Frankfurter article as answers, was signed by twenty-six Boston leaders. Although the text was sectarian—a franker discussion with less of the advocate's logic might have been more effective—the twenty-six were not. They included a Cabot, a former speaker of the Massachusetts House of Representatives, the president of the Boston Women's City Club, the president of the Massachusetts League of Women Voters, and some members of the Harvard faculty. All these notables and all the other letter writers together could not match the persuasions of a Bishop Lawrence, but they contributed a useful supplement to the arguments for a review.

Boston was divided, but most unequally. Most conservatives,

* Reported in *Boston Globe*, May 27, 1927, p. 1.

** Published in *Official Bulletin of the Sacco-Vanzetti Defense Committee*, May 1927, p. 1.

getting angrier all the time, had the immovable opinion that the prisoners were guilty. Bullard, who had been profoundly shaken by the effects of his editorial, described the situation in an article for the *New York Times* of June 26. Entitled "Boston Cleft," it saw the two sides: "In the main, labor and liberal opinion in Boston and that large body of students of current problems loosely called the intelligentsia are pro-Sacco. The very large conservative element, representing much that in attainment and tradition is best in Boston in finance and society as well as law, are predominantly anti-Sacco." Thus Moorfield Storey, a distinguished lawyer and, as a supporter of Negro rights, head of the N.A.A.C.P., said: "Our system of administering the law in Massachusetts is on trial." The result was a bitter family quarrel: "Some clubs by general consent have prohibited discussion of the case; the members have nearly come to blows. At social gatherings, men of both years and eminence grow apoplectic in denunciation of the 'Communists who think they can run this country.' " Sadly, Bullard observed that few persons based their opinions on the facts of the case, the conservatives upholding the conviction "on the ground that nothing must be permitted to damage the judicial system of Massachusetts," and the liberals denouncing authority as generically prejudiced and heartless.

In his novel *The Late George Apley*, John P. Marquand defined the two types as individuals, each authentically Bostonian. Horatio Willing, the suitable Boston biographer he created as narrator, writes of the case: "Apley's position was eminently the right one— . . . the two men were radicals, who had been found guilty under the laws of Massachusetts, whose case was delayed solely through the efforts of fellow radicals and of emotionally unbalanced sentimentalists. . . ." Willing then personified the other position in Henry Joyce, the smartest boy in his class in a proper Back Bay school: "What might have been a brilliant and successful career has been clouded over by an unbalanced preoccupation over social injustices. . . . he has dissipated his notable abilities in an unbalanced espousal of various lost causes, which led to his arrest while picketing the State House in the unfortunate Sacco-Vanzetti dispute. . . ." In the minority along with Mrs. Elizabeth Evans, Henry Joyce was as true to type and tradition as George Apley.

In fact, all Boston, conservative and liberal, was proud of the city's revolutionary and reformist traditions. It hallowed the relics of the American Revolution; there was Faneuil Hall, for example, known as the Cradle of Liberty for having served as the meeting place of the revolutionary patriots. It virtuously recalled that the city had gone on to become an abolitionist center despite its financial interest in the cotton trade. It gave honored places in its history to the fanatical abolitionist William Lloyd Garrison and his proselyte, Wendell Phillips, the son of the first mayor. It even suffered Phillips when he went on to become a thorough radical, expounding an angry revolutionary socialism with the encouragement of his wife, another of Boston's reformist ladies, who would say: "Wendell, don't shilly-shally." Nineteenth-century Boston, furthermore, had defended Henry Thoreau, who was, lest we forget to attach the proper definition, an anarchist, albeit a nonviolent one. Oscar Handlin, the Harvard historian, has written about its citizens: "Naturally, they were democrats. They gloried in the Constitution, valued its blessings, and hoped its principles would spread to all the peoples of the earth. They sympathized with the revolutionary struggles of the French, Greeks, Poles, Magyars, Italians, and Irish, and, when they could, aided materially and generously." The case of Sacco and Vanzetti was not so alien to Boston as it might seem.

It was actually stranger to Boston's recent immigrants. By the third decade of the twentieth century, the old Anglo-Saxon stock, although still dominant, had become a minority, representing just one-third of the population. There were as many Irish, with the other third divided among Italians, Jews, and Slavs. The Italians themselves, suspicious of their anarchist brethren and socially insecure, refused their solidarity until the very end. Only then, with the world's encouragement, would they let their relation to the prisoners warm to life. The Irish, conservative and Catholic, were perhaps the hardest enemies of these atheistic anarchists. They were not, however, in a position to do much more about it than communicate their resentment over the defense efforts. (The Defense Committee's Irish radicals were, of course, isolated exceptions.) The other immigrant groups, who had less reason for engagement than the Italians, but also correspondingly less reason for embarrassment, preferred not to associate their real problems with the fantasies and doubts represented by Sacco and Vanzetti. Thus the case was thrown back upon that part of Boston which was inclined to see itself, with the passive cooperation of the others, as the whole of Boston.

At the approach of the summer solstice of 1927 you could anatomize the case on the body of physical Boston: certain parts of the city stood for certain positions on the issues. Henry Adams had anticipated that in his *Education*, where he told of his birth "under the shadow of the State House . . . a nest of associations, so colonial—so troglodytic—as the First Church, the Boston State House, Beacon Hill, John Hancock and John Adams, Mount Vernon Street and Quincy. . . ." He inquired: "What would become of such a child of the seventeenth and eighteenth centuries, when he should wake up to find himself required to play the game of the twentieth?" The Sacco-Vanzetti case was a twentieth-century game. In the intricate play, the State House represented the neutral position. There the Governor pursued his thought processes under the portraits of the conservative John Hancock and the radical Sam Adams. Appropriately located, the State House marked the eastern point of Beacon Hill, the home of many of the Brahmins. Back Bay, just to the west of Beacon Hill, harbored more of them, and 90 per cent of all of them were instinctive defenders of the authority that would kill Sacco and Vanzetti. From the State House or a Beacon Hill domicile, the

Governor or any one of his Brahmin neighbors could look down, toward the south, upon the green of the Common and the contiguous Public Gardens, which damped for them the restlessness of the city. On the Common, British and American troops had answered mustering call, and, during the summer solstice of 1927, men would make speeches about Sacco and Vanzetti; and, at all times, unqualified people would take a grateful ease. From the State House, if you turn your back on Beacon Hill and Back Bay, a few minutes' walk to the east will take you through the business and financial districts to the North End. The late George Apley, who owned a Back Bay house, had an indigene's interest in Boston history which he expended on conscientious papers for his scholarly society. One of them took a North End property through 115 owners from the seventeenth century, from Jonas Good to Luigi Martinelli; the Italians had taken over the North End. (Playing cards and communicating liquidly, they sun themselves today in the square that leads from Hanover Street to the old North Church, where Paul Revere had hung his lanterns in 1775.) Here, one flight up at 256 Hanover Street, the Sacco-Vanzetti Defense Committee had its headquarters.

In the State House the Governor, spending fourteen hours a day on the case, was experiencing more and more pressure as April passed into May. Most of it was from the sympathizers. However, on April 25, the *Boston Transcript*, organ of the Brahminate and specialist in genealogical tables (it would die of its laggard preoccupations in 1941), attempted to redress the balance by putting forward a champion to annihilate Frankfurter. He was Dean John H. Wigmore of the Northwestern University Law School, a Harvard Law graduate, a liberal jurist according to the twenties' lights, and a highly respected legal scholar whose writings are basic texts in law faculties today. Unfortunately for his dignity and purposes, Wigmore tripped over a detail and compromised his generally sound arguments with bad manners. The detail concerned the "approved"-"affirmed" question in

Thayer's Medeiros opinion. Wigmore had argued correctly enough that Thayer was claiming only an "affirmation." Failing, however, to note the one "approved" that had crept into the opinion, he innocently denied that it existed. The manners appeared in the references to Frankfurter as a "prominent pundit" and, for anyone who missed the point, a "plausible pundit." All this made Wigmore vulnerable fore and aft. The *Herald* was glad to hold up its presses as Frankfurter wrote out a rebuttal that made him look silly. Massachusetts justice was being wretchedly served by its friends.

Wigmore had made another point by trumpeting the trade secret that review courts violated the law. This had to do with the questions of error of fact and error in law. As everybody knew by this time, the Supreme Judicial Court reviewed only errors in law and not errors of fact. Nevertheless, Wigmore argued, courts subject to such a restriction have a way of getting around it when they want to. They could simply make a wilful misinterpretation of some imprecise section of the record, language and human fallibility always providing the opportunities, and call it an error in law. The Massachusetts Supreme Court had not done this because it was confident that no error of fact had occurred, the Dean concluded. To this argument, Frankfurter could simply retort that the law forbade such illegal actions by the reviewing judges. Of course, he ignored the fact that there was no one to review the reviewers, but he won his point by sheer deftness. Another *Transcript-Herald* exchange two weeks later, in which Wigmore returned with sounder reasoning and unexceptionable facts, failed to change the first effect. Once more the Sacco-Vanzetti defense had triumphed in the area of public relations.

These were only a few of the arguments hurled at the Governor. Moreover, some sympathizers of anarchistic persuasion were expressing themselves with threats. One of the latter was embodied in a fuseless bomb sent by a "citizen of the world," who promised to follow it with a fully equipped one if the Governor were not merciful. This was warning enough for the police to station guards at his offices and home, where they would remain until 1929. The barrage would have moved another man to quick agreement with the petitions, so that an advisory committee might share the dangerous problem with him. Possessed of a hard sense of duty, however, the Governor sought information from everyone and kept his own counsel. Rumors attempted to interpret his silence, and the *Herald* reported on May 24 that "all doubt was removed" and that there would be no advisory committee to review the case. Appalled, the sympathizers protested, but they were quarreling with air. More temperate judgments advised waiting for better authority, but no one escaped the tension.

Meanwhile, the other events of 1927 called for attention. On May 17, a month after he got the Lawrence petition, the Governor attended the formal opening of the Ritz-Carlton Hotel, eighteen stories of "elegance rather than splendor" overlooking the Public Gardens. Among the guests was Mayor James J. Walker of New York, who might have been imagined by F. Scott Fitzgerald: a light-hearted person unburdened by his responsibilities and always willing to have a good time. Three days later, Charles Lindbergh set off on his non-stop flight to Paris. In Boston, caught up with the rest of the world in the pure adventure of it, Sacco and Vanzetti were driven back into the inside pages of the newspapers.

On May 27, A. Lawrence Lowell, president of Harvard, visited the Governor in the State House. On June 1, Lowell came again, this time accompanied by Samuel W. Stratton, president of the Massachusetts Institute of Technology, and Robert Grant, a probate court judge and minor novelist. Later in the day the Governor announced that the three men would form an advisory committee to study the case. He also said that he would conduct his own investigation separately from that of the committee. The sentencing speeches of Sacco and Vanzetti, the world's protests and the actions of the intellectuals, and perhaps a sense of justice or mercy, had moved the Governor.

Now, four men held the absolute and unquestioned responsibility for judgment. It had once been exercised by twelve men who had been protected by their number and anonymity, while the courts had further blurred the relation between the individual and his decision. The choice of Judge Thayer as the villain had been a literary tour de force which could not withstand the facts. After June 1, 1927, however, the judgment belonged, in the first and last instance, to the Governor; and to Lowell, Grant, and Stratton. What character and competence did they bring to it?

Governor Alvan T. Fuller was forty-nine when the case came upon him, the perfect model of the self-made man. The early death of his father, a *Boston Globe* compositor, set him early to earning his living. He began by building on the athletic attainments that made him the New England bicycle champion at sixteen; at eighteen he was operating a successful bicycle sales and repair shop. Three years later he went off to Europe—it was 1899—and returned with two automobiles, the first imported into Boston. He later became the New England sales agent for Packard and still later, still prescient, a General Motors dealer. Fuller's fortune in the twenties was estimated at about forty million dollars.

Fuller got along well with the Brahmins without seeking their favor. Although he resided in a Back Bay Renaissance mansion stocked with Gainsboroughs and Romneys, he had never attempted to deny his origins. Politically, he had followed Theodore Roosevelt into the Bull Moose revolt and entered the Massachusetts legislature as its only Progressive representative in 1912. He then served two terms in Congress, where he won the respect and liking of Fiorello La Guardia, at the time a progressive Republican representative and a man who knew where to put forty million dollars on the scale of character judgment. In the 1924 governorship election Fuller defeated the great James M. Curley by the largest majority in the Commonwealth's history. Fuller's incumbency represented a period of passage from the Brahmin leadership to the time when people named Curley, Furcolo, and Kennedy would win command.

To the extent that the decision would be Fuller's, the great responsibility for the lives of Sacco and Vanzetti did not rest with Brahmin Boston. On the Advisory Committee, however, the Brahmins were appropriately represented by two of the three members. We pass quickly by Stratton, who was not Boston at all; he had been born in Illinois and had spent most of his professional life in Washington as the first director of the U.S. Bureau of Standards. He was a man of some achievement, but it was in physics, and he rarely spoke at the Advisory Committee hearings. Friends of his two associates told me that he let them guide his judgment, a fact borne out by Grant's account in his autobiography, *Fourscore*. Grant and Lowell were purely Boston.

With his moderately rounded vest Lowell stood midway between the unambiguously large Stratton and the frail Grant. A Boston classic of great format at seventy-one, he had known how to fall out of frame loudly. He was a conservative but his own kind of conservative. Thus he had taken a reactionary position on child labor and opposed the nomination of Louis Brandeis to the U.S. Supreme Court, but he supported American membership in the League of Nations and held like a rock on the question of academic freedom. Lowell had, for example, acted as counsel for the uncomfortably liberal Professor Zechariah Chafee, Jr., when Chafee was put on trial by the Committee to Visit the Law School for calling a Supreme Court decision "a disgrace to our law." He won his case by a six-to-five vote, and Chafee dedicated his book, *Free Speech in the United States,* to Lowell, "whose wisdom and courage in the face of uneasy fears and stormy criticism made it unmistakably plain that so long as he was president no one could breathe the air of Harvard and not be free." Lowell himself explained his support of Chafee by referring to the principle of "an unfettered search for truth on the part of those who devote their lives to seeking it in their respective fields." He made no exceptions on the subject, not even for the future Labor Party intellectual eminence, Harold J. Laski. Teaching at Harvard Law School, Laski achieved a perfect discord by expressing his sympathy with the Boston police strikers in 1919. Laski was a foreigner and it was a law-and-order issue; the conservatives demanded his head. Lowell replied: "If the Overseers ask for Laski's resignation they will get mine!" Lowell further distressed the conservatives when he did fire a professor. In this case the man had made speeches for the railroad interests; it seemed almost unfair. The best of Boston had the sense to recognize those actions of Lowell with which it disagreed as proof of his superiority according to its standards.

Unlike Governor Fuller, Lowell had taken a long time getting his feet under him. After seventeen years at it, "I was a failure at the practice of law." He began lecturing in government at Harvard in 1897, becoming Professor of the Science of Government two years later. He won scholarly reputation with his sound studies, and influence through his character, pure as ice made of distilled water, and the Harvard presidency seemed an inevitability even before he was named to it in 1909.

The more modest figure of Robert Grant also compounded the law with more humane interests. After studying Dante as a Harvard doctoral student, Grant followed his sense of family responsibility into a judgeship. Once established with a professional competence and family, however, he again yielded to the romantic, and adding a reformist element, began writing novels *à thèse* of a feminized gentility of style. Without attempting to shake social foundations, his books attacked child labor, the subordinate role of women, and the rigor of the divorce laws. In prewar Boston, Grant took on the pastel hue of an acceptable radicalism that made him an interesting dinner guest. Indeed, the *Nation* kindly reviewed his book of elderly reminiscences, *Convictions of a Grandfather:* "It is a patriarch with a very young heart. . . . He is a Radical grandfather much more Radical than his grandchildren. . . ." This gentle reformer could be expected to have an open heart for the prisoners. Moreover, he had distant Italian relations through a cousin who had married into an aristocratic family and he remembered his dancing teacher: "An Italian . . . a pattern of deportment. . . . I had a liking and respect for him, but was never more than a respectable waltzer." If the accused were of a different class of Italians, Grant had proved his Boston noblesse oblige.

The nomination of the Advisory Committee was just one phase in Fuller's preoccupation with the case, and he went on, almost without interruption, in his efforts to find out what had happened at the crimes and trials. A stream of lawyers and witnesses moved through his offices, more than a hundred witnesses of the South Braintree holdup alone. He also made a point of getting all he could out of the prisoners. Although Sacco hopelessly refused to talk, Fuller had two friendly interviews with Vanzetti, commenting to the warden, "What an attractive man." Vanzetti, for his part, reported in a letter: "An honest man, as he understands it, and sincere, courageous, stubborn man but well intentioned at bottom and, in a way, clever. And I like to tell you that he gave me a good heartfull sake hand, as I lef. I may be wrong, but I don't believe that a man like that is going to burn us on a case like ours." Vanzetti, however, soon changed his mind.

The Advisory Committee got only slowly to work, since Lowell was occupied with such university duties as the June commencement. This delay, coming after Fuller's long thoughts, had let the execution date—July 10—move impracticably close. Fuller ignored the rising suspense, participating himself at the commencement on June 23 and showing perturbation neither from the strain nor from the eighty-nine-degree temperature. On June 29, however, he granted a thirty-day respite, putting off the execution date to August 10. The arguments and strains quickly expanded into the new chamber of time.

The Advisory Committee then fixed itself in State House offices and began. After long interviews with the prisoners, Sacco permitting himself some intercourse on this occasion, it organized most of its study in the form of extended hearings. In effect, the Committee constituted itself as an informal court. The hearings lasted from July 11 until July 25.

Judge Thayer, already tried by world opinion, endured almost a trial before the Committee on July 12. Grant later wrote: "It had fallen to me, at the request of my two associates, to examine Judge Webster Thayer. The evidence that he had been grossly indiscreet in his remarks off the bench was cumulative. I was amazed and incensed that any Massachusetts judge could have been so garrulous."* Dominating his humiliation, Thayer settled his Panama hat squarely on his head, faced the press as squarely, and returned to his vacation place in Maine. The chastening had legal limits, however, Grant concluding in the Advisory Committee report that "the Judge was indiscreet . . . a grave breach of official decorum. But we do not believe he used some of the expressions attributed to him. . . . Furthermore, we believe that such indiscretions . . . did not affect his conduct at the trial or the opinions of the jury. . . ." On the real point at issue, the Committee decided that Thayer had given no evidence of prejudice. With Thayer defined, it turned to the whole disorder of the case.

Much of the Committee's work was inevitably duplication of Fuller's inquiry in quite a different style. Reviewing all the evidence with extreme care, it spoke with nearly all of the important witnesses as well as with ten members of the Dedham jury. (The summer, which treats Boston as cavalierly as the winter does, was boiling up, and the temperature was ninety-two degrees at 3 P.M.

* Robert Grant, *Fourscore*, (New York: Houghton, Mifflin, 1934), p. 371.

on July 13 and ninety-five degrees at its peak the next day.) The Committee did not take official cognizance of the Goddard ballistics test, which had been carried out the month before, although it might have heard of the results. It listened to Moore's expert, Albert Hamilton, and studied the Van Amburgh testimony and the ballistics arguments of the appeals period. Besides this attention to old facts and witnesses, the Committee members ranged far enough to hear out one addle-pated woman whom Katzmann had not dared to put on the stand. She told them: "My head is too full of music to remember." Intriguingly, she was the only person claiming to have seen both Sacco and Vanzetti at South Braintree. She said she had known Sacco at an earlier job of his, and she quoted Vanzetti as saying: "Hurry up, there, I have got to get through at half-past three. I have clams to dig." Irritated by the Committee's demands for coherence, however, she returned: "You have got my character sticking in your old crop that I am a low woman." That kind of sincerity impressed the Committee members, who found her testimony more credible than not, in spite of her "eccentricity." There was also a long tangle about the date of the banquet mentioned by two of Sacco's alibi witnesses, a matter requiring the study of newspaper files and arousing Thompson's uncertain anger, this time against one of his own witnesses at the hearing. And then there were the questions left open because of the absence of a few important persons. Thus, although Thomas McAnarney spoke at length, his brother Jeremiah, who had been the active and articulate of the two at Dedham, did not appear at all. Assistant District Attorney Ranney asked: had he given up the cause? Unanswerable questions threatened every provable fact.

Fred Moore was the most prominent absentee. Thomas McAnarney had spoken about him at length, and the Marquis Agostino Ferrante, the Italian consul, who had attended the trial, testified: "I dislike Moore because he asked me once to do something I do not consider right." But Moore, specifically uninvited by Thompson and under attack for arousing Thayer's prejudice, had no chance to defend himself. Now, with the Frankfurter-Thompson team and the intellectuals in charge, the sour memory of the man was his best argument for the defense.

The prisoners themselves fought back with all their desperate resources. They wrote letters and received visitors bearing encouragement and new help. Georg Branting, son of a former prime minister of Sweden, brought the support of Europe's non-Communist Left and, on June 11, flowers for Vanzetti's thirty-ninth birthday. Sacco had been in Dedham jail since the arrest as a prisoner awaiting sentence, while Vanzetti had spent the years in Charlestown prison as a properly convicted man (for the Bridgewater holdup) until he was brought back to Dedham for his second sentence. Now, at last, they were united. Vanzetti could also appreciate the easier atmosphere of Dedham jail, writing to a woman correspondent: "My window is all leaves and flowers; a plant of giranium in bloom; a tulip in bloom; a bundle of mayflower; white pinks and red pinks and fern. That is great in its everlasting greetings." This comfort, however, could not last, the passing of sentence having canceled out the reason for the stay in Dedham. After receiving new easement on June 29 from the thirty-day respite, Sacco and Vanzetti were shaken out of their sleep the next night forty minutes after midnight and transferred stealthily—to avoid a demonstration—to Charlestown prison, which was in Boston in a rundown Irish neighborhood near the Bunker Hill monument. (The prison has since been torn down.) Sympathizers protested the cruelty of the move, and the prisoners regretted their flower-banked cells. In Charlestown, however, they could fight back all the harder, and as the Advisory Committee hearings droned on across the Charles River, they began a hunger strike on Sunday, July 17.

On Friday, July 22, a great crowd eddied about the State House, while the lawyers inside were arguing before the Advisory Committee in their last efforts to interpret the completed testimony. The crowd was there to see Charles Lindbergh, whom Fuller had invited to Boston on his tour of the United States. Boston and the country found it much easier to give their attention to Lindbergh's accomplishment than to the gritty matter of what Sacco and Vanzetti had or had not done seven years before. Everyone agreed that Lindbergh was important; only the most engaged sympathizers thought the prisoners were important, and the rage of their enemies began with the feeling that these shabby lives could not matter that much.

Meanwhile, as the intellectuals began to come to Boston, the Communists also entered the city with their organization, techniques, and noise. Still hopeful about stealing the cause, they opened a Boston branch of the International Sacco-Vanzetti Committee, one of their several ad hoc groups. On Sunday, July 24, they took advantage of the facilities of the Common to hold an open air meeting. The speakers were Earl Browder, who would become the party's frequent presidential candidate, and Harry Canter, a young man who would support Sacco and Vanzetti with more sincerity than the organization wanted. A mild and wondering *Globe* reporter, who had never seen or heard anything of the sort before, described the outlanders' manners and vocal excesses—the Communists naturally spoke of world revolution and Massachusetts injustice in the same breath—with the attention to curious detail he would have given to a circus or a lodge convention. Boston found these odd radicals to be as dull as they were baffling, less than 200 persons listening to the speakers. Nevertheless, they added to the force of the defense.

The new judgments were taking form under all these effects. On the next day, Monday, July 25, the Advisory Committee heard the last of the lawyers' arguments. On Wednesday afternoon Lowell, Grant and Stratton, each carrying a brown folder, entered Fuller's offices for a conference, the first official meeting between the Committee and the Governor since the beginning of their separate inquiries. Whatever conclusions they drew then, the three men and Fuller compared their answers to the important questions: Were Sacco and Vanzetti guilty, did they have a fair trial, did the new evidence change anything? Outside, the rumors were bad, and the defense, now that the Advisory Committee had stopped listening, turned a final force on the Governor. On Friday, July 29, Thompson roused himself to talk to Fuller for nearly eight hours. Every last moment had to be used.

On Sunday, July 31, the Defense Committee, refusing to be outdistanced publicly by the Communists, held a meeting on the Common. The size of its audience, some 5,000 persons, was reassuring. Moreover, the Committee was better equipped to engage in a dialogue with Boston, its speakers including Gardner Jackson, whom any Brahmin recognized as one of his own kind, and another not unfriendly figure, the patrician Alfred Baker Lewis, a wealthy Socialist and hopeless aspirant to the governorship. In addition to the usual arguments, Mary Donovan called attention to her own problem: she said she had been fired as a state labor inspector because she had been trying to make the employers obey the labor laws. The Labor Commissioner, however, had come to the conclusion that she had been neglecting the employers, a judgment that any student of the Sacco-Vanzetti case would be inclined to accept. This Sunday, the Communists, seeing that they could not compete with the Defense Committee, marched off the Common and tried to compensate for their weakness by defying the law. They brushed past a few resisting policemen and established themselves in City Hall Plaza, a short distance away. Boston authority refused to react, and the police, guarding their limited strength, chose to let the Communists have their demonstration. Boston was officially tolerant this Sunday.

The weekend had been the final strain before the decision. Fuller himself had sought some relief at his summer place in New Hampshire; on Monday, the first day of August, he told the press he would make an announcement in two days. That Monday he saw more witnesses, more representatives of the defense and, for a bitter last, Judge Thayer. Queer hopes emerged from rumors and the *New York Times* labor reporter, Louis Stark, who had been writing pro-defense articles, predicted that Fuller would somehow maneuver toward a new trial with the help of the Massachusetts Legislature. Stark had doubtless got the idea from Defense Committee strategists, who wanted to suggest a way out to the Governor. Yet, as the wiser sympathizers well knew, Fuller would never take it. In an interview with another *Times* reporter two months before he had recalled his first inaugural in 1925: "I experienced a thrill such as I had never felt before in my life. I then and there resolved that I would not fail." It would be Fuller's decision.

On Tuesday, August 2, a routine act of the prison administration suggested a frightening metaphor of the next day's decision. At five that morning, a month and a day after they had come to Charlestown Prison from Dedham jail, Sacco and Vanzetti, and Medeiros as well, were led across the prison yard to the block of death cells. Medeiros was placed in cell number one, Sacco in cell number two, and Vanzetti in the third of the block's three cells, the death order if everything was lost. The warden had simply been obeying regulations, which put the condemned men into those cells a specified number of days before the execution, and the execution date was still August 10. The transfer, however, had a creative effect on Vanzetti, who settled into his new habitation and wrote an eleven-page letter to Thompson: "Here are a few suggestions on things of which we spoke last evening. . . ."

That Tuesday President Coolidge, on vacation in the summer White House in the Black Hills of South Dakota, called in reporters at noon and handed out fifteen copies of the statement: "I do not choose to run for President in nineteen twenty-eight." The Boston morning newspapers were still carrying the Coolidge headlines on Wednesday, August 3—and also the statement by Fuller that he would announce his decision on the prisoners at eight or nine in the evening. To prepare it, he retired to a suite at the Ritz-Carlton, laboring there with a Boston reporter named Edward Whiting. As the sun went down a crowd began gathering in Newspaper Row in front of the *Globe* building. The delays plucked at men and resisted time, the waiting people went over old arguments, and the evening held motionless. In the Defense Committee headquarters twenty-five persons sat about the two rooms on boxes, bundles of pamphlets, tables, and asthenic chairs; reporters, photographers, professors, Italian laborers and anarchists, and a half-dozen women sympathizers. One young man, fortunate in his world until now, said: "If they electrocute Sacco and Vanzetti, my ideas of human nature are false. I'll become a complete cynic."

The decision was announced at 11:25 P.M. In agreement with the Advisory Committee, the Governor refused clemency.

The decision would have Sacco and Vanzetti die in one week.

It was not, however, absolutely final. A vast effort had ended in failure, and the best hope, executive clemency, had been crushed. Admitting the absolute nature of his defeat, William Thompson resigned as chief defense counsel. Yet, three days later, the Supreme Judicial Court ordered Thayer to hear a motion for a new trial by Thompson's successor. This suggested a repetition of old failures, but the law could always tease men with vague hope. Sacco and Vanzetti had won time, and time had created new human situations. The world had been speaking to the courts of Massachusetts during all these weeks. The courts were human; they might have been moved to new insights. The defense would go on trying.

17. Movers and Shakers I

IN these last weeks a number of intellectuals were gathering in Boston. They would be movers and shakers, to use the title phrase of a volume of Mabel Dodge Luhan's autobiography. Before the war Mabel Dodge had brought together radicals, reformers, writers, and editors in her lower Fifth Avenue salon: the I.W.W. leader Big Bill Haywood, the anarchists Emma Goldman and Alexander Berkman, the future Secretary of Labor of the thirties Frances Perkins, Lincoln Steffens, Walter Lippmann, and the radical journalists Mary Heaton Vorse and John Reed. With John Reed she put on a pageant in Madison Square Garden to collect funds for an I.W.W. strike in New Jersey; it was one of the first occasions when intellectuals joined union activists. The pageant, however, attracted too few sympathizers to pay expenses, and Mabel Dodge and Reed embarked for Paris together the next day. Reed went on to become a significant figure in intellectual radicalism, covering the Russian Revolution and introducing it to American readers in his *Ten Days That Shook the World*, helping organize the Communist Party in this country, and then dying of typhus in Russia after fighting to keep the American party free of rigid Comintern control. Now in Boston the intellectuals had another opportunity to move from theory to action. They helped out in the Defense Committee offices or founded new defense committees, demonstrated in the streets and on Boston Common, and went to jail. On August 3, with the announcement of the Governor's decision, they would call upon themselves for greater efforts.

The group in Boston included Ruth Hale, Heywood Broun's wife; Ellen Hayes, a retired Wellesley professor of astronomy and mathematics; Jeannette Marks, a Mount Holyoke professor of literature; Lola Ridge, a poetess; Paula Halliday, a Greenwich Village restaurant proprietor; Louis Bernheimer, a Malraux figure who had been a war pilot, hermit, and philosophy student in China; John Howard Lawson, a playwright who would become a successful writer of screen plays and a victim of the Hollywood anti-Communist hysteria; Powers Hapgood, a young Harvard graduate who had become a professional proletarian by working in Welsh and Russian coal mines, who would marry Mary Donovan at the end of 1927, and who would become a C.I.O. leader in New England; the Communist Michael Gold, who would write columns for the *Daily Worker* in the thirties; another Communist intellectual, Bertram D. Wolfe, later a Trotzkyite, and, still later, a respected scholar of Soviet phenomena; the then radical and later conservative journalist Isaac Don Levine; Michael A. Musmanno, a young Pittsburgh lawyer who had attached himself to the Defense Committee as an unpaid runner of legal errands, and who would rise to the bench of the Pennsylvania Supreme Court; Ella Reeve Bloor, an elderly woman used by the Communists as a propaganda figure under the title of "Mother"; Robert Morss Lovett, a *New Republic* editor and University of Chicago literature professor; and Dorothy Parker, Edna St. Vincent Millay, and John Dos Passos.

In her book, *Thirteen Days,* Professor Jeannette Marks has left a record of an intellectual's thoughts and emotions during those August days. Miss Marks had come down from her vacation on Lake Champlain to give what help she could. In Boston, against the denials of conservative authority, she could draw hope from the character and ability of the Defense Committee leaders: the "fine, dark-looking Celt" Mary Donovan, Aldino Felicani with the "childlike spirituality" of an Italian painting, and "Felix Frankfurter . . . compact, human, friend of justice and of these breaking hearts." The issue, however, overwhelmed the persons of the prisoners: ". . . already as individuals Nicola Sacco and Bartolomeo Vanzetti were being lost sight of . . . already they were gone from our midst . . . symbolic." For Miss Marks, their symbolic character represented the essence of the contemporary problems of justice, tolerance, and progress in the country.

Another intellectual has given perhaps the most precise definition of the psychic situation of his class in 1927. The literary critic Granville Hicks, then on the faculty of Smith College, had been one of the organizers of the Sacco-Vanzetti meeting that listened to Professor Landis in April. Up to that point he thought he had solved the problem of the intellectual's alienation in American society. At Smith he had found a "sense of belonging," he wrote in a book published in 1946. "This is the crucial experience for the intellectual, that moment when he finds his milieu. . . . This was life as I had dreamed it might be." The reaction of the Northampton townspeople, however, made him realize that he had achieved only half a solution to his problem: "But the moment when the intellectual feels that at last he belongs is the moment when his divorce from society becomes absolute. . . ." It was not only the rich and powerful, Hicks saw, that opposed the cause of Sacco and Vanzetti: ". . . it was also the doctors, the lawyers, the shopkeepers, the farmers, the workers. . . . the battle was between the intellectuals and everybody else. . . ." Hicks had to admit: "In the first community in which I had set myself up as a householder . . . I was an outsider, even an enemy." For the moment the young woman who taught literature at Mount Holyoke still had her sense of belonging.

Now the prisoners' lives were invested with a breathless immediacy. For more than seven years the most important element in their struggles had been delay. The end of everything had existed theoretically, but it had seemed as insubstantial as any other geometrical point. Now people had to face the fact that Sacco and Vanzetti could die in a few days.

A new climax began building. Bombs exploded in two subway stations in New York, killing two persons and injuring a dozen more. Other bombs damaged a Philadelphia church and the home of the mayor of Baltimore. The police responded with extraordinary measures. In New York, all 14,000 members of the police force, including 1,200 detectives, were ordered on bomb duty. In Washington, officials worked out plans to rush Army troops from Fort Mayer and Marines from Quantico in case of need. Boston's 2,000-man force was on twenty-four-hour duty in the most drastic action of the department's history. At headquarters, armorers prepared 56 shotguns, 12 submachine guns, 24 bulletproof vests, and 15,000 rounds of ammunition, while a special squad of 464 men, trained to use all kinds of weapons, was posted to the city's twenty-one police stations.

The Governor's decision roused both prisoners. Sacco had been expecting the worst, but he fought back. On August 4, he wrote his anarchist friends: "My Dear Friends & Comrades. . . . From the death cell, we are just informe from the Defense Committee that the governor Fuller has descide to kill us Ag. the 10th. . . . It is up to your know [you now] o, brothers comrades! . . . we have never had faith. . . . for we have always know that the gov. Fuller-Thayer and Katzmann are the murder. . . ." But then he fell back into his old attitude of resignation. More volatile, Vanzetti was reacting so sharply that his friends feared a new loss of sanity. He mastered himself, however, and wrote farewell letters to Elizabeth Evans, Mary Donovan, and another woman correspondent, trying to express the depth of his feelings but also aware that those letters would help the defense.

Meanwhile, the new chief defense counsel, Arthur D. Hill, called a legal strategy meeting on August 5. Associated with the defense since 1923 as a sympathetic consultant, he was a cultivated, attractive Brahmin, educated in France, who had been a progressive ally of Theodore Roosevelt. With Frankfurter contributing new ideas, the lawyers decided on a five-point program that comprised an attack on various courts, ranging from Dedham Court to the Commonwealth's Supreme Judicial Court and, beyond, to the United States Supreme Court. In view of the closeness of the execution date, now only five days off, they also planned to ask the Governor for a new stay. The strategy was simple in essence. The defense needed a writ of habeas corpus or other redress that would prepare the way for another review and a new trial. It offered one argument: Thayer's judicial unfitness. The case now dropped away from all the other questions that had been fought so hard through the trial and the appeals. Thayer's prejudice, brought up by Thompson in 1927, was the only legal hope left, and the debate about witnesses, motivations, guns, and alibis subsided into a background murmur.

Sunday, August 7

The demonstrations, which had slacked off during the waiting period, were resumed in greater force. The police reacted by breaking up a meeting of 5,000 on the Common, silencing Artur M. Giovannitti, a favorite anarchist author of Vanzetti's, and the Communist Harry Canter. There was little resistance, the 100 policemen making only four arrests to carry their point.

Larger demonstrations were taking place abroad. In London, a crowd of 10,000 led by English Communists listened to three hours of speeches in Trafalgar Square and roared at a mock electrocution acted out by a British war veteran, his medals flashing in the sun. Almost half of the group then marched to the American Embassy in Grosvenor Gardens, but only the British caretaker was there to listen to them, the ambassador and his staff having gone to the country this summer Sunday. In Paris, 5,000

Communists and sympathizers paraded in the Bois de Vincennes behind Luigia Vanzetti, who was on her way to the United States to join her brother. From Italy the *New York Times* correspondent reported that Americans were being insulted and threatened.

Monday, August 8

With the execution two days away Judge Thayer arrived at Dedham courthouse to deal with Sacco and Vanzetti once more. The *Globe* found him cheerful as he descended from his automobile "with a hop, step and a jump," but Michael Musmanno, who wrote a book on the case, thought he was depressed and "very pale."

That afternoon Thayer presided at one of the most complex maneuvers in the case's history. A nightmare reflected unendingly in a series of mirrors, it began with an effort by Hill to persuade the judge that he was too prejudiced to continue, that he should step down at this moment. No one believed that Thayer would accede, and then Hill would bring forth his motion, which said the same thing, that Thayer's prejudice has denied the prisoners a fair trial. Again, no one believed that Thayer would admit prejudice; he would reject the motion. Only at this point would an element of sense emerge. When Thayer actually denied the motion, Hill could appeal that denial to the Supreme Judicial Court. It was necessary that the judge himself permit the appeal, but Thayer was bound to do so in order to avoid carrying the onus alone.

Hill began with the first stage, arguing for Thayer's immediate withdrawal. He quoted the Advisory Committee's report on the judge's out-of-court conduct: "grave breach of official decorum." From this he argued: "Every consideration of sound sense, good morals and intelligent administration of law impels you to withdraw." Hill measured his attack carefully; he must not annihilate

Thayer, he must combine shock and seduction, opening the way for graceful withdrawal: "No one can criticize your motive; no one can challenge your courage in the matter."

Thayer refused that relief. He would take no action that could be construed as an admission of prejudice. He defended himself: "For nearly seven years I have been placed in a position where I could not say a word. I have declined every interview for publicity. This is the only time when I have had a chance to say a word publicly." But then, when he tried to speak for himself, he could only repeat the old arguments of the appeals, although he took some strength from the rebuttal to Hill by the Massachusetts Attorney General, Arthur K. Reading: "I have just heard the most preposterous argument that I have ever heard from an able lawyer." Hill had not been able to support his charge of prejudice, as Reading pointed out, and Thayer had the law on his side when he rejected the motion. In the area of public opinion, once more, that was not enough.

The second stage having been traversed, Hill could now appeal Thayer's decision, and he duly filed his exceptions.

Hill had argued the same logic, Thayer's prejudice, before Justice George A. Sanderson of the Massachusetts Supreme Judicial Court that morning. As in the case of Thayer's hearing, the defense expected nothing except a denial, but a denial that would permit more action. Hill was dealing with one judge; a denial would give him the right to appeal to the entire bench. As expected, Judge Sanderson denied the petition, the defense filed its exceptions, Sanderson granted the exceptions, and the case went to the full court.

Thus the Supreme Judicial Court would hear appeals from two decisions, from Thayer's denial as trial judge and Sanderson's denial as its single representative. One might find reasonable hope in the situation. In the first place, something was better than nothing, and something now filled in the blank after Fuller's denial, when nothing stood between the prisoners and the electric chair. They were still due to die on August 10, but no one expected that Fuller would permit it while legal action was pending. The defense could hope for more time and, beyond that, for some extralegal force to move Massachusetts. The world was reacting more vigorously every day. Perhaps the assembled judges would find reasons, reasons of humanity or reasons of state, to save the men.

Fuller remained silent. He would not be hurried; a popular song that year was "The Whole World Is Waiting (For Dreams to Come True)." Lindbergh was still flying around the country, and the Defense Committee wired him at one of his halts, vainly asking him to use his great and irrelevant prestige to help the cause.

The Advisory Committee was being heavily attacked, although a few persons had been persuaded to change their minds by its report. Thus Dr. Morton Prince, a Harvard psychiatrist, now disavowed his old prodefense arguments, and Arthur N. Holcombe, a Harvard professor of government, wrote Fuller: "As one who asked you to review the evidence, I am satisfied with your decision."* Few persons on either side, however, made the effort to follow the reasoning of the denials.

Tuesday, August 9

During the evening the intellectuals in Boston attempted to extend their protest by breaking the law. Specifically, they demonstrated without a permit. Led by the Communist Bertram D. Wolfe, who had attached himself to the Defense Committee rather than to the party organization, some 125 persons paraded just above the Common on Beacon Street before the State House. A police captain, dressed in uniform trousers but with a citizen's suit jacket and Panama hat, acted with the same easy ambivalence and gave the demonstrators seven minutes to leave. Most of them,

* Associated Press report, August 4, 1927, in *Sacco-Vanzetti Collection*, Scrapbook S219n (Treasures Room, Harvard Law Library), vol. 1.

including Wolfe, accepted that advice, but the police found thirty-nine persons available for arrest. Fuller was watching from the State House as the demonstrators were brought into the Joy Street police station nearby.

Wednesday, August 10

With the execution time still fixed for midnight, Fuller continued to study the question of a respite. He had been seeking the advice of the Commonwealth's former attorney generals. By eleven in the morning he had spoken with seven of the eight then alive. He then called his executive council to get its concurrence for whatever decision he would make.

Defense Counsel Hill, meanwhile, hurried about on his legal paths. He was joined temporarily by William Thompson, who had returned to Boston to see the prisoners and make one more effort on their behalf. Thompson was with Hill when he visited U. S. Supreme Court Justice Oliver Wendell Holmes in the afternoon. At his summer home in Beverly, a coastal town north of Salem, the old man listened tolerantly as Hill went over old arguments about habeas corpus. His refusal, kind but inflexible, sent Hill back to Boston, where the lawyer carried his desperation to another federal instance, the United States Circuit Court. The same arguments getting the same response, Hill moved on to the State House at nine that evening to talk to the executive council. It was rumored that Fuller had made up his mind to grant the respite, but the council wanted more information, and Hill had to deny his fatigue and spend almost two hours in hard pleading. It had been a long day for everyone.

It was the second period of waiting, unpleasantly similar to the events of the week before. On August 3, after all the hard anticipation, the Governor had denied clemency. Now he was trying to make a decision on a respite that might permit another kind of clemency to appear. Those concerned with the decision were jerking about in patterns that had already been traced. Sympathizers were marching again before the State House as the executive council talked and waited for Hill. Throughout the United States and the world more demonstrations were erupting. There were small protest strikes in Rochester, Indianapolis, Baltimore, Scranton, and Tampa. In New York, mounted and foot police broke up parades that had been formed at a meeting attended by 15,000 protestants, while the Chicago police used tear gas to quell small riots. In South America, a general strike caused some disturbances in Montevideo and two bombs were exploded in Buenos Aires. In Europe, thousands of Parisians were holding meetings and, across the Channel, London police routed 10,000 persons demonstrating again at the American embassy. The world waited.

In Paris, more privately, the dancer Isadora Duncan debated the case with a Chicago judge on the sidewalk terrace of the Café Select, where much of Hemingway's *The Sun Also Rises* takes place. Isadora Duncan was vehement about official murder, and the judge was defensive about American judicial integrity. The café auditors gave the victory to the dancer.

Awaiting the decision, Sacco and Vanzetti heard a soft humming: the electric chair was being tested. Celestino Medeiros was in an adjoining cell. The case had moved on past him, leaving him in utter irrelevance, since the "other gang" theory, which he embodied, was forgotten legal debris. It was, however, impossible to separate Medeiros so abruptly from the fate of the anarchist prisoners, and he would partake of the reprieve, if there was to be one. Vanzetti, specifically human in his solidarity, refused to abandon the man, having never accepted the distinction his sympathizers drew between criminal and rebel prisoners of the state. All three were bound within the same condemnation, according to the gospel of an anarchist Saint Luke.

While the people waited, the sun went down and floodlights lit up the walls and roofs of Charlestown prison. Nearby, in the Church of St. John the Evangelist, Michael Musmanno noticed that the parishioners were praying for Sacco and Vanzetti. Everyone expected a reprieve, and the sympathetic Warden William Hendry was so certain of it that at 10:22 P.M., while Hill was still talking to the executive council, he told reporters that there would indeed be one. He reflected, however, and hastily retracted his statement. The waiting continued.

The reprieve came. It came an hour after Hendry had given his assurance, but now that it had come, everyone knew that it had been a certainty. After this moment of relief, however, the sympathizers would have to face an absolute threat with no more room for maneuver.

Reported in the *New York Times* with an eight-column headline and four columns of news stories on the front page, the reprieve gave the prisoners another twelve days. Now, sympathizers began to stare at another date: August 22. The very neatness of the last legal steps—the exceptions granted symmetrically by Thayer and Sanderson—had been frightening; the Supreme Judicial Court would consider them at the same time. A single decision rendered at one sitting could blow them both away.

The prisoners were moved from the death cells to the ordinary part of Charlestown prison, and the world offered its opinions to Massachusetts. Europe's left-wing press continued to condemn American justice, while the conservative newspapers, equally persuaded of innocence, tried to suggest a way out to the Commonwealth. The London *Evening News* used a logic of time that avoided a study of the facts: "We can see no conceivable reason for executing these men. If they are guilty they paid the penalty many times over, and if they are innocent, it is difficult to find words to describe their treatment." *Le Soir,* also emphasizing the long delays, hopefully concluded that the execution was now impossible. It seemed inconceivable that Massachusetts would carry out its worst purposes.

The question of violence suggested another subject to editorial writers who were baffled by the processes of American justice. Some newspapers accused the American police of setting off bombs to discredit the defense. On the other hand, the conservative Paris *Liberté* argued that the intellectuals of the left were inciting radical fanatics to commit murder. A few days after the reprieve a bomb completely destroyed the home of Lewis McHardy, one of the Dedham jurors. Miraculously, the man, his wife, and their three children escaped with bruises.

Thursday, August 11

Vanzetti gave up his 26-day hunger strike.

Friday, August 12

Vanzetti wrote to a correspondent: "Being still alive I renew to you my best regards and good wishes." He wrote it economically on the same scrap of paper which carried this note of August 10, just before the reprieve came: "I bless you and bide you with great heart my last goodby."

Saturday, August 13

Fuller, whose son was recovering from an appendectomy, sent off his two daughters, aged eleven and thirteen, to have their tonsils removed.

Sunday, August 14

Police stopped a protest meeting on the Common that drew 10,000 persons, some to demonstrate and more to observe.

Monday, August 15

The newspapers were reporting the death at eighty of Judge Elbert H. Gary, board chairman of U. S. Steel and the man who had broken the 1919 steel strike.

This was the thirtieth day of Sacco's hunger strike. The prison doctor entered his cell with an apparatus for forcible feeding, three feet of red tubing attached to a bulb. Urged to cooperate by Rose Sacco and Vanzetti, Sacco balanced the alternatives and addressed himself to a bowl of soup. A guard refilled it and Sacco took more, saying: "Good health to all of you."

Tuesday, August 16

Policemen, smiling apologetically, searched through the bags and briefcases of people entering Pemberton Square courthouse, where Defense Counsel Hill argued the exceptions to Thayer's and Sanderson's rulings before the Supreme Judicial Court. Hill spoke about justice and prejudice in the morning, while Attorney General Reading spent much of the afternoon on such legal points as the impossibility of appealing after sentence has been passed. In effect, Hill was pleading for mercy against the technical requirements of the law as represented by Reading. Ignoring most of Hill's plea, the Attorney General did, however, argue that Thayer's opinions had not been communicated to the Dedham jury.

Thursday, August 18

Early in the evening the decision of the Supreme Judicial Court was locked in a courthouse safe. Again the world waited.

Friday, August 19

When the safe was opened at the release time of 9 A.M., reporters ran to their telephones and called in their bulletins: "Exceptions Overruled," "They Lose," "They Must Die," and "Sacco and Vanzetti Must Die in Chair."

Sacco took the news stolidly. Vanzetti broke. He cried: "Get the million men! Get the million men!" Remaining incoherent most of the day, he demanded a radio so that he might talk to the world. Musmanno, who had brought the news, tried to reduce its effect by emphasizing one more chance, the possibility of another appeal to the U.S. Supreme Court. He failed to move the prisoners.

The three men—Medeiros was still joined to Sacco and Vanzetti—were brought back to the death cells; it was the second return for the anarchists and the sixth for Medeiros. On the walk of a few hundred feet Sacco suddenly called out: "They crucify me! I am so weak!"

If Vanzetti had no one at this moment, Sacco was also without his wife, who was in New York. The public relations demands of the case had brought her there to welcome Luigia Vanzetti, arriving on the *Aquitania.* Rose Sacco, accompanied by Aldino Felicani and 200 sympathizers, greeted her: "Dear sister in misfortune." Luigia Vanzetti was taken to a radio station, where she read an Italian speech someone had handed her: "My brother . . . most tragic hour of his life . . . in the hope that this powerful nation . . . will prevent a ghastly miscarriage of justice." More privately, she indicated a desire to bring her brother back to Catholicism.

The opinion that would send the men to the electric chair was purely technical, the *Transcript* admitting that it "may not be of particular value as an enunciation of broad principles." The Supreme Judicial Court said it could not intervene for two reasons: the exceptions had come improperly after the sentencing, as Attorney General Reading had argued; and Thayer's judicial fitness was a matter of "fact" and not "law," and thus outside the court's jurisdiction. In other words, the Court refused to admit having thought about the one argument which Defense Counsel Hill had brought before it, that Thayer's prejudice had denied the defendants a fair trial.

In a talk with me Charles P. Curtis, the lawyer who had helped with the petition to Fuller, ironically paraphrased the opinion: "If the trial court has followed the rules (a) its decision must be just, (b) probably is just, and (c) we have no right to question it." Yet the Supreme Court had studied the question of Thayer's prejudice and could have given an indication that it had absolved him. Thus, Curtis said, it could have supported the technical reasons for its denial with a common-sense explanation replying directly to Hill's accusation. That opportunity was missed while, as Curtis recalled, "Felix's article gets around the world." Curtis described Senior Associate Justice Henry K. Braley, who wrote the opinion, as an admirable judge but an "over-educated, over-sound lawyer" unable to communicate with laymen. He added: "Never crossed Braley's head, never crossed any of their heads. And it was the same way with Fuller. Fuller said: 'Not for me to interfere,' and there they were, a handful of technicalities in their hands and the world wanting to know what it was all about." By this default, the intellectuals could win another victory in the area of public opinion.

The Court would have intervened, Curtis said, if it had felt that there had been a real question of injustice. It would have found some reason to turn a question of fact into one of law, with which it could deal. In their innocence, the Court and the Boston authorities thought the world would realize this.

With the exception of the *Transcript,* the Boston press refused to take a clear position. In effect, it accepted the Court's decision as it had accepted the Governor's and the Advisory Committee's: they knew best. Robert Lincoln O'Brien, who had enlisted his *Herald* in the service of the defense strategy, felt he had done all he could and, moreover, had arrived at a belief in the guilt of the prisoners. The *Globe,* which had permitted Sibley to write his sympathetic articles, failed to say anything about the Court's decision on its editorial page. The *Transcript,* however, took the decision as a final vindication of its views: the men were guilty, they must pay the penalty.

The *World* continued its efforts to save the men. Walter Lippmann, in a full-page editorial under the title, "Doubt That Will

Not Down," argued for commutation: "There remains in the minds of uncounted multitudes the gravest doubt as to whether [Sacco and Vanzetti] have had an unprejudiced trial on all the available evidence." Some of the defense people thought the *World* could have been more forceful.

Charlestown prison seemed the quietest place in a protesting world. Musmanno returned there later in the day. Earlier he had mentioned the United States Supreme Court; now he would give substance to the hope by the fact of his movements. He was taking the train that evening to see what could be done in Washington. The prisoners, joined by sympathetic prison guards, allowed themselves to be somewhat cheered.

Meanwhile, the Boston police began mobilizing again. Headquarters strengthened the special unit assigned to Charlestown prison, alerted the bomb and riot squads, canceled vacations and free days, ordered policemen to spend their off-duty hours in their station house, and sent special police guards to the homes of the threatened principals of the case. Sacco and Vanzetti were to die in three days.

18. Movers and Shakers II

> "Funerals he found the most satisfactory of social occasions, because there you expressed your human attachments without unnecessary chatter."
>
> —GEORGE SANTAYANA
> *The Last Puritan*

August 19–August 22:
Friday–Saturday–Sunday–Monday

AUGUST 19, the date of the Supreme Judicial Court's last denial, had been a Friday; August 22, the execution date, would be a Monday. The weekend set the limits for the last attempts to save the men.

The intellectuals led the world against Boston, which George Santayana had earlier seen "self-banished from the great human caravan," and Boston continued to ask what the difficulty was. The misunderstanding was complete on both sides. Most observers abroad still believed that the force of active sympathy in the world was bound to take effect on that city.

In the little time remaining, the lawyers continued to play their game skilfully. Laymen learned the meaning of a new word, *writ of certiorari*, describing the last possibility. Since he entered the case Defense Counsel Hill had been trying to appeal beyond the Commonwealth by means of a writ of habeas corpus; the alternative might be better. Certiorari is, by definition, an exception. Federal courts have no jurisdiction over criminal cases in state courts, except when the U.S. Supreme Court decides that a given case is of overriding importance to the nation at large.

Thus the effect of the exception is to permit the Supreme Court to intervene almost at will, a license which it exercises with great caution.

There are two steps to the process of intervention. The Court must first decide whether it will consider a case brought to its attention. If it decides negatively, the matter ends there. If, however, it proposes to intervene, it will grant the writ of certiorari, study the matter, and then confirm or reject the lower court's ruling. Now, during the vacation period, a complication of time offered a possible extra chance. Normally, the whole bench would decide whether or not it would grant the writ of certiorari. Between sessions, however, any one justice could order a stay of execution, if he felt his associates would seriously consider the writ when they reconvened in October. To approach the Court in these circumstances, you first filed a petition asking for the writ; this was Michael Musmanno's errand in Washington after he had left the prisoners on Friday. The petition was almost nothing of itself, a request for action of a court that would not meet until two months after the execution date. Yet it gave Hill some substance with which to confront the individual justices. He could say that the petition was awaiting legal action in the fall; would it not be proper to keep the defendants alive up to that point?

The new effort upon the Supreme Court, moreover, permitted other legal combinations. Hill got back to the Massachusetts Supreme Judicial Court on August 19, the day its denial had been announced. He asked Chief Justice Walter Perley Hall for a stay of excution, pending his appeal to the U.S. Supreme Court. He argued for nearly three-quarters of an hour and got an absolute negative. Attempting the same argument, one of Hill's associates, Elias Field, got the same answer from a federal Circuit Court judge. It appeared that the defense would have to make do with the writ of certiorari standing alone.

Hill's other associate, Richard C. Evarts, was probably the least affected among the defense group, although he accepted the challenge with sympathy and professional enthusiasm. In recent years a gray and prosperous Boston lawyer of high standing, he remembered racing from place to place in automobiles chauffeured by Harvard volunteers during the last days. "It was tense and hopeless and I suppose you would call it moving," he told me. It was an American version of Kafka's *The Trial,* where the crime had never been listed, the charge never written, and justice was to be found in the hands of nameless judges hidden in dark corners. If Massachusetts thought everything was clear enough, most persons had the impression of falling into a Kafka nightmare. Like the guilt of Josef K, the guilt of Sacco and Vanzetti had attached itself to everyone connected with the case, the jurors, judges, state's attorneys, the administrators, those who had not helped or helped enough, those who were not aware of what was going on and should have known, everyone.

Evarts tried to approach Justice Louis D. Brandeis, whose wife and daughter had been helping the defense, but the connection was too close to permit him to take official action. Evarts recalled: "He shooed us away." The defense attempted Justice Holmes once again. Now, ten days after refusing to entertain a petition for a writ of habeas corpus, he also denied a stay of execution on the certiorari writ. The lawyers went on trying.

Meanwhile, beyond the courts, new efforts were being made by a new group of intellectuals, the Citizens National Committee for Sacco and Vanzetti. The Defense Committee, troubled by allies as well as by enemies, had found itself flanked by another rival. Called into life by Isaac Don Levine and Robert Morss Lovett on the theory that the original group was incapable of success or amelioration, the National Committee set up its headquarters in the Bellevue Hotel, on Beacon Street and facing a wing of the State House. It comprised an impressive sum of 500 members, including such notable persons as John Dewey, the institutional economist John R. Commons, the old muckraker Ida M. Tarbell, Oswald Garrison Villard of the *Nation,* the settlement leader Jane

Addams, the novelist Katherine Anne Porter, the former Amherst College president Alexander Meiklejohn, and John Haynes Holmes, the reformist pastor of the Community Church in New York. John F. Moors, the State Street broker who had helped with the petition to Fuller, had become unhappy with the Defense Committee and also joined the new group, as did a Boston mother-and-daughter pair formerly devoted to antivivisection. The Citizens National Committee represented a new and superior element of respectability for the cause. Unlike the first defenders, most of its members were more than intellectuals. From positions in recognized institutions, they could hope to exert greater influence. But they were late.

Among the people affected by the case, Justice Oliver Wendell Holmes was able to see it both as a responsible jurist and as an intellectual. His relation to it was given the aesthetic form of a dialectic in his famous correspondence with Harold Laski.* On November 21, 1926, attempting to provoke his Socrates into agreement, Laski wrote: "I had a long note from Felix Frankfurter yesterday, full of his crime survey of Boston and the incredible Sacco-Vanzetti case. I hope that the latter is settled, for, otherwise, the working classes will disbelieve in Massachusetts justice." When Holmes failed to react, Laski returned to the charge five months later, on March 20, 1927: "But I read Felix's little book on Sacco and Vanzetti and thought it a neat, surgical job." The first Holmes response, in his letter of March 31, was sympathetic but noncommittal: "I take it that Felix's book is a bit of heroism on his part—and I vaguely hear that it has brought criticism upon him." Another pair of letters followed in April, Laski still assuming his correspondent's agreement and Holmes still remaining neutral.

On August 9, after the Advisory Committee decision, Laski returned to the subject with somewhat less restraint: "I agree

* Mark De Wolfe Howe (ed.), *Holmes-Laski Letters* (2 vols., Cambridge: Harvard University Press, 1954), vol. 2, pp. 900–999.

fully with all that Felix says of Lowell in this case. Loyalty to his class has transcended his ideas of logic and of justice." Instead of moving toward Laski's view, however, Holmes responded in his next letter, dated August 18, with an instructive rendering of the effects of the intellectuals' activities: ". . . but the result has been already some letters telling me that I am a monster of injustice in various forms of words, from men who evidently don't know anything about the matter but who have the customary willingness to impute evil for any result that they don't like." Quite suddenly the realities of the situation and the different characters of the men revealed the cleft between them. In the first place, Holmes' function carried a responsibility that classified him as an enemy of the defense sympathizers, Laski among them. Moreover, Holmes was an unqualified liberal. Laski, functionally irresponsible as a European observer, was essentially no liberal but an idealist and a dogmatist of the Left: he could be intolerant for the sake of his vision of a better world. Ideologically, the distance between the two men was unbridgeable; but they were friends.

Laski, meanwhile, wrote another letter on August 19, one day after Holmes had sent his letter off, thus unaware of his correspondent's reaction. Still assuming Holmes' agreement, Laski revealed his European assumption that Frankfurter was the final authority on the case: "I need not tell you how much I sympathized with your difficulties in the Sacco-Vanzetti case. I cannot see that you had any alternative, and I suppose that the event must move to its tragic end. But I wish I could make people like Fuller realize the immense damage his action has done to the good name of America. This case has stirred Europe as nothing since the Dreyfus case has done. And to me, at this instance, and with the reliance I have on the substantial accuracy of Felix's picture, it seems that it is indeed another Dreyfus case."

In his next letter, dated August 24, Holmes made two illuminating points. The first is relevant to the civil rights issues of our time: "I cannot but ask myself why there is so much greater interest in red than black. A thousand-fold worse cases of negroes come up from time to time, but the world does not worry over them. . . ." Holmes then got to the intellectuals: "But I see no adequate available reasons for the world outside the United States taking up the matter and I think your public and literary men had better have kept their gentle mouths shut. . . ." He went on: ". . . my prejudices are against the convictions but they are still stronger against the run of the shriekers. The lovers of justice have emphasized their love by blowing up a building or two and there are guards in all sorts of places, including one for this house for a few days. . . ." Laski never commented on these points.

Holmes also made a careful definition of Felix Frankfurter's role: "I also appreciate what I believe was the generous knight-errantry of Felix in writing the book." For his own part, however, Holmes sagely refused to have an opinion on the case itself: "I have never read the evidence except on the limited points that came before me. . . ."

In a letter of September 1 the great liberal returned to the intellectuals: "It isn't a matter of reason, but simply shrieking because the world is not the kind of world they want—a trouble most of us feel in some way." Near the end of November he made his last judgment on the intellectuals: "I had a letter from A. Hill saying that Frankfurter will write nothing more about Sacco and Vanzetti for a year. I hope it will be longer than that, as I think all those who were interested in that side seem to have got hysterical and to have lost their sense of proportion."

Meanwhile, the hope relating to a writ of certiorari, which Holmes and the eight other Supreme Court justices had represented, was exhausting its small credibility with the loss of hours. After Holmes himself had refused to act upon it, Musmanno tried to persuade Chief Justice William Howard Taft by telephone. The line was poor—Taft was on vacation in Canada—and Taft saved his voice and wired his reply. It was another fragment from

Kafka: Taft said he could not act in Canada, and he suggested that the defense approach three justices, two of whom—Holmes and Brandeis—had already refused to grant the writ. The third was Harlan Stone, and Hill was desperate enough to go up to Maine, where Stone was spending his vacation, to get another refusal. This was the end of the certiorari effort.

The defense could only keep on assailing all the instances and offices of authority. U.S. Attorney General John G. Sargent, on vacation in Vermont, listened to a three-hour argument on the connection of the Justice Department with the case. He refused to make its records public, but, in Washington, the Acting Attorney General, George R. Farnum, was moved to release a "synopsis" of the department's file on the men; it contained a single notation mentioning Sacco and Vanzetti as subscribers to an anarchist publication. President Coolidge was beleaguered by telephone and telegraph, most particularly and most insistently by Musmanno, but he would not come to the telephone or reply. And Fuller was receiving petitions, six more in the last few days. All these attempts, as the defense lawyers knew, were very nearly hopeless. Their best strengths had been used up.

The defense could only try to increase the sheer power bearing upon Boston. Europe and the rest of the world responded on Sunday with massive demonstrations that would grow larger and angrier the next day. In Boston on Sunday, 20,000 persons went to the Common, most of them to see what the sympathizers would do. The mayor had withdrawn eighteen permits for that day, interdicting meetings of such groups as the Animal Welfare Association in the general ban, but it was expected that the friends of the prisoners would defy the prohibition. The police, however, dominated the Common so absolutely that the result of the day's resistance comprised a few scuffles and seven arrests.

Some sympathizers were able to hold a protest meeting, but it was in the Scenic Temple on the South Side. There 1,000 persons heard a series of speakers dominated by the Communists. In a broad condemnation they denounced Brandeis and Holmes, as well as Fuller and the Advisory Committee, for representing various shadings of middle-class deceit. With Rose Sacco and Luigia Vanzetti present, the meeting was the most successful of the Communist efforts to identify themselves with the cause. They were not, however, closer to capturing it. In fact, they were not sure they wanted to have it. While they continued their propaganda, they were preparing to turn on the Defense Committee and disassociate themselves from a defeat. In any case they would claim the martyrdom of Sacco and Vanzetti for the world proletariat.

So ended the dispirited Sunday of August 21 in Boston. Monday was the day of execution.

The prisoners remained in character. Sacco was almost serene as the last hours fell away. Vanzetti, recovered from his breakdown, fought acutely for his life. On that Monday he wrote to Dante Sacco: "I tell you now that all that I know of your father, he is not a criminal, but one of the bravest men I ever knew. Some day you will understand what I am about to tell you. That your father sacrificed everything dear and sacred to the human heart and soul for his fate in liberty and justice for all. . . . Remember, Dante, each one who will say otherwise of your father and I, is a liar insulting innocent dead men who have been brave in their life. Remember and know also, Dante, that if your father and I would have been cowards and hypocrits and rinnegators of our faith, we would not have been put to death. They would not even have convicted a lebbrous dog; not even executed a deadly poisoned scorpion on such evidence as that they framed against us. They would have given a new trial to a matricide and abitual felon on the evidence we presented for a new trial. . . ."

The struggle for their lives overwhelmed their real worth. Sacco's long withdrawal indicated how little value he put on his own. On the other hand, Vanzetti had been deriving his emotional force from the perils of his situation. One might ask how he could exist in more normal circumstances. And to Professor Marks and most of the intellectuals those lives had been reduced down to symbols.

Vanzetti approached his death like a statesman. He made a last demand to see Thompson, who came down from his summer place in New Hampshire to spend fifty minutes with the prisoners. In return, the lawyer asked a service of Vanzetti. Would he advise his friends against violence? Vanzetti was an idealist who might take a broader view of his own execution. He was a political idealist but not a saint; Vanzetti refused. As Thompson later recalled the episode,* Vanzetti said he had identified his fate with a humanity fighting "for existence against entrenched power and wrong." Accordingly, Vanzetti went on in official idiom, he would give no such "sweeping advice" not to act. "Now, for the first and only time in conversation, Vanzetti showed a feeling of personal resentment against his enemies," Thompson wrote. Vanzetti asked how he could be expected to forgive the men who were destroying him. To this Thompson could only reply with the example of another enemy, Jesus Christ; the prisoners had twice refused to see the prison chaplain that day. "There was another pause in the conversation. I arose and we stood gazing at each other for a minute or two in silence. Vanzetti finally said that he would think of what I had said."

Rose Sacco and Luigia Vanzetti saw the prisoners three times on that last day. Passionate enough to be jealous in his earlier prison days, Sacco had little emotion left for the wife from whom he had been separated for seven years, while Vanzetti and his pious sister were strangers to each other. A newspaper report attempted to describe the scene: "Both condemned men, with but few hours to live, stretched their arms through the bars of the death cells in their efforts to embrace the women they loved."

At 8:50 that evening Warden Hendry told the prisoners that

* William G. Thompson, "Vanzetti's Last Statement," *Atlantic Monthly*, February 1928, pp. 254–57.

Justice Holmes had refused an execution stay for the third time, this time when attorneys of the Citizens National Committee had come to him with a new habeas corpus argument. Hendry said: "It is my painful duty to inform you that you must die tonight." Sacco and Vanzetti moaned but then contained themselves. Medeiros had eaten so much at his last meal that he lived out the hours in a stupor. Sacco, in the best mental condition of the three, calmly went on writing letters.

A monstrous rotary engine of mass and energy rumbled around the prisoners. One newspaper counted a total police force of 735 men at Charlestown prison: besides detectives and riot squad personnel, 300 patrolmen, 50 state troopers, 70 mounted police, 20 motorcycle officers, and 75 Boston & Maine railroad police from the nearby railroad yards. To help locate possible trouble, light played baldly about the prison walls from great searchlights on the prison tower and the roof next to the main gate. Guards manned the walls, while police, making their purpose clear with fixed bayonets and machine guns, established a forward line a thousand feet from the prison. Beyond, a police boat with a twenty-five-man squad patrolled Boston Harbor in anticipation of the fantastic.

Prepared to fight off a major assault, the police found themselves in easy control of a hopeless demonstration. In their resignation the sympathizers called their protest the death march. They marched before the State House and outside the Charlestown prison police line, and the police efficiently arrested 172 of them. But then Sacco and Vanzetti had expected nothing more from their nonanarchist allies. Among the death marchers arrested, all charged with loitering and sauntering, were Edna St. Vincent Millay, Professor Ellen Hayes, John Howard Lawson, Mother Bloor, the Negro Communist leader William L. Patterson, and Miss Katherine Huntington of Beacon Hill, whom *Time* magazine identified as a gentlewoman. While the other arrestees pleaded guilty silently and paid fines of five dollars, the notables pleaded guilty, made speeches and paid ten-dollar fines, the Misses Millay and Huntington emphasizing their long American ancestry.

The force of the protest was in inverse proportion to its proximity to the old crime. The quietest area was the Sacco-Vanzetti home region south of Boston. Riordan of the *Brockton Enterprise* recalled that only a handful demonstrated in Brockton, although it had a large Italian population.

Europe was violent on Monday. In Paris, hundreds of protestants and forty-three policemen were injured during the course of the day, while 250 persons were arrested in a rougher manner than in Boston. A mob of 15,000 gathered in the working class area on the Right Bank near the Place de la Bastille, where it fought police, tore up street benches, overturned kiosks, broke windows, and sacked shops of the Boulevard de Sebastopol. Five thousand Communists, divided into five columns, converged on the American Embassy, just off the Place de la Concorde, where they were dispersed by Republican Guards, three of whom were stabbed in the encounter. In Montmartre other rioters, defending themselves against police with café chairs, broke windows of restaurants and night clubs, with particular attention to the Moulin Rouge. Police said the demonstrations were the worst since the May Day riots of 1920 and 1921.

Expatriate Americans, and particularly American intellectuals, found themselves completely defenseless against the protests of the French. This attitude was explicitly remembered by Elliot Paul in his *The Last Time I Saw Paris*, published in 1942:

> The only occasion on which I felt utterly ashamed and lonely in the rue de la Huchette [in the Latin Quarter] was the night of August 22, 1927. For in distant Massachusetts that evening, my native State, a "good mason [sic] and a poor fish peddler" were put to death, after seven years of mental torture, for a crime they had not committed. . . . What had been confused and distorted in Beacon Hill was perfectly clear to the inhabitants of my little

> street, and to the workers of Paris generally, namely, that Sacco and Vanzetti were being murdered because they had been "anarchists" and foreigners and that Judge Thayer and Alvan T. Fuller destroyed them for the good of their privileged kind.

In another comment, Paul indicated one reason for the anger of the Europeans, the feeling that America was betraying their trust in it as a land where the usual injustices did not exist: "It was no new thing to the French to have undesirables railroaded and executed on one flimsy pretext or another. But, somehow, they had hoped it was different in America. . . ."

Colonel Alfred Dreyfus, vacationing on the Normandy coast, was persuaded to violate his old refusal to express an opinion. Betrayed by his fellow officers, he had never denied his old corps nor his own conservative views. Previously he had refused to support the Sacco-Vanzetti defense. Now, on the basis of his own experience, he was willing to move this far: "When doubt exists, it is fighting providence to commit the irreparable."

Other demonstrations were comparable to the Parisian riots. The Swiss, fired into an uncharacteristic violence, formed mobs and attacked the American Consulate and the League of Nations Palace, giving way only when firemen and police counterattacked with high-pressure hoses and drawn swords. In London, after a Sunday gathering of 12,000 in Hyde Park, mounted and foot police charged a group attempting to start up a parade in the park on Monday; forty persons were injured. Police in Berlin were ruthless enough to control their rioters, but one person was killed and several wounded in Leipzig. In Johannesburg, not well known for its interest in civil liberties, demonstrators burned the United States flag on the Town Hall steps. More protests and riots were reported from Gothenburg, Copenhagen, Helsingfors, Sydney, Buenos Aires, Nancy, Lyons, and scores of other cities.

Mussolini kept Italy quiet. As leader of an aggressively nationalistic Italy, he had been embarrassed by the Italian origins of the prisoners. Under pressure from public opinion, however, he indicated to the American government that he would welcome an "act of clemency." Less discreetly, the controlled press broke precedent to report the case developments on the front page, heretofore reserved for articles on Italy and Fascism. The newspaper *Il Tevere* mentioned the "satanic pride of the United States" and the *Tribuna* called the case "one of the blackest judicial events that man can recall."

As night came in Boston the lights went up on Beacon Street and the Common, but the dome of the State House remained dark. While it was no time for the illumination of Commonwealth pride, the police found the lamps of a lower altitude useful in dealing with the death marchers. At his desk since eleven in the morning, the Governor spent thirteen hours considering reasons that might justify stopping the execution. Not content with his own vision, moreover, he had ordered Attorney General Reading to hear legal arguments separately. The Governor saw, among many, Waldo L. Cook, publisher of the *Springfield Republican* and an old defense supporter; Arthur Garfield Hays, attorney for the American Civil Liberties Union, and other lawyers; and, late in the evening, Musmanno and Rose Sacco and Luigia Vanzetti, the last three arriving after the women had made their third and last visit to the prison. He leaned over his desk as if to communicate his body warmth and said: "It is these ladies that move me most."

The fact of the Attorney General's working presence in another office was, for Fuller, a final chance of averting an event that had become more and more inevitable in his own chambers, and he asked Musmanno to wait until Reading's report arrived. Anticipating nothing that would contradict his own conclusions, however, Fuller must have decided that it was more merciful to end the suspense for Rose Sacco and Luigia Vanzetti. At about eleven he told them formally but feelingly that he could appreciate their pain but that his conscience required him to let the law take its course. Musmanno waited hopelessly for the Reading report.

When reporters caught him as he left the State House, the Associated Press sent a flash: "Attorney Musmanno says it all over—Boston 11:07 P.M."

The momentum of Fuller's mercy had not stopped. Continuing to receive callers, he saw Thompson and Ehrmann, and, for the irrelevant last, a Philadelphia lawyer. Then, one minute before midnight, he quit the State House and his responsibility in the Sacco-Vanzetti case.

With hope guttering out in Boston, the case reached out again to President Coolidge, who was on a sightseeing trip in Yellowstone National Park. Prominent members of the Citizens National Committee for Sacco and Vanzetti telegraphed a new appeal to him, but it got the expected reaction: nothing. That evening, however, the chief ranger of the park, aware that President McKinley had been killed by an anarchist, stationed guards around the President's hotel and even persuaded him to change his room.

About a hundred persons gathered in the Defense Committee headquarters. Lola Ridge, who had escaped arrest in a scuffle at the Charlestown prison police line, arrived there about eleven. Freed after their arrest, John Howard Lawson and Mother Bloor also came in, Mother Bloor receiving cheers for her spirited defiance of the police. At this, Mary Donovan demanded silence with the authority of a schoolteacher, the group complying like a chastened classroom. Jeannette Marks also noted the "quiet entrance of Felix Frankfurter" and John Dos Passos "flitting about cheerful, charming." Louis Bernheimer was whispering to himself, sending and receiving messages. With Ruth Hale, Miss Marks fed the defenders sandwiches, coffee, and milk.

Warden Hendry came for the prisoners a few minutes before midnight. Sacco, who had been writing a letter, asked Hendry to see that it was mailed. Vanzetti and Medeiros had been sleeping. On awakening, Vanzetti told the Warden he was ready for the inevitable; Medeiros rose but then fell back into his cot. Someone had counted out the steps from each death cell to the death chamber: for Medeiros, thirteen; Sacco, seventeen; and Vanzetti, twenty-one. (On leaving the State House Musmanno had come directly to the prison, but Hendry refused to let him see the prisoners. On the verge of a breakdown Musmanno said: "Tell them that I just wanted to tell them there is more mercy in their hearts than in the hearts of any who profess the orthodox religion.") Nearby, in a room hastily equipped with telephones, 100 reporters waited. Outside, the streets of Charlestown were quiet.

"The lights were glaring and everybody looked extremely unhappy," the Associated Press reporter, who was one of the seven official witnesses in the death chamber, recalled in an article in 1952.* "I was standing next to Warden Hendry. He was more affected than anybody. I thought he was going to cave in. . . ."

It was after midnight, no longer August 22, officially the execution date, but an illegal August 23. Sacco, Vanzetti, and Medeiros had the right to all of August 22; the perfect response to rights of the accused and the law would have been an execution precisely at midnight. The law granted a few minutes.

The first to enter the death chamber was Celestino Medeiros: "He came out stolidly. . . . They strapped him in. And that was that."

The prison records listed the time for Medeiros: entered death chamber, 12:02:47; electricity applied, 12:03:37; pronounced dead, 12:09:35.

"Nicola Sacco was a small man, peppery, quarrelsome and bad tempered. . . . He spoke of his wife and children [the *Boston Herald* reported: He said in broken English, 'Farewell my wife, my child, and all my friends!' As the straps were adjusted across his face he said to the witnesses, 'Good evening, gentlemen.'

* Associated Press article by W. E. Playfair, *Boston Herald*, August 22, 1952.

Then, 'Farewell, mother!'] and then his last words were in Italian: 'Vive l'anarchia.' . . . he was defiant.

"Bing, they stepped on the juice."

The prison records for Sacco: entered death chamber, 12:11: 12; electricity applied, 12:13:10; pronounced dead, 12:19:02.

"Vanzetti was a very lovable guy, mild, gentle, humorous," the *Associated Press* man continued. "Everybody liked him, including the Warden." Vanzetti shook Hendry's hand warmly, thanking him for his kindness.

Then Vanzetti measured out his last words: "I wish to forgive some people for what they are now doing to me."

It was a perfect leavetaking. Vanzetti would forgive some of his enemies—but not all of them. As he had earlier made clear to Thompson, he took his cause too seriously to give up his right to judge those who would destroy him. One anarchist journal, *L'Adunata dei refrattari,* tried to improve its portrait of Vanzetti by eliding the "some," but fortunately for the real man, better witnesses heard his statement.

The prison records for Vanzetti: entered death chamber, 12: 20:38; electricity applied, 12:21:33; pronounced dead, 12: 26:55.

August 23–August 28:
Tuesday–Wednesday–Thursday–
Friday–Saturday–Sunday

At midnight in the Defense Committee offices, as they waited and stared at their watches, Aldino Felicani said softly: "What are two lives? It is the ideal." Mary Donovan said desperately or reminiscently: "What if the finger of God should stay the execution this night?" (In the Boston Psychiatric Hospital, where the police had imaginatively brought him, Powers Hapgood quarreled with the tolerant guards. In her police station cell one deathmarcher, a Boston gentlewoman, stood at attention from midnight.) At 12:20 A.M., a few seconds in advance, someone said: "It must be over." Several people wept. Mary Donovan told Joseph Moro, the secretary-treasurer: "Lock the doors, Joe. The work is over." Malcolm Cowley wrote: ". . . after the execution, their mood changed. They fell silent, they separated, and many of them marched the streets alone, all night. Just as the fight for a common cause had brought them together, so the defeat drove them apart, each back into his own orbit."

In Union Square in New York a crowd of 10,000 got the news from a bulletin of the *Daily Worker:* "SACCO MURDERED!" (It was followed by an attack on the A.F. of L. and the Socialists: "WOLL-GREEN AND THE SOC PARTY BETRAYED THEM.") A *Time* magazine man reported: "Loud but orderly cries of indignation, boos, catcalls. But no fiercer than a 10,000 baseball-crowd makes when a favorite disappoints. Flares and the *Internationale,* which soon died." A *World* reporter, however, sent this account: "The crowd responded with a great sob. Women fainted in fifteen or twenty places. Others, too, overcome, dropped to the curbs and buried their heads in their hands. Men leaned on one another's shoulders and wept. There was a sudden movement in the street to the east of Union Square. Men began to run around aimlessly, tearing at their clothes and ripping their straw hats, and women ripped their dresses in anguish."

In Italy the Sacco family got the news after receiving this telegram from the office of Pope Pius XI: "The Holy Father . . . has done everything possible with the competent human authorities, after having prayed to God according to your desire and as he will continue to do so." When the elder brother Sabino told his widower father, according to an Associated Press reporter: "Screaming inarticulately and trembling in every limb, the aged man finally managed to say, 'They have killed my innocent son,' and he then fell back into his chair, weeping and muttering maledictions." Lighting a lamp, Sabino placed it before an image of the Madonna. The women of the household wailed.

A flare of reactions darted about the world like heat lightning. The Paris rioters demonstrated a second time on the Boulevard de Sebastopol. Reduced in energy and numbers, down to 1,000, they were swept away by the police. French momentum was not spent immediately, however, and the Associated Press was reporting an attack on the American Consulate in Cherbourg on August 26. By then, protests against the execution were spilling over into demonstrations marking the funeral of Sacco and Vanzetti.

Despite the final expression to come, Boston and the United States were trying to forget quickly. Under the headline, "Back to Normalcy," the *Boston Herald* asked for an amnesty of ill feeling: "Let us get back to business and the ordinary concerns of life. . . . The chapter is closed. The die is cast. The arrow has flown." The *World* withdrew from its exposed position among the radical outcroppings: "The *Evening World* strongly opposed the carrying out of the sentence. It now hopes with equal earnestness that there may be no bitterness, no recrimination, no rancorous harping on what might or should have been, in after-discussion of the event." Representatives of the extremes, however, would not retreat. On the Right, the *Transcript* stated firmly: "Massachusetts has narrowly escaped a lynching. . . . That it was the community and not the individual that was to be lynched in no wise affects the principle of this case. . . ." The sympathizers, for their part, would use the funeral to give their meaning to the event.

The Boston authorities, deciding to be tolerant about the last ritual of revenge, negotiated cooperatively with the Defense Committee over the planning. According to city regulations the funeral would have to be held within four days, but the Health Commissioner extended the time to Sunday, when the traffic problem would not be so great. Meanwhile, on Wednesday, the bodies of Sacco and Vanzetti, dressed in blue serge suits, white shirts, and figured ties, were yielded up to mourning and curiosity in the undertaking parlor of John Langone at 385 Hanover

Street, a few store fronts down from the Defense Committee headquarters and adjacent to the New North Meeting House. A line of workingmen, Italian matrons, children, and clerks from the nearby business district began to wind through Langone's. Other visitors came by sight-seeing buses. Vendors of frankfurters and balloons did an excellent business; thirty policemen patrolled the street. The people of the neighborhood, although not truly committed to the men, nevertheless accepted the tragedy as their own. Giving no evidence of anger, Hanover Street was solemnly unhappy. The only expression that moved the police was an initiative of Mary Donovan, who brought placards carrying the words attributed to Thayer, "Did you see what I did to those anarchistic bastards?" When she posed for newspaper photographers with the slogan at her breast, a policeman intervened, the protesting Powers Hapgood was slapped, and she was taken off to the station. Quickly released, she was cheered on her return. For three days the people came to see the bodies of Sacco and Vanzetti.

On that Wednesday Celestino Medeiros was buried in the Pine Grove Cemetery of New Bedford. A handful of family friends and 2,000 others attended.

About 200,000 persons lined the streets to watch the Sacco-Vanzetti funeral procession in a mood that began with an easy curiosity and ended with a touch of concern. About 7,000 or 8,000 persons, eight or ten times as many as had demonstrated earlier, marched for the dead.

For most persons the case had been a summer affair, and now it was August 28, and the summer was slipping away. August 28 was gray, rainy, and windy, a day out of November.

Forming up for their march in North End Park, at the harbor end of Hanover Street, the celebrants set down their floral wreaths in the mud and waited among drifts of fog. At about two o'clock they moved down Hanover Street to Scollay Square in the business district. From there they were led off by the two horse-drawn hearses of the cortege, followed by Defense Committee members. The police had refused to permit a routing that would have taken the procession down Beacon Street past the State House, and now coveys of angry men tried to revert to it, but they were blocked by barricades and police squads. Permitting themselves to be shunted down Tremont Street, with the Common protecting the State House from their last protest, the marchers linked their arms, thirty or forty abreast, in the convention of solidarity.

The marchers wore black-lettered scarlet arm bands, kept hidden until the parade had got under way, which read: "Remember, Justice Crucified, Aug. 22, 1927." They also carried scarlet flowers which they began throwing into the street despite the admonitions of the Police Superintendent not to dirty up the city. At moments they expressed their rage by throwing stones and, more frequently, with catcalls and jeers a *Herald* reporter found typical of baseball spectators. He found the parade "more picturesque than solemn" with its raucous cries, crushed flowers, inexpertly flung missiles, and clottings of awkward bodies at police-disputed corners.

The objective of the cortege was the Forest Hills Cemetery, eight miles to the southwest of the starting point. It had been assumed that the mass of the paraders would disperse in the South End, but the marchers broke through the police lines in a series of spasms and ran after the leaders. In the disorders the head of the parade was taken by the Socialist Albert Baker Lewis, who remained immaculate, soft-voiced, and unconsciously aloof to the sweaty violence of his fellows. Taxis followed the parade, picking up the weary, as it continued, shambling and inexorable, torn occasionally by mounted police but reforming and delivering counter blows of stones and cries. At one point the marchers stalled a streetcar and, at another, they stopped a truck whose driver had insisted on carrying out his business. When the driver protested the paraders attacked him with umbrellas and canes, forcing him to take refuge atop the cab. Heavy rain and another encounter with the police finally reduced the parade numbers, the police attacking with clubs and knocking down a dozen marchers. Making no arrests, the police preferred to keep the demonstration under control by limited attacks at key points. In view of its size and anger they achieved an eminent success in preventing fatalities and even serious injuries, not to mention damage to property. But then, the paraders, getting their maximum of protest expressed, had their success.

When the cortege arrived at the cemetery shortly after four o'clock, six pallbearers, the ubiquitous Edward H. James among them, bore the coffins into the chapel. One hundred and fifty persons crowded after them, while 5,000 got moist on the grass slopes outside. Mary Donovan, haggard and white, read the eulogy. Written by Gardner Jackson, it began with a statement of protest against "one of the blackest crimes in the history of mankind." Mary Donovan addressed Nicola Sacco and Bartolomeo Vanzetti: *

"Massachusetts and America have killed you—murdered you because you were Italian anarchists. Two hundred and fifty years ago the controlling people in this state hanged women in Salem—charging them with witchcraft. . . . The minds of those who have killed you are not blinded. They have committed this act in deliberate cold blood. . . . You, Sacco and Vanzetti, are the victims of the crassest plutocracy the world has known since ancient Rome. . . ."

Mary Donovan closed with the famous Vanzetti citation: "If it had not been for these thing. . . ." Reciting its last phrase, "that agony is our triumph," she continued: "By that triumph we are fired with an everlasting fire. . . . In your martyrdom we will fight on and conquer!"

At five o'clock the bodies were cremated.

* *Boston Globe,* August 29, 1927.

19. Movers and Shakers III

> "But I must tell you, this repetition of my ideas in the past makes a very disagreeable impression on me."—Nicolai Stavrogin in
>
> DOSTOEVSKY'S *The Possessed*

MARY DONOVAN was right. The Sacco-Vanzetti case became a legend of innocence betrayed. It became more: a parable about betrayal in American society.

Let us now trace out the main lines of the small and the great betrayal. What do they mean of themselves? How are they related? How did the intellectuals conceive and develop them? We are seeking our own sense of the case for use today.

About the small betrayal, we have seen how the intellectuals identified themselves with the prisoners. Were they not all—accused and defenders—outcasts, astray in the villages, spoken against? The intellectuals arrived at their belief in innocence and betrayal through a burst of revelation; they began with pure emotion and applied their best intelligence to the proof of it. George Santayana has said of the intelligent man that "his knowledge is an ideal figment, painted with vegetative oils and dramatized by his private emotions." The case became the private drama of the intellectuals.

Despite its private character, the case showed that the intellectuals were not as isolated from the rest of American society as they thought. One indication was their ability to achieve power effects through organization and public relations. Moreover, they were acting out the faults they condemned in their middle-class, business-oriented neighbors: loosely associational thinking, sentimentality, class conformity, and intolerance. Also, like the editorial writers for conservative newspapers, they had to make things simple. This meant destroying some of the best truths about the case and the nation. It also meant destroying reputations. Thus they laid a heavy condemnation upon everyone representing a different opinion on the case: jurors, Judge Thayer, prosecutor, Governor Fuller, the Advisory Committee, the citizens of Massachusetts, and other nonsympathizers. Some of the intellectuals did not rest content with the charge as made, going on to discover more proofs of their enemies' evil. Lowell, for example, was accused of anti-Semitism and the exploitation of the Harvard cleaning women. In 1935 a group of Harvard alumni, including Malcolm Cowley, John Dos Passos, and Osmond K. Fraenkel, published a pamphlet to bring their fellow alumni to "an awareness of the incredible and destructive twists of men's minds—even the mind of the President of Harvard University." Lowell's associate on the Advisory Committee, Judge Robert Grant, was accused of prejudice against Italians because he wrote a humorous account of having his pocket picked in Rome. Thayer got the worst treatment. He had to endure an unremitting denunciation the rest of his life, and in 1932 a bomb wrecked his house and severely injured his wife. After that, it became his custom to call home every day at noon to see if he still had wife and house. Demanding their private justice, the intellectuals could be as unjust as corporation presidents. Only in this way could they maintain the purity of their small betrayal.

The intellectuals then made the leap from the case to the great betrayal they saw pervading American society. Surely there was a great deal that deserved the best brimstone. It was a time when businessmen were making too many of the important decisions for the country; their high-profit philosophy was both too reckless and too narrow. It was a time of the Ku Klux Klan, the Tennessee monkey trial, the company towns, and union-busting practices.

Moreover, it was a time when the United States was causing great damage in world affairs by rejecting its international responsibilities. Since criticism was their prime function, the intellectuals can be forgiven for dwelling on the evils and denying the evident good things. Reality, however, had a better balance than they were willing to admit. In the twenties the country was doing well in many ways. It was improving its productive efficiency and generalizing many benefits for all classes. Between 1880 and 1920, furthermore, it was assimilating 23,500,000 immigrants, and if the process inevitably resulted in frictions and various shadings of discrimination, it was nevertheless a remarkable social accomplishment. What other nation has done as much? Nor could anyone deny that the government was a reasonably responsive democracy, whatever unexpressed needs it failed to hear. The country was immense with potentials in all directions. No one could quite make sense of it.

The intellectuals understood their country as badly as the Sacco-Vanzetti case. If we study their writings of the period, we can see that they had little more insight than the business minds. Most of them, playing with the dull explosives of Marxism or Thorstein Veblen's reversals of reality, failed to see the real evils and advocated either irrelevant revolution or trivial solutions. Some gave up their duty as critics. Thus in 1928, a year after he strove for Sacco and Vanzetti, the former Socialist Walter Lippmann was writing: "The more or less unconscious and unplanned activities of business men are for once more novel, more daring; and in general more revolutionary, than the theories of the progressives." A year later Lincoln Steffens, while admiring Soviet Russia and Mussolini's Italy, wrote: "Big business in America in producing what the Socialists held up as their goal. . . ." Accepting or rejecting this business society, the intellectuals never saw the economic maladjustments that would lead to the depression. In 1932 a group of intellectuals issued a manifesto reading: "If I vote at all, it will be for the Communists.

. . ." The signers included John Dos Passos, Edmund Wilson, Malcolm Cowley, Lincoln Steffens, Theodore Dreiser, Sherwood Anderson, and Sidney Hook. It took the intellectuals a long time to learn from the depression itself—and then they needed help from the Englishman John Maynard Keynes and the nonintellectual Franklin Delano Roosevelt.

Seeking to understand, the intellectuals reduced the impossible complexities to an impossibly simple parable of good and evil. The providential appearance of Sacco and Vanzetti on the scene provided their stock figures. Thus John Dos Passos puts into the mind of the sympathetic social worker in his *U.S.A.* trilogy: ". . . the slums, the shanties with filthy tottering backhouses, the miners' children in grimy coats too big for them, the overworked women stooping over stoves, the youngsters struggling for an education in night schools, hunger and unemployment and drink, and the police and the lawyers and the judges always ready to take it out on the weak; if the people in the pullmancars could only be made to understand how it was. . . ." Maxwell Anderson generalizes in similar terms in *Winterset,* the play he constructed from the Sacco-Vanzetti material: "In fact, at the moment, I don't think of anything you can't buy, including life, honor, virtue, glory, public office, conjugal affection, and all kinds of justice, from the traffic court to the immortal nine. . . ." The specific of all this is the tragedy as seen by Anderson for his play, expressed in these words by the Dos Passos character: "If the State of Massachusetts can kill these two innocent men in the face of the protests of the whole world it'll mean that there never will be any justice in America again." With the depression assisting, the logic arrives at its full circle: a nation ridden by injustice and error produces a Sacco-Vanzetti case, and this means more injustice and error.

Afterward, the truths of the American situation slowly forced themselves on the intellectuals. Learning from the New Deal and time, they would eventually come to accept at least some of the contradictions of the twenties. About Sacco and Vanzetti, however, they would maintain the old simplicities. Virtually all comments on the case in serious historical and cultural studies as well as in reference works define it as judicial murder or, at the mildest, as a miscarriage of justice. One can find such notes in the *Dictionary of American Biography;* F. L. Allen, *Only Yesterday;* Alfred Kazin, *On Native Grounds;* J. J. Hoffman, *The Twenties;* Edmund Wilson, *The American Earthquake;* Cleveland Amory, *The Proper Bostonians;* and Arthur M. Schlesinger, Jr., *The Crisis of the Old Order*. The Schlesinger treatment, for example, mentions the "murder of a paymaster" but not that of the guard, and has the police arresting "two Italians in an automobile filled with the innocent and febrile literature of anarchistic propaganda." (Note the errors of fact and misleading omissions: the men had neither automobile nor literature; they did have arms.) Referring to "a time of hysteria," "gaps in the testimony" and the "predilections of the judge," Schlesinger concludes: "But the last moment belonged to Sacco and Vanzetti"—quoting the "If it had not been for these thing. . . ." citation. G. Louis Joughin, co-author of *The Legacy of Sacco and Vanzetti,* could write: ". . . the literary verdict is unanimously sympathetic to the executed men. Prosecution, judges, and the hostile public majority have not in twenty years found a single literary defender of their position."

The intellectuals won their profoundest effects in a creative reworking of the case in verse, novels, and the drama. I have cited several examples already; here are others: James T. Farrell's autobiographical novel, *Bernard Clare,* sends its hero to a brothel and a Sacco-Vanzetti protest meeting, his stream of consciousness recording: "The flesh of that Harlem whore. The murdered, martyred flesh of Sacco and Vanzetti." A collection of verse on the case, *America Arraigned,* mourns "You Vanzetti, with the marching blue in your eyes. . . ." and concludes: "But shame on folk of the printed word/Who raise no cry that rich men plunder!/Come, let our voices be heard/In revolutionary thunder."* In the 1941 play by James Thurber and Elliott Nugent, *The Male Animal,* the citation "If it had not been for these thing. . . ." is used as a casus belli between underdog liberals and businesslike Pharisees. After a faculty member reads it to his class as an example of distinguished expression, the reactionaries rise up in an attack that threatens academic freedom. The case always represents a struggle between unqualified good and evil.

The most important and illuminating use of the case occurs in Maxwell Anderson's poetic drama, *Winterset,* which opened on Broadway in 1935 and later became a film. Like the other writers dealing with the case, Anderson tells the simple story of innocence betrayed. Unlike the others, he knew the facts so well that he had to take great care to keep it simple. In point of fact, he had learned his lesson in his earlier play on the case, *Gods of the Lightning,* which failed because it had got too close to the event. In *Winterset,* he started out at a safe remove in time and place, locating the drama in New York after the execution. With the prisoners retrospectively fused into a single martyr, the hero is the martyr's son and the *primum mobile* is vindication. To complete the logic of innocence, Anderson provides a confessor on the Medeiros model, a real killer of his own imagination and a defending lawyer after Felix Frankfurter. He persuades his depression audience to identify with the defeated and adds a romantic interest: "Why, girl, the transfiguration on the mount/ was nothing to your face. It lights from within—a white chalice holding fire, a flower in flame,/ this is your face." Offering something for everybody, Anderson was able to stir a wide range of emotions.

All this, however, was not enough: it was defeat but not tragedy. Anderson had to steal that from the enemy. For his tragic figure is no proletarian martyr; it is Judge Thayer. Anderson got the idea from a Boston lawyer named Robert H. Montgomery, who was a friend of his but a supporter of the guilty

* Poem by Ralph Cheyney entitled "The White Terror," p. 24.

verdict. Indeed, Montgomery later wrote a book on the subject. Arguing his point with Anderson, Montgomery had suggested that the embattled Thayer was the real victim. This kind of tragedy was useless to Anderson's thesis, but it lent itself to dramatic translation. The playwright went on to change Thayer from Montgomery's victim of bombs to a Shakespearean victim of conscience. Wandering about in the great city, seeking absolution for the crime he committed upon an innocent man, the judge becomes Anderson's King Lear, the largest, most human, most credible figure in the play. The enemy carries the play.

Anderson draws upon Lear quite obviously. One can, however, find a better reference to his judge in another Shakespearean play, in the character of Shylock. Jew and judge begin as conventional villains. In both cases the playwrights bring their characters to life by using truths that contradict their conscious prejudices. Thus Shakespeare gives Shylock the great speech: "Hath not a Jew eyes? Hath not a Jew hands, organs, dimensions, senses, affections, passions. . . . If you prick us, do we not bleed? . . ." For his part, Anderson needed no universal truths to strengthen Thayer; he had a number of mediocre ones available to him, those facts suggesting a less than perfect martyrdom. Thus his judge is permitted to argue against the image of Vanzetti: ". . . men have come before me perfect in their lives,/ loved at home,/ and gentle, not vicious, yet caught so ripe red-handed/ in some dark violence there was no denying/ where the onus lay." And Anderson gives him the truest line in the play: "Can it not be . . . that the great injustice lies/ on your side and not mine?" Under the force of the play's overt message, however, the audience is led away from the thought. It suffers with the judge and believes with the playwright.

Anderson perfected the Sacco-Vanzetti legend. His timing was just right: the middle of the depression and eight years after the men were executed. The depression was seeking scapegoats; there were no new facts to upset the arrangement according to Anderson. The legend became part of American folklore.

But it is a false legend. We can see this without getting into the question of guilt or innocence. It denies the humanity of Sacco and Vanzetti, difficult and complex persons with a wide range of possibilities, while refusing all good will to those who would not believe them. In its logic, furthermore, the legend blanks out the very contradictions that made the case. And beyond the case itself, its message of defeat is simply not in accord with the American experience; our immigrants and workingmen, by and large, are victors on the installment plan. Some legends produce better truths by altering the facts. This does not.

Moreover, the legend is a commonplace. Telling us nothing new or unique, it is indistinguishable from a thousand other wretched stories. In terms of art, most of its uses show up its poverty. *Winterset* succeeded only because of the depression and the playwright's additives; critics found it incredible and impossibly sentimental in a recent television revival. The Sacco-Vanzetti episodes in the Dos Passos *U.S.A.* are among its weakest. We can do nothing with the legend today.

Yet the legend had it valuable uses in the past. One of the finer ironies of the case is that it did more good than harm, whatever encouragement it gave to nonsense. In the first place, it taught tolerance for foreigners and strange ideas. Moreover, it made people think. It was the only significant intellectual occurrence in the United States between the first World War and the depression. Through the intellectuals, it forced itself on the nation when Americans wanted to sleep in the static promise of a perfected capitalism. Something was wrong, and the questions raised by the case were helpful in attacking the failures in the national leadership. The fact that the criticism was widely off the mark does not negate its value. Progress often requires the grossest of stimuli.

The case was perhaps even more important because of its effect on the intellectuals. It gave them a unity and an esprit de corps to prepare them for the more profound and responsible situation into which the depression thrust them. True, it infected them with a false disillusionment by a false symbol of what was wrong. They went on, however, to use that disillusionment to apply better questions about the system when the depression later made its real demands. Tamed by responsibility, the intellectuals gave up their Marxist or nihilistic dreams and accepted the reasonable solution in the theory of Keynes and the practices of the New Deal. In fact, they became the best defenders of the free enterprise system. In the thirties they were the realists, while the businessmen were clinging to their own legends of the balanced budget and sound fiscal policy. By then the intellectuals had moved in from the helpless fringe of American society to the power centers. With the New Deal, university degrees achieved working force, Felix Frankfurter was sending his students into government offices, and the liberal intellectuals could now compensate for the inadequacies of the businessmen with their own more imaginative failures. The Sacco-Vanzetti case had helped make them movers and shakers.

The Sacco-Vanzetti legend has been enormously valuable as a vehicle of protest and an inspiration to the intellectuals. In view of all this, we might be sorry for knowing what we do about the facts of the case. For, knowing them, we cannot live with the legend today. We might well regret its passing. Among other things, we still require its lessons of tolerance for strange ideas and strange people.

Like other legends it was called into life to fill a need. Religions have the miraculous lives of saints and martyrs to strengthen faith. Military units tell stories of courage and sacrifice to give men a reason for attacking or holding on when there is no good reason. In American history, the legend of the Alamo fitted into our expansionist policy. Closer to the problem of justice, compare the history of John Brown's raid on Harper's Ferry with the legend of John Brown. The man was a fanatic who murdered innocents to carry out his arbitrary justice. But his legend told a great truth about the crime of slavery in a free country. We might very well regret the passing of the Sacco-Vanzetti legend.

Nevertheless, its sentimentality and childlike character are no longer appropriate to the way the nation thinks and feels about the issues it raised. Having got through the depression, World War II, and two decades of the postwar period, we have learned to live more comfortably with irony; we have learned to qualify many of our absolutes. We have seen the disadvantages of union militancy and the uses of economic royalists in organizing a war industry to defeat the Axis powers. Afterward, we discovered that the enemy became a useful ally against the ally turned into our most dangerous enemy. By now we are learning to live with Soviet Russia while taking note of a possibly more dangerous enemy over its shoulder. To master our situation we need a better guide than a parable teaching that the underdog and irresponsible ideas have a unique virtue. The truer Sacco-Vanzetti story, a lesson in contradictions and disorder, should serve our understanding better today.

About other issues, however, we are not obliged to reject the values of militancy and uncompromising action. The civil rights struggle will need its heroes and martyrs. Perhaps we should believe them absolutely, at least until that battle is won. Afterward, we can try to understand with the help of irony.

APPENDIX

Within the frame of coherent narrative it was impossible to deal with every rumor and incident. As Clarence Darrow, the great labor attorney, has said: "But the number of irresponsible stories that come to a lawyer in the preparation of a press-agented case is almost beyond belief." Following are details on some of the stories, irresponsible or not:

The Sacco Alibi

Sacco's alibi—that he had been in Boston seeking a passport—was actually articulated several months after his arrest; originally he claimed to have been at work on April 15, 1920. In any case, a former consular clerk named Giuseppe Adrower, who had returned to Italy, signed affidavits on April 13 and 15 and May 11, 1921 which supported the Sacco alibi but which differed in detail, depending on whether Adrower was being questioned by representatives of the defense or the prosecution. Sacco had claimed he had brought an impracticably and memorably large passport photograph and that Adrower had told him to return with one of the proper size. The clerk, who said his memory had been prompted by a defense volunteer, admitted that a normal day's business brought in 150 to 200 persons and that there was no official record of Sacco's visit. Furthermore, Sacco had used a passport before and should have known the permissible photograph size.

The Vanzetti Citation

The "If it had not been for these thing . . . ." citation has had a confusing history. It has often been called a part of Vanzetti's sentencing speech. The original edition of *The Letters of Sacco and Vanzetti,* edited by Marion D. Frankfurter and Gardner Jackson, used the citation as an epigraph with this note: "From a statement made by Vanzetti after receiving sentence, April 9, 1927." I asked Gardner Jackson about it and he insisted that he wasn't trying to mislead anybody. A recent paperback edition of the letters has dropped the original epigraph and carries a specific reference to the jail interview.

Many other mentions, however, place the citation in a Vanzetti letter. This was the way it was introduced in the play, *The Male Animal,* for example, and Ruth McKenney's Communist novel, *Jake Home,* has a party member say: " 'I have a letter here. . . . Bartolomeo wrote it just after the decision to a friend of mine. . . .' " The speaker continues: " 'I thought there are writers, poets among you. Perhaps you could suggest some manner of using this letter to further this case.' "

Stong's subsequent references to his interview add to the confusion. He makes a number of errors in an account of the case appearing in the book, *The Aspirin Age.* Thus he writes ironically: "It was 'proved' at the trial that the bullets in Berardelli's body came from Vanzetti's revolver." Of course, Stong here confuses Vanzetti's silent weapon, which the prosecution said he got from the dying Berardelli, with Sacco's pistol, the issue of all the ballistics argumentation. Furthermore, Stong misquotes his original quotations of the prisoners. When he attempts to repeat them in 1949, he changes Vanzetti's "These thing" to "this thing" and reduces "I might have live out my life, talking at street corners to scorning men" to "I might have live out my life among scorning men," among other discrepancies. The Sacco quotation shows even more change.

The Story of the Cap

At the Advisory Committee hearings in 1927, Jeremiah F. Gallivan, the Braintree police chief in 1920, testified about the cap found at the crime scene, the one that Sacco had tried on in court. Katzmann had argued that the cap belonged to Sacco, who had had the habit of hanging it on a nail near his work bench. That habit, Katzmann argued, explained a hole in the cap's lining. Now Gallivan testified that he had torn the cap's lining to see if he could find a name inside. It seems a doubtful story. Would even a provincial police official tamper with evidence? In any case it is too trivial to influence a judgment.

The Department of Justice Files

Two former agents of the Federal Bureau of Investigation, Lawrence Letherman and Fred J. Weyand, accused the Department of Justice of having conspired with the prosecution to incriminate Sacco and Vanzetti. They also claimed that the Department's files contained information that would help exonerate the accused. They could not substantiate their statements, although there was a connection of sorts between the Department and the local prosecution. The Department, hoping to get information on the Wall Street bombing of September 16, 1920, secured Katzmann's cooperation in placing an informer in the cell next to Sacco's. The informer learned nothing and was quickly withdrawn. About the files, the Department, according to the Attorney General, did not even have a record of the arrest of Sacco and Vanzetti.

The Governor

Michael A. Musmanno and Louis Stark, the *New York Times* labor reporter at that time, argued that Fuller had revised an original decision to commute sentence. The motive, they suggested, was presidential ambitions. They pointed out that Coolidge's announcement about not running preceded the release of Fuller's decision. The Coolidge statement was given to reporters at noon on August 2 in South Dakota; Fuller's decision became public shortly before midnight on August 3, 1927. Yet the Advisory Committee's negative report had been in the Governor's hands for a week. Had Fuller held another opinion, we can be sure he would have discussed it with the Committee members. He did not do so. It is also impossible to imagine that his opinion, which a Boston newspaperman is credited with having drafted, had not been prepared some days previous to its release and shown to the Governor's intimates for final corrections. The thesis, moreover, requires a singularly unkind judgment of Fuller's character.

Lowell's Discomfiture

Sacco's alibi had been supported by two witnesses who said they remembered the date because of a banquet held in Boston. However, one put the banquet at noon and the other said it was in the evening. Lowell went through the files of the *Gazetta di Massachusetts* and found no mention of a banquet on April 15, 1920. He did find a report of a banquet in the issue of May 14, a month later. When he asked Felice Guadagni, one of the two witnesses, about it, Guadagni admitted he must have been mistaken. Yet his testimony was followed by that of Albert Bosco, editor of another Italian-language newspaper, who insisted that there had been a banquet on April 15. The next day he came to the Advisory Committee hearing with a copy of his newspaper which reported on the banquet. Lowell apologized, but the matter remains in doubt. It would not have been impossible for the editor to have produced a counterfeit copy. Furthermore, the issue refers back to the contradictory testimony of two defense witnesses, both anarchist friends of Sacco.

A NOTE ON SOURCES

The Sacco-Vanzetti case lacks important mysteries and arcane sources. In my narrative, while I have largely avoided the footnotes of a more formal scholarship, I have attempted to indicate the principal origins of my information. This note on sources gives more specifics.

Of all sources, one must be placed first. This is *The Sacco-Vanzetti Case: Transcript of the Record of the Trial of Nicola Sacco and Bartolomeo Vanzetti in the Courts of Massachusetts and Subsequent Proceedings, 1920–7.* 5 vols. *With a supplemental volume on the Bridgewater case* (New York: Henry Holt, 1928–29). These six volumes of more than 6,000 pages give the most nearly complete record of what was said at the trials and hearings as well as what was written in the appeals. Also included are such oddments as the reports of Pinkerton detectives, affidavits, and statements. To the extent that the *Transcript* provided undisputed facts of the record I have used it to confirm all information received from other sources.

Interviews and Correspondence

I am grateful to all those who endured my questions so tolerantly. The interviews included talks with Alfonsina Brini, Beltrando Brini, Lefevre Brini (Wager), Charles P. Curtis, Herbert B. Ehrmann, Richard C. Evarts, Aldino Felicani, James M. Graham, Oscar Handlin, Gardner Jackson, G. Louis Joughin, Dexter Keezer, Harry E. King, Charles J. Lewin, Walter Lippmann, Eugene Lyons, George Minot, Robert H. Montgomery, Arthur S. Nickerson, Lt. Robert Pardua of the New York City

Police Department, Dudley P. Ranney, Robert E. Riordan, Edward B. Simmons, Michael E. Stewart, Harold P. Williams.

Correspondents included Bruce Bliven, John Dos Passos, Felix Frankfurter, J. D. Gunther, Michael A. Musmanno, Virginia Stong, Bertram D. Wolfe.

The Sacco-Vanzetti Collection

The Treasures Room of the Harvard Law Library has a Sacco-Vanzetti Collection of material built around a nucleus of press scrapbooks and documents from the Sacco-Vanzetti Defense Committee. These include:

Original letters of Sacco and Vanzetti: the published edition of the letters is a carefully edited fraction of the prisoners' epistolary production, which is crueler, rawer, less grammatical, more violent, and more vital.

Other original letters: writers include Fred Moore, Mrs. Lola Moore, and others connected with the defense.

Official Bulletin of the Sacco-Vanzetti Defense Committee. Boston. July 1926–March 1928. (17 issues at irregular dates; several other libraries, including the New York Public Library, have bound copies.)

Miscellany under classification number S219pb: purported interview with Governor Fuller in *Berliner Weltbuehne* originally and translated in *Living Age* of November 1930; mimeographed report of interview with Mario Buda (Mike Boda) by Edward Holton James, plus supplementary note on details of case history by James, dated February 21, 1928; March, April, May, June, and August 1929 copies of *The Lantern,* magazine published in Boston by Gardner Jackson.

Captain Charles J. Van Amburgh (with Fred Thompson): "The Hidden Drama of Sacco and Vanzetti," six-part magazine article in *True Detective Mysteries,* April–September 1935.

Copy of speech: Edward Holton James, "An Interpretation of History," given at Winter Garden, Lawrence, Massachusetts, May 27, 1927.

Scrapbook of letters and telegrams, including a letter of Felix Frankfurter accepting congratulations on his rebuttal of Dean Wigmore.

Scrapbooks classified under S219n2, ten volumes: news clippings, August 6 to 10 and August 11 to 31, 1927; majority of articles from *Boston Herald,* including Associated Press and United Press reports, and also articles from *Boston Traveler* and *Brooklyn Eagle.*

Scrapbooks classified under s219n2, ten volumes: news clippings,

May to August 1927; *Boston Herald, Transcript,* other Boston newspapers, AP and UP reports, also *New York Times, World,* and other non-Boston newspapers.

Pamphlets:

Collin, Fernand. *L'Affaire Sacco et Vanzetti.* Louvain. 1927.

Ellis, Fred. *Case of Sacco and Vanzetti in Cartoons.* New York. Daily Worker Publishing Co. 1927.

Grabhill, E. V. *Sacco and Vanzetti in the Scales of Justice.* Boston: Fort Hill Press. 1927.

Massachusetts State House Library

Massachusetts: Governors: 1925–1929 (Alvan Tufts Fuller). Boston: Commonwealth of Massachusetts. 1928.

Story of the Sacco-Vanzetti Case. Roxbury: Progress Printing Company. 1921 (?).

Massachusetts Documents

Copy of a letter from W. J. Burns, Director of Federal Bureau of Investigation, to Lawrence Letherman re Silva confession; Statement of Frank Silva, alias Paul Martini, and Jacob Luban.

Books

Adamic, Louis. *Dynamite.* New York: Viking. 1934.

Adams, Henry. *Education of Henry Adams.* New York: Book League. 1928.

Adams, Samuel Hopkins. *Incredible Era.* Boston: Houghton Mifflin. 1939.

Allen, F. L. *Only Yesterday.* New York: Harper. 1931.

Amory, Cleveland. *The Proper Bostonians.* New York: E. P. Dutton. 1947.

Anderson, Maxwell, and Harold Hickerson. *Gods of the Lightning.* New York: Longmans, Green. 1927.

——. *Winterset.* In John Gassner (ed.). *Twenty Best Plays of the Modern American Theater.* New York: Crown. 1939.

Asch, Nathan. *Pay Day.* New York: BWPC Ltd. 1930.

Bakounine, Michel. *Confession.* Paris: Rieder. 1932.

Bakunin, Michael A. (ed. G. P. Maximoff). *The Political Philosophy of Bakunin: Scientific Anarchism.* Glencoe: The Free Press. 1953.

Baldwin, H. W., and Shepard Stone. *We Saw It Happen.* New York: Simon & Schuster. 1938.

Beard, Charles A. *An Economic Interpretation of the Constitution.* New York: Macmillan. 1935.

Belin, Jean. *Secrets of the Sureté.* New York: Putnam. 1950.

Bergstresser, Genevieve. "History of the Haymarket Riot." University of Chicago thesis. 1917.

Berkman, Alexander. *Prison Memoirs of an Anarchist.* New York: Mother Earth Publishing Association. 1912.

Borchard, Edwin M. *Convicting the Innocent.* New Haven: Yale University Press. 1932.

Bourne, Randolph S. *Youth and Life.* New York: Houghton Mifflin. 1913.

Brogan, D. W. *Proudhon.* London: Hamish Hamilton. 1934.

Brooks, Van Wyck. *The Flowering of New England.* New York: Dutton. 1936.

——. *New England: Indian Summer.* New York: Dutton. 1940.

——. *The Confident Years.* New York: Dutton. 1952.

Broun, Heywood. *Collected Edition.* New York: Harcourt, Brace. 1941.

Busch, Francis X. *Prisoners at the Bar.* Indianapolis: Bobbs-Merrill. 1952.

Bryce, James. *The American Commonwealth.* New York: Macmillan. 1919 (1888).

Canby, Henry Seidel. *American Memoir.* Cambridge: Houghton Mifflin. 1947.

Chafee, Zechariah, Jr. *Freedom of Speech.* New York: Harcourt, Brace & Howe. 1920.

Commager, Henry Steele. *The American Mind.* New Haven: Yale University Press. 1950.

Cooke, Alistair. *A Generation on Trial.* New York: Knopf. 1950.

Cowley, Malcolm. *Exile's Return.* New York: Norton. 1922.

Curtis, Charles P. *It's Your Law.* Cambridge: Harvard University Press. 1954.

——. *Oppenheimer Case.* New York: Simon & Schuster. 1955.

Darrow, Clarence S. *The Story of My Life.* New York: Scribners. 1932.

David, Henry. *History of the Haymarket Affair.* New York: Farrar & Rinehart. 1936.

Denarques, Edmond. *Ravachol: Crimes anarchistes.* Paris: Bernardin-Bechet. 1931.

Devlin, Patrick. *Trial by Jury.* London: Stevens. 1956.
De Voto, Bernard. *We Accept with Pleasure.* Boston: Little, Brown. 1934.
Dos Passos, John. *U.S.A.* New York: Modern Library. 1950.
——. *District of Columbia.* Boston: Houghton Mifflin. 1952.
Dostoevsky, Fyodor. *The Possessed.* New York: Macmillan. n.d.
Dostojewski, Fyodor. *Memoiren aus einem Totenhaus* (Deutsch von Nadja Strasser). Potsdam: Gustav Kiepenheuer. 1924.
Draper, Theodore. *The Roots of American Communism.* New York: Viking. 1957.
Ehrmann, Herbert B. *The Untried Case.* New York: Vanguard. 1933.
Farrell, James T. *Bernard Clare.* New York: Vanguard. 1946.
Faulkner, Harold U. *The Quest for Social Justice.* New York: Macmillan. 1931.
——. *American Political and Social History.* New York: Crofts. 1941.
Fitzgerald, F. Scott. *The Great Gatsby.* New York: Scribners. 1925.
—— (ed. Edmund Wilson). *The Crack-Up.* New York: New Directions. 1945.
Forbes, Edward W., and John W. Finley (eds.). *The Saturday Club.* Boston: Houghton Mifflin. 1958.
Fraenkel, Osmond K. *The Sacco and Vanzetti Case.* New York: Knopf. 1931.
Frank, Jerome. *Law and the Modern Mind.* New York: Brentano. 1930.
——. *Courts on Trial.* Princeton University Press. 1950.
——, and Barbara Frank. *Not Guilty.* New York: Doubleday. 1957.
Frankfurter, Felix. *The Case of Sacco and Vanzetti.* Boston: Little, Brown & Little. 1927.
——. *Law and Politics.* New York: Harcourt, Brace. 1939.
—— (with Dr. Harlow B. Phillips). *Felix Frankfurter Reminiscences.* New York: Reynal. 1960.
Frankfurter, Marion, and Gardner Jackson (eds.). *The Letters of Sacco and Vanzetti.* New York: Viking. 1928.
Gassner, John (ed.). *Twenty Best Plays of the Modern American Theater.* (including: Anderson, Maxwell. *Winterset*). New York: Crown. 1939.
Goldberg, Harvey. *American Radicals: Some Problems and Personalities.* New York: Monthly Review Press. 1957.
Gompers, Samuel. *Seventy Years of Life and Labor: An Autobiography* (2 vols.). New York: Dutton. 1925.
Grant, Robert. *The Convictions of a Grandfather.* New York: Scribners. 1912.

——. *Fourscore.* New York: Houghton Mifflin. 1934.
Gunther, Jack D., and Charles O. Gunther. *The Identification of Firearms.* New York: John Wiley. 1935.
Halas, Nicholas. *Captain Dreyfus.* New York: Simon & Schuster. 1955.
Handlin, Oscar. *Boston's Immigrants.* Cambridge: Harvard University Press. 1941.
——. *Race and Nationality in American Life.* Boston: Little, Brown. 1948.
Hapgood, Norman (ed.). *Professional Patriots.* New York: Boni. 1927.
Hart, W. C. *Confessions of an Anarchist.* London: Richards. 1906.
Hatcher, Maj. Gen. Julian S., Lt. Col. Frank J. Jury, and Jac Weller. *Firearms Investigation, Identification, and Evidence.* Harrisburg: Stackpole. 1957.
Hicks, Granville. *Small Town.* New York: Macmillan. 1946.
Hoffman, J. J. *The Twenties.* New York: Viking. 1949.
Hofstadter, Richard. *The Age of Reform.* New York: Knopf. 1955.
——. *Anti-Intellectualism in American Life.* New York: Knopf. 1963.
Holmes, Oliver Wendell. See Howe, Mark De Wolfe.
Hook, Sidney (ed.). *John Dewey.* New York: Dial. 1950.
Howe, Helen. *We Happy Few.* New York: Simon & Schuster. 1946.
Howe, Mark De Wolfe (ed.). *Holmes-Laski Letters* (2 vols.). Cambridge: Harvard University Press. 1954.
Hunter, Robert. *Violence and the Labor Movement.* New York: Macmillan. 1919.
James, Henry. *The Bostonians.* New York: Macmillan. 1886.
——. *American Scene.* New York: Scribners. 1946 (1907).
James, William (ed. H. M. Kallen). *Philosophy of William James.* New York: Modern Library. 1925.
Josephson, Matthew. *Portrait of the Artist as American.* New York: Harcourt, Brace. 1930.
Joughin, G. Louis, and Edmund M. Morgan. *The Legacy of Sacco and Vanzetti.* New York: Harcourt, Brace. 1948.
Kazin, Alfred. *On Native Grounds.* New York: Reynal & Hitchcock. 1942.
Kropotkin, Piotr A. *Conquest of Bread.* New York: Putnam. 1907.
Krutch, Joseph Wood. *The Modern Temper.* New York: Harcourt, Brace. 1929.
Leighton, Isabel (ed.). *The Aspirin Age.* New York: Simon & Schuster. 1949.
Lerner, Max. *Ideas Are Weapons.* New York: Viking. 1939.
Leuchtenburg, William E. *Perils of Prosperity.* University of Chicago Press. 1958.

Lippmann, Walter. *A Preface to Morals*. New York: Macmillan. 1929.
——. *The Good Society*. Boston: Little, Brown. 1943.
Lord, Walter. *The Good Years*. New York: Harpers. 1960.
Luhan, Mabel Dodge. *Intimate Memories* (4 vols.). New York: Harcourt, Brace. 1933.
Lyons, Eugene. *The Life and Death of Sacco and Vanzetti*. New York: International Publishers. 1927.
——. *Assignment in Utopia*. New York: Harcourt, Brace. 1937.
MacLeish, Archibald. *The Irresponsibles*. New York: Duell, Sloan & Pearce. 1940.
Madison, Charles A. *Critics and Crusaders*. New York: Henry Holt. 1957.
Marks, Jeannette. *Thirteen Days*. New York: A. & C. Boni. 1929.
Marquand, John P. *North of Grand Central* (*The Late George Apley, Wickford Point, H. M. Pulham Esquire*). New York: Doubleday. 1956.
Mason, Alpheus T. *The Supreme Court from Taft to Warren*. Baton Rouge: Louisiana State University Press. 1958.
Massachusetts General Court. *Record of Public Hearing before Joint Committee on the Judiciary of Massachusetts Legislature on the Resolution . . . Recommending a Posthumous Pardon for Nicola Sacco and Bartolomeo Vanzetti*. Boston Committee for the Vindication of Sacco and Vanzetti. 1959.
May, Henry (ed.). *The Discontent of the Intellectuals: A Problem of the Twenties*. Chicago: Rand-McNally. 1963.
McKenney, Ruth. *Jake Home*. New York: Harcourt, Brace. 1943.
Mencken, H. L. *The Days of H. L. Mencken* (*Heathen Days: 1890–1936*). New York: Knopf. 1947.
Montgomery, John. *The Twenties*. London: Allen & Unwin. 1957.
Montgomery, Robert H. *Sacco-Vanzetti: The Murder and the Myth*. New York: Devin-Adair. 1960.
Morris, Joe Alex. *What A Year*. New York: Harpers. 1956.
Morris, Richard B. *Fair Trial*. New York: Knopf. 1952.
Musmanno, Michael A. *After Twelve Years*. New York: Knopf. 1939.
Parrington, Vernon L. *Main Currents in American Thought*. New York: Harcourt, Brace, 1927.
Partisan Review. *America and the Intellectuals: A Symposium*. New York: Partisan Review. 1953.
Paul, Elliot. *The Last Time I Saw Paris*. New York: Random House. 1942.
Post, Louis F. *The Deportations Delirium of Nineteen-Twenty*. Chicago: C. H. Kerr. 1923.
Profiles from the New Yorker. New York: Knopf. 1938.

Pyzur, Eugene. *The Doctrine of Anarchism of M. A. Bakunin.* Milwaukee: Marquette University Press. 1955.

Raby, R. Cornelius. *Fifty Famous Trials.* Washington: Washington Law Book Co. 1937.

Reed, John. *Ten Days That Shook the World.* New York: Boni & Liveright. 1919.

Reynolds, Quentin. *Courtroom.* New York: Farrar, Straus. 1950.

Riesman, David. *The Lonely Crowd.* New Haven: Yale University Press. 1950.

Rogge, O. John. *Why Men Confess.* New York: Nelson. 1959.

Runyon, Damon. *Trials and Other Tribulations.* New York: Lippincott. 1933.

Russell, Francis. *Tragedy in Dedham.* New York: McGraw-Hill. 1962.

Santayana, George. *Character and Opinion in the United States.* New York: Scribners. 1920.

——. *The Genteel Tradition at Bay.* New York: Scribners. 1931.

——. *The Last Puritan.* New York: Scribners. 1937.

——. *Persons and Places.* New York: Scribners. 1944.

——. *Dominations and Powers.* New York: Scribners. 1951.

Schaak, Michael J. *Anarchy and Anarchists.* Chicago: F. J. Schulte. 1889.

Schlesinger, Arthur M. *The American as Reformer.* Cambridge: Harvard University Press. 1950.

Schlesinger, Arthur M., Jr. *The Crisis of the Old Order: The Age of Roosevelt.* New York: Houghton, Mifflin. 1957.

Seldes, George. *Witch Hunt: The Technique and Profits of Redbaiting.* New York: Modern Age. 1940.

Sinclair, Upton. *Boston.* Pasadena: Upton Sinclair. 1928.

Stearns, Harold E. (ed.). *Civilization in the U.S.* New York: Harcourt, Brace, 1922.

——. *America Now.* New York: Scribners. 1938.

Thurber, James, and Elliott Nugent. *The Male Animal.* New York: Random House. 1940.

Tocqueville, Alexis de. *De la Démocratie en Amérique.* Paris: Librairie de Medicis. (Original edition: 1835).

Trent, Lucia, and Ralph Cheyney, *America Arraigned.* New York: Dean. 1928.

Van Passen, Pierre. *Days of Our Years.* New York: Dial. 1940.

Veblen, Thorstein B. *Theory of the Leisure Class.* New York: Macmillan. 1899.

——. *Instinct of Workmanship.* New York: Macmillan. 1914.

Viereck, Peter. *Shame and Glory of the Intellectual.* Boston: Beacon. 1953.

Vorse, Mary Heaton. *Footnote to Folly.* New York: Farrar & Rinehart. 1935.

Weeks, Robert P. (ed.). *Commonwealth vs. Sacco and Vanzetti.* Englewood Cliffs, N.J.: Prentice-Hall. 1958.

Wells, H. G. *Mr. Blettsworthy on Rampole Island.* New York: Doubleday, Doran. 1928.

——. *The Way the World Is Going.* London: Ernest Benn. 1928.

West, Rebecca. *The Meaning of Treason.* New York: Viking. 1947.

Wigmore, John H. *The Principles of Judicial Proof.* Boston: Little, Brown. 1931.

Wilson, Edmund. *To the Finland Station.* New York: Harcourt, Brace. 1940.

——. *Axel's Castle.* New York: Scribners. 1954.

——. *The American Earthquake.* New York: Doubleday. 1958.

White, William Allen. *Forty Years on Main Street.* New York: Farrar & Rinehart. 1937.

——. *A Puritan in Babylon.* New York: Macmillan. 1938.

Yeomans, Henry A. *Abbott Lawrence Lowell.* Cambridge: Harvard University Press. 1948.

Yrondy, Pierre. *Sept ans d'agonie.* Paris: Editions Prima. 1929.

Zelt, Johannes. *Proletarischer Internationalismus im Kampf um Sacco und Vanzetti.* (East) Berlin: Dietz Verlag, Institut fuer Gesellschaftswissenschaften beim Zentralkomitee der S.E.D. 1958.

Articles

The most important articles and other expressions were:

Bagdikian, Ben. H. "New Light on Sacco and Vanzetti." *New Republic,* July 13, 1963.

Baldwin, Roger. "The Capital of Men without a Country." *Survey,* Aug. 1, 1927.

Beffel, John Nicholas. "Eels and the Electric Chair." *New Republic,* Dec. 29, 1920.

Berle, A. A. "Commonwealth vs. Sacco and Vanzetti." *Survey,* Sept. 1, 1927.

Bliven, Bruce. "In Dedham Jail." *New Republic,* June 22, 1927.

Callahan, Jack. "How I Found Frank Silva." *Outlook & Independent*, Oct. 31, 1928. One of five articles in that issue, all concerning the Silva confession to the Bridgewater crime.

Cook, Fred J. "Sacco-Vanzetti: The Missing Fingerprints." *Nation*, Dec. 22, 1962.

Cowley, Malcolm. "Echoes of a Crime." *New Republic*, Aug. 28, 1935.

Dewey, John. "Psychology and Justice." *New Republic*, Nov. 23, 1927.

Dos Passos, John. Open Letter to A. L. Lowell. *Nation*, Aug. 24, 1927.

Eastman, Max. "Is This the Truth about Sacco and Vanzetti?" *National Review*, Oct. 21, 1961.

Ernst, Morris E. Review of Frankfurter book on case. *Yale Law Journal*, June 1927.

Evans, Elizabeth G. "Sacco and Vanzetti." *Survey*, June 15, 1926.

Evans, Ernestine. Review of book on case by Eugene Lyons. *Nation*, Dec. 14, 1927.

Frankfurter, Felix. "Case of Sacco and Vanzetti." *Atlantic Monthly*, Mar. 1927.

Franklin, Fabian. "The Logic of the Sacco-Vanzetti Case." *McNaught's*, June 1927.

Grossman, James. "The Sacco-Vanzetti Case Reconsidered." *Commentary*, Jan. 1962.

Jackson, Gardner. "The Power of Two Ghosts." *Nation*, Aug. 21, 1929.

Kallen, H. M. "Fear, Freedom and Massachusetts." *American Mercury*, Nov. 1929.

Lyons, Eugene. Review of *The Legacy of Sacco and Vanzetti*, by G. Louis Joughin and Edmund M. Morgan. *New Leader*, Dec. 25, 1948.

Morgan, Edmund M. Review of *The Untried Case*, by Herbert B. Ehrmann. *Harvard Law Review*, Jan. 1934.

Riddell, William R. "The Sacco-Vanzetti Case from a Canadian Jurist's Viewpoint." *Current History*, Mar. 1928.

Stark, Louis, "The Grounds for Doubt." *Survey*, Oct. 1, 1927.

Stern, Samuel R. Letter. *Outlook*, Sept. 7, 1927.

Sutherland, Sidney. "The Mystery of Sacco-Vanzetti." *Liberty*, Mar. 8, 1930. *Liberty* took the occasion of this article, a stale recounting of the case, to offer a $10,000 reward for a solution; nothing was forthcoming.

Thompson, William G. "Vanzetti's Last Statement." *Atlantic Monthly*, Feb. 1928.

Warner, Arthur. Untitled editorial on Sacco-Vanzetti case. *Nation*, Sept. 28, 1921.

——. "A Sacco Revolver Expert Revealed." *Nation,* Dec. 7, 1927.

The *New Republic* and the *Nation* carried a number of editorials on the case. *Time* and the *Literary Digest* also carried unsigned accounts.

Pamphlets (*New York Public Library*)

Bernheimer, Louis. *The Trial of Sacco and Vanzetti.* 1927.

Chase, Stuart. *Are Radicals Crazy?* New York League for Industrial Democracy. 1926.

Dos Passos, John. *Facing the Chair.* Boston: Sacco-Vanzetti Defense Committee. 1927.

Evans, Elizabeth G. *Outstanding Features of the Sacco-Vanzetti Case.* Boston: New England Civil Liberties Committee. 1924.

Fuller, Alvan T. *Decision of Governor Alvan T. Fuller.* 1927.

Guernut, Henri. *L'Affaire Sacco et Vanzetti.* Paris: Ligue des Droits de l'Homme. 1927.

Marcantonio, Vito. *Labor's Martyrs.* Workers Library. 1937.

Les Martyrs du proletariat. Paris: Librairie Hayard. 1927.

Moerder Massachusetts. New York: Verband Internationaler Arbeiter der U.S. 1928.

Story of the Sacco-Vanzetti Case. Boston: Sacco-Vanzetti Defense Committee. 1922.

Thinet, Louis. *Le Drame Sacco-Vanzetti.* Paris: Librairie Baudenière. 1927.

Vanzetti, Bartolomeo. *Background of the Plymouth Trial.* Road to Freedom Group. 1926.

——. *The Story of a Proletarian Life.* Boston: Sacco-Vanzetti Defense Committee. 1924.

Walled in His Tomb. Boston: Excelsior Press. 1936.

Newspapers

Newspapers were consulted *sur place* or in the New York Public Library and the Boston Public Library. They included *New York Times;* the Boston *Globe, Herald, Traveler, Transcript, American; Brockton Enterprise; Old Colony Memorial* (Plymouth); *New Bedford Standard-Times.* Copies of the important New York *World* editorials are part of the Sacco-Vanzetti Collection in the Treasures Room of the Harvard Law Library.

INDEX